D0615628

★ AMERICAN IDOL ★

AMERICAN IDOL

IDOL

The Untold Story

RICHARD RUSHFIELD

HYPERION

NEW YORK

Copyright © 2011 Richard Rushfield

All rights reserved. No part of this book may be used or reproduced in any manner what-soever without the written permission of the Publisher. Printed in the United States of America. For information address Hyperion, 114 Fifth Avenue, New York, New York, 10011.

Library of Congress Cataloging-in-Publication Data has been applied for.

ISBN: 978-1-4013-2412-4

Hyperion books are available for special promotions, premiums, or corporate training. For details contact the HarperCollins Special Markets Department in the New York office at 212-207-7528, fax 212-207-7222, or e-mail spsales@harpercollins.com.

Book design by Renato Stanisic

FIRST EDITION

10 9 8 7 6 5 4 3 2 1

THIS LABEL APPLIES TO TEXT STOCK

We try to produce the most beautiful books possible, and we are also extremely concerned about the impact of our manufacturing process on the forests of the world and the environment as a whole. Accordingly, we've made sure that all of the paper we use has been certified as coming from forests that are managed to ensure the protection of the people and wildlife dependent upon them.

FOR NICOLE

The children sing in far Japan,
The children sing in Spain;
The organ with the organ man
Is singing in the rain.

—ROBERT LOUIS STEVENSON

If you were to ask me what I would be when I grow up
when I was little, I would've been, like, I want to be famous.

—CARRIE UNDERWOOD

ACKNOWLEDGMENTS

★

Sometimes it takes a village to cover a television show, particularly when that show exists on the epic scale of *American Idol*. I stumbled onto the *Idol* beat four years ago, and since then my work has been just a piece of a larger puzzle, fitting together at every stage with the work of some of the most talented people I've ever known.

First of all, I never would have gotten into this whole mess without the support and encouragement of two wonderful editors who knew I had a rendezvous with destiny under the *Idol* dome long before I accepted it myself. To Kate Aurthur and Maria Russo I owe it all.

In my three years covering this for the *Los Angeles Times*, I was part of a great team who in a host of ways contributed to our coverage and allowed us to take it beyond the daily news churn and rumor chasing. I will always be grateful to my comrades who at various moments joined our *Idol* team; in no particular order, a million thanks to Lora Victorio, Jevon Phillips, Patrick Day, Joseph Kapsch, Todd Martens, Denise Martin, Stephanie Lysaght, Leslie Wiggins, Rebecca Snavely, Martin Miller, Ann Powers, Maria Elena Fernandez, and Scott Collins. Supporting me from above and giving me time to pursue this crazy obsession, my thanks and apologies for the many missed meetings while off in *Idol* land to Meredith Artley, Rob Barrett, and Russ Stanton. And many thanks to two great editors of the Calendar section, Lennie Laguire and Betsy Sharkey, for letting me share this with the *Los Angeles Times* readers.

At the Daily Beast, where I've been lucky enough to take my *Idol* journey to the next level, I am indebted to Gabe Dopplet, Edward Felsenthal, and Tina Brown.

One of the pleasures of life on the *Idol* beat has been working with some of the finest reporters in Hollywood. Through judging mishaps and grand finales, in an incredibly competitive reporting environment, the collegiality of this group has been a delight to work with, and one of the great pleasures of heading to the *Idol* dome each week was seeing each of them, competitors but never foes. Thank you to my fellow *Idol* dome survivors, and most especially Shawna Malcom, Adam Vary, Whitney Pastorek, Steve Gidlow, Antonia Blyth, Carita Rizzo, Lisa Ingrassia, Shirley Halpern. And a million thanks to my colleagues in the rest of the *Idol* press corps, who over the years have let me pick their brains, test my crazy theories, and swap tales, most especially to Fred Bronson, Brian Mansfield, and Lyndsey Parker, and to my fellow bloggers MJ Santilli, Rickey Yaneza, and Melinda Greene.

Within the *Idol* family, the PR team has, through the years, been nothing but a delight to work with and to know, and my eternal thanks go out to them for all the help they've given and the trust they've shown in allowing me to roam their empire. To Jill Hudson, Eric Green, Julian Henry, Shannon Ryan, Manfred Westphal, Chloe Ellers, Michael Cilnis, Erica O'Connor, Dru Libby, Stephanie Molina, Roger Widynowski, Leslie Fradkin, Jenifer Sprague, Alex Gillespie, Michael Roach, Jason Clark, Erin Lawhorn, and Molly Heintz, thank you so much for everything.

Writing this book was a dream of mine for years, and to the people who made it come true and have seen this project from proposal to proofreads, I owe more than you can imagine for helping me get this out of my system. Enormous thanks as ever to my agents Daniel Greenberg and Monika Verma, and at Hyperion to my editor Brenda Copeland and Kate Griffin, who made this whirlwind process completely painless, and to Elisabeth Dyssegaard for bringing it in out of the cold.

Many thanks are also due to my fellow historians who have helped me along the path: William Georgiades, Chris Lee, Matthew Tyrnauer, John Travis, Ryan Shiraki, and Vanessa Grigoriadis.

And of course, no family deserves to have this much *Idol* brought into their lives, but they have stood with me through it all. My thanks to Ali, Len, and Karen Rushfield and to Justin and Renee LaPorte for all their support, and of course to my *Idol* widow, Nicole LaPorte, who is the wind beneath my wings every day of my life.

What inspired me to write this book, and to take seriously this little singing contest in the first place, was witnessing up close the stories of two groups of people. The first are the incredibly talented professionals who put together the *Idol* circus week after week. Seeing them work and getting to talk to them about their various crafts—from construction to design to photography to securing the vast production—has been an education and an inspiration, and the hours I've spent being able to look over their shoulders have been some of the most fulfilling of my career. Over the years, I've spoken to so many members of the crew, some of whom would prefer their names not be mentioned, and I will always remember their skill and dedication. Special thanks to Miles Siggins, Debbie Williams, Kieran Healy, Bruce Gowers, Andy Walmsley, Mezhgan Hussainy, Michael Orland, Debra Byrd, Rickey Minor, Raj Kapoor, and Michael Boschetti for opening their worlds to me over the years. And for this book, I am especially grateful to Simon Fuller, Cecile Frot-Coutaz, Simon Cowell, Nigel Lythgoe, Gail Berman, Mike Darnell, and Preston Beckman for sitting down and sharing their stories and their insight.

But most of all, what has inspired me and kept me going at every stage of this journey has been the experience of, every year, watching a dozen singers step forward and have the guts to go after their dreams. To get to know many of these talented people and their families and to see all they experience during their *Idol* journeys and beyond has been the reporting experience of a lifetime, and I am forever grateful that so many of them through the years have opened their lives to me and shared those journeys. In particular, I am immensely grateful for their trust to, in chronological order, Nikki McKibbin and Craig Sadler, RJ Helton, Justin Guarini, Kimberley Locke, Kim Caldwell, Jon Peter Lewis, Ace Young, Phil Stacey, Carly and Todd Smithson and Marie Stephens, Brooke White and Dave Ray, Michael Johns and Stacey Vuduris, Joanna Pacitti, Kristin Holt, the entire amazing family Castro, Stephanie Baisey, David and Jeff Archuleta, Alexis Grace, Andrea Perry and Laura McKenzie, Matt Giraud, Jackie Tohn, Alex Wagner Trugman, Megan Joy, Michael Sarver, Scott MacIntyre . . . and really every last member of seasons 7 and 8. The producers will often make the case that "it's all about the talent" and truly, your stories, your heartbreaks and incredible triumphs, have been what has kept me and millions of people coming back. Thank you for sharing them with us all.

CONTENTS

★

★ AMERICAN IDOL ★

Chapter 1

CREATOR

I n a nation where every child dreams of being a star, it was a moment millions had imagined for themselves, but few would ever come close to experiencing. Six months before, Fantasia Barrino had been a high school dropout. Functionally illiterate, she was struggling to overcome a background of abuse and raise her child alone. At seventeen, Diana DeGarmo was a high school junior, a former Miss Teen Georgia, and a popular performer in local pageants.

On the face of it, these two young women had nothing in common. And yet, on May 24, 2004, they stood side by side while an audience of thirty-three million, second only to the Super Bowl, watched them compete to be the third champion of *American Idol*.

When the little singing contest had debuted as a summer replacement on the U.S. airwaves, it was packed between reruns and low-cost filler. The promise that the show would be a game changer for the Fox network, that it would find America's next pop star, produced a hearty round of guffaws from the country's media critics. Three years, two stars, and millions of records later, no one was laughing.

American Idol had completed its conquest of the American airwaves.

With the eyes of the nation and its superstar panel of judges upon them, Fantasia and Diana competed for the biggest prize America has to offer. The currency is fame, and it's bigger than money, more desired than power. This wasn't *Survivor* handing out a cash reward to be squandered before the year was out, or *The Bachelor* bestowing dubious promises of romantic bliss. This was stardom, genuine, durable stardom, the coin that participants in church choirs and high school plays and beauty contests everywhere yearn for.

Before the result was announced, Fantasia and Diana joined the previous winners in a swelling rendition of "The Impossible Dream." The lyrics were no hyperbole, however. Not tonight. Not for the two finalists whose lives had been transformed in mere months, not for the Dallas waitress who had become *Idol's* first champion and America's biggest pop singer in years, and not for the judges who sat in review and had themselves become enormous stars, their blunt verdicts transforming our cultural tongue. If there was to be another member in this illustrious group, it would be the show itself, which, in a few short years, had achieved the truly impossible, building an empire in a tottering industry, the likes of which had not been seen for decades.

As unlikely as the story was, even more unlikely were its origins, half a decade before, and a world away, at the bottom of the globe.

IF *AMERICAN IDOL* was to be the show that changed entertainment, it seems appropriate that the road to its creation should have begun with the man who, as much as anyone in our age, changed the face of civilization: South African President Nelson Mandela. And it seems appropriate that it started on a day Mandela himself called "one of the greatest days of my life."

The day he met the Spice Girls.

November 1997: The pop group had been summoned to perform a private concert at the Mandela residence to entertain thirteen-year-old Prince Harry, who had accompanied his father on his first trip abroad since his mother's death some three months earlier. The event was a huge success. "Girl Power Engulfs a Worshipful Mandela" was the headline of the *Calgary Herald*. "Nelson's Really Really Spice" proclaimed London's *Sunday Mirror*. Mandela was, as reported, charmed. Prince Charles was charmed. As for Harry—*charmed* doesn't even begin to cover it.

This intersection of politics and pop occurred when the Spice Girls were all-powerful, dominating a recording industry that was at the height of its success, the fall to come not even a rumor. In their three years together, the Spice Girls had been transformed from a semi-ludicrous collection of out-of-tune Bananarama clones into the most successful female group in history. Their first album had sold an unbelievable (even for those golden days) thirty million copies, making them arguably the most explosive British band debut since the Beatles. In fact, the single "Wannabe" debuted in America at number eleven, at the time the highest-ever U.S. debut by a British act, beating the previous record held by the Beatles for "I Want to Hold Your Hand."

Industry insiders had estimated that the Spice Girls' empire, which included a perfume line, deals with Pepsi and Cadbury, a PlayStation video game, a collection of dolls, and an upcoming film, would earn nearly a billion dollars before the decade was out.

But it had been a lot of work. Dashing from recording sessions, to filming endorsements, to their current yearlong world tour, the Spice Girls had been in perpetual motion since they had exploded onto the pop scene. "He's been flogging them to death," a source close to the group said of the workload their manager had placed on them.

So on this magical night, flirting with a man who survived decades in prison to liberate the majority of his nation from their chains, the thought may have occurred to the young singers, why couldn't the Spice Girls be liberated?

And when the Spice Girls envisioned breaking their chains, they saw them held by the man the press had dubbed "Svengali Spice," their manager, Simon Fuller.

At that moment, Fuller was in Italy recuperating from back surgery. He had planned the Spices' world tour with the double benefit of capitalizing on a loophole in British tax law that allows citizens a break on taxes provided they go a full year without stepping foot on British soil. He had made extensive plans to spend the year ahead traveling with the band, as well as overseeing the empire from his homes on the Mediterranean and in the Caribbean. However, just two weeks after the Mandela evening, watching from his recovery bed as his troop picked up an armful of trophies at the British MTV awards, Fuller received a phone call. His band—the band whose empire he had built from nothing, whose five monikers were known in every corner of the planet, whose success had turned into not just a recording career but a genuine multimedia empire—*that* band would no longer be requiring his services. The Spice Girls were sacking their Svengali, Simon Fuller.

There must, he thought, be a better way.

. . . .

ALREADY A LEGENDARY éminence grise in the British music world by the time he was in his early thirties, Fuller had risen by seeming force of will, shunning the traditional routes for advancement at the major labels and finding his own way up the ladder. Succeeding in a music industry that he found snobbish, cut off from its public, and obsessed with "cool" over popularity, the thirty-seven-year-old had pulled off perhaps the biggest coup of any independent manager. Now, it seemed, he was right back where he started.

The few profiles that have been written on Simon Fuller give the impression of two completely different people. On the one hand, there's the Wizard of Oz, the man behind the curtain, the shadowy creator of a vast international multimedia empire who lives a life divided between seven homes on four continents; the ruthless negotiator and the Spice Girls mastermind whose interests today extend from sports (managing the career of David Beckham) to fashion (a joint venture with designer Roland Mouret and a stake in a modeling agency) to films (producing a project featuring heartthrob Robert Pattinson titled *Bel Ami*) to the perhaps most elaborate Internet launch in history.

Then there are the other reports from those who know him, who repeat terms such as "low key," "soft-spoken," "courteous," and "down to earth." These reports talk of a man who, while living at the epicenter of Planet Earth's pop culture, shuns the limelight and hasn't sat for a formal interview in the better part of a decade.

When you step into Fuller's world, you're instantly transported to the sleekest edge of modern entertainment. The Sunset Boulevard offices of 19, the two hundred–plus person management and production firm Fuller built, are a study in California whites, punctuated by shards of a WWII-era jet fuselage. The receptionist sits in the circle of a jet engine. Sheets of re-buffed antique gun metal form the countertop and walls. The effect gives a playful touch to what would otherwise be clean, minimalist, high-powered showbiz chic, complete with jaw-dropping view of the city from the twentieth floor above the Sunset Strip. As if playing into legend, the offices themselves are suggestive of a certain baton passing. The suite was formerly occupied by Playboy Enterprises. Fuller now sits in the corner suite where Hef himself once kept his chambers.

Fuller stands to greet his visitor, offering a drink and then reminding me of the one time we had previously met, an introduction that had lasted all of ninety seconds three full years earlier. He projects an impressive self-contained confidence, paired with down-to-earth diffidence. At fifty, he could easily pass for ten years younger, his face soft but without the bagginess of age. He speaks in a gentle soothing lilt, and throughout our interviews seems perpetually alert for fluctuations in his visitor's mood and schedule. In contrast with the typical in-your-face music biz manager, Fuller is all politeness and reserve.

The tale of Fuller's ascent to this peak is one of those Horatio Alger–type stories of luck and perseverance that these days only seem to happen in the entertainment industry. The man who would create *Idol* was born the youngest of three sons to a schoolmaster on the Mediterranean island of Cyprus, where his father was founding the first of several schools he would create, before moving the family to Africa, where Fuller would spend much of his early life.

Ultimately, the family settled in Hastings, a seaside town of 100,000 on the southern tip of England. While far from the main arteries of the entertainment world, the town is actually celebrated by its inhabitants as the "Birthplace of Television," thanks to the fact that John Logie Baird, the Scottish inventor who crafted the first working prototype, spent a few critical years living there.

Off the showbiz map though it may have been, Hastings was not immune from the revolutions that shook the music world in the years following Fuller's birth in 1960. Among his earliest memories are his guitar-playing elder brothers infusing the house with music. "My first ten years were spent listening to some of the greatest music ever played, particularly the Beatles. . . . I'd been hearing music all the time and it was a big part of my life." When he got a little older, young Simon picked up a guitar but found, much to his frustration, that he "probably wasn't going to be a musician. So I kind of moved on but my love for music continued to grow."

As any frustrated young would-be rock star can tell you, a passion for music with no outlet can be a dangerous thing. Searching for an outlet to make his stamp through music, Fuller channeled his impulses into a form of empire building that would soon shake the world. At his high school, a formal boys' school fairly rigid even by the standards of the day, he took the unlikely first step on a trail that would lead to *Idol*. "We used to have loads of after-school societies. There was the poetry society. The *this* society and the *that* society. Then there was the music society but they only played classical music. I was kind of thinking, *Well, this is not cool.* So I set up the record club and once a week we'd play the latest hot album."

The enterprising Fuller charged members fifty pence (about fifty cents) to join the record club, which he used to buy a record player.

"From the record club we played rock records and we'd get up amidst all the other societies, the historical society, like, 'The record club. Today we'll be playing the Stranglers' new album or the Clash.'"

By the time Simon reached sixteen, the record club's renown had spread to the point where he was charged with booking the talent for school dances. "This kind of got me into the world of bands. . . . So I ended up knowing all the local bands and they all wanted to play." By seventeen, Fuller had taken his relationships with the local talent to the next level, helping them get booked not only for the school dances, but at the other clubs and venues in the area. "In essence, at seventeen I called myself the manager."

Once out of high school, he expanded his reach, venturing up to London to book his bands there. "This is little old me at seventeen. I was speaking to all these agents, trying to come off as being a big shot. But in the end it worked really well and I booked in all the clubs in London like the Marquee and the Palace. All of those, and a couple of them on that alternative club scene were pretty big. But to me that was management and then it was like getting into record demos because you needed a demo to get the gigs. So I used the money we earned from playing to pay for demos. So I was a proper little manager, but the difference was that I didn't really know what a record company was particularly. I was more of a tour manager than what I now know to be a manager."

It was while studying at art college and working with his stable of Hastings bands that Fuller first bridled at the limitations thrust upon a manager. "It was frustrating for me because I had real drive and passion and ambition, but as a manager you really are only as good as the artists you manage."

In a fluke, one of his bands, a mod revival group called the Teen Beats, was signed to a tiny label, getting as its first single a cover of the 1960s Troggs song "I Can't Control Myself." The song got radio play in Canada, where, to Fuller's shock, it became the first hit in his career. "To me, it was like, 'You're huge in Montreal.' To me Montreal was kind of North America. It felt like it was actually more people than Montreal, than literally Quebec and Toronto."

Not one to take the slow road, Fuller dropped out of school to accompany his band on tour, where after a few months of playing, they promptly broke up. Chalk up an early lesson on the tenuousness of the traditional manager's position.

"My dreams were shattered. I was kind of thinking, *Shit*. . . . I didn't really know what the real music business was, record companies. I hadn't entered that world. But I knew that to really make it I had to move to London. That was my big decision."

Fuller hit the big city, taking a tiny apartment and working as a waiter, trying to hustle some sort of contracts for his Hastings roster. One day, he was talking with an executive at a music publishing company, trying to push one of his bands. "He was a great guy, very sort of interested in what I was doing. After a while he said, 'Look, Simon, I've got to tell you, I think your band sucks. But I think you're brilliant. I think the best advice I could give you is to get a proper job working for a proper music company.'

"I swear to God this was a revelation to me. I just hadn't thought like that. To me, I'd always been working for artists. I'd always been hustling."

It's at this point that the wunderkind through lines begin to appear in Fuller's story. Suddenly informed of the existence of a traditional industry, with traditional ladders to climb, Fuller interviewed for most of the major U.K. labels. He was offered three separate entry-level positions, but was ultimately offered a job at Chrysalis as a sort of talent scout, bringing in performers and songwriters and servicing the company's clients.

Fuller's face lights up while telling of that first job. "It was a really proper job, to work the catalogue and get covers. It wasn't a lot of money. It wasn't a high-paying job. But the fact that I was being paid and I had expenses. I'd go and see bands and sign people. People tell me that I've had a great career, and I've always said to myself, almost, that the happiest I've ever been was then because I was young, doing what I loved and being paid for it. I had no care in the world. It was not about the money. I'd have done it all for nothing."

In a very short time, Fuller had earned an impressive reputation as a spotter of talent and material, having brought an array of hits, including Madonna's "Holiday," into the company. At the age of twenty-four, Simon Fuller was being considered for the executive track, complete with expense account, company car, assistant, and the high-flying lifestyle of a music industry player in those halcyon days—not the sort of offer that many twenty-four-year-olds would lose much sleep over, particularly those who had been waiting tables just three years before. But those years of scraping by had implanted something in Simon Fuller that apparently had not vanished during his brief stint under the establishment roof. So instead of saying, "Thank you, that sounds incredible," Fuller's response was "Hmmmmm. . . ."

His thinking at the time demonstrates just how the wheels were turning even at that preposterously early point in his career.

"I said, 'Okay, I've had a few hit bands. I'm generating a lot of money here for my company. What's my next challenge? What do I do next? I just moved to A&R. So head of A&R probably ain't going to happen tomorrow.' . . . So I was thinking, *If my next step isn't going to happen here, maybe I should move to another record company and maybe that could be my next career move. I could be paid more money, given more responsibility, maybe be head of A&R.* Then I thought, *If I move to another record company I leave all my artists behind and I have to start from scratch. If my new acts were successful that would be great. If they weren't successful, then, shit, I might be fired.* Then I thought, *If I stay here and I don't have any success I'm going to get fired. If I have lots of success then I can get another job but I'm still working . . . I'm still an employee.*"

He decided to leave. "Because the truth is that if I leave and I start my own company, if I'm rubbish at it then I'm in no worse a position because they'd kick me out of there anyway and if I'm successful then I could be very successful."

And so at twenty-four years old, Simon Fuller said good-bye forever to a life on the traditional rungs of the recording industry and left to set up his own company.

He phoned Chris Morrison, an industry mogul he knew, and brazenly asked him to fund a management company, saying all he wanted was an office, a car, and a guaranteed salary. Morrison, no doubt impressed by the boldness of the proposal, agreed to fund him for 3½ years. In April 1985, Fuller set up shop and signed a young singer named Paul Hardcastle as one of his first clients. He was still unpacking the new office when his first client's first single was released. A pop/dance anthem about the Vietnam War, "19" instantly went to number one on the U.K. charts and sold six million copies worldwide. Fuller's firm was a million pounds in the black—instantly.

"Chris Morrison never invested one cent, never had to. That was the beginning of 19 [the firm, named after the song]. I remember Chris said, 'Simon, it's not always like this. It doesn't always go like this.' It was true. It took me a while to have my next number one."

The road, however, moved steadily upward. When Annie Lennox left the Eurythmics, Fuller signed her, seeing her potential to move beyond her 1980s pop star roots and become a true solo sensation. By the time the Spice Girls appeared, almost a decade later, Fuller was chomping at the bit to create something more than just a hit album—an empire.

The Spice Girls came to Fuller after defecting from Bob and Chris Herbert, a little-known father-and-son team who held auditions to cast a girl group, originally to be called Touch. When they appeared on Simon Fuller's doorstep, the Spices had tired of fruitlessly attempting to break out and staged the first revolt of their career. The possibilities for a bubblegum collection of mini-skirted warblers in the age of Alanis Morissette seemed dim. Nonetheless, Fuller took them on and readied them for the public eye. Following the release of their first single, the soon-to-be-ubiquitous "Wannabe," he formed the first truly modern media empire based around a pop group. Fuller used the publicity generated by the music and the assertive personalities of the girls themselves, with their vaguely defined "girl power" rallying cry, and soon built the Spices into an empire.

Svengali Spice found himself roundly criticized in the press for the shameless commercial exploitation of the phenomenon, as though it were possible to commercialize something so inherently of the marketplace. But no amount of oversaturation seemed to slow them down. The Spice Girls had the highest debut any U.K. band has ever had on the U.S. charts, taking the crown from the Beatles. As their second album hit the marketplace, as tickets sold out in moments for their impending yearlong world tour, as their film became a hit in the United

Kingdom (and not badly reviewed, for that matter, as pop acts went), there seemed no end to where the Spice empire might go.

And then all of a sudden, for Simon Fuller, it was over.

After climbing as high as any manager had ever gone before he was forty, he was back at square one.

Still bedridden from his back surgery, Fuller looked back on it all and thought, "Next time, we have to think much much bigger."

Chapter 2

LIGHTBULBS

t starts with an idea that's sometimes kind of random, but comes into your head and then you sort of reflect and develop," Fuller recalls of those first stirrings that led him to *Idol*.

Reeling from the breakup with the Spices, recovering from surgery, and locked out of his country on self-imposed tax exile, Simon Fuller's road to *Idol* first had to run through a rebound relationship. Before *Idol*, there had to be *S Club*.

"That year was so significant in my life. It's hard to believe that so much can come out of one year. The thing that came out of it was that while I loved managing, I didn't want to be totally beholden to the fragility of an artist's management contract. I wanted to come back and build 19 into a much more ambitious proposition."

The day after the breakup, Fuller rolled up his sleeves and began sketching out what would essentially be the bigger, better version of the Spices. *Better* from his perspective because it wouldn't be based on the unpredictable talents and personalities of a group of performers. The star of his new project would be the concept itself, a concept that would be big enough to start life as a multimedia empire rather than evolving into it.

Fuller's next project launched as a TV show targeted for the tween audience loosely modeled on *The Monkees*. Entitled *Miami 7* on its original British run and *S Club 7* when it ran in the United States on ABC Family, the show featured the adventures of seven singing and dancing telegenic young people. The septet quit odd jobs at Miami resorts to play together in a band called S Club 7, breaking into song at the slightest provocation. The on-screen band, of course, released real-world albums and merchandise. Seven years before *Hannah Montana* would make Miley Cyrus an international sensation by cross-pollinating a fictional on-screen rock star's life with a real-life music career, *S Club 7* revived the model once used by novelty band the Monkees for a much more ambitious media age.

The show became a staple of tween culture and the teenybopper press, their second single reaching number one on United Kingdom charts. The band soon had its tour, its singing dolls, and its commercial endorsements lined up, the full marketing machine perfected for the Spice Girls. This, however, wasn't a band that had come in looking for guidance, but a concept imagined, owned, and operated by Simon Fuller. And it was the concept itself—the teens, the outfits, the music, the TV show—that was the selling point and star, above and beyond any of its cast members.

Dreaming up *S Club* was just the throat-clearing, the warm-up. Almost as soon as that concept was out of his head, Fuller had charged off beyond it, thinking about how he could take the idea of a self-contained, fully operating music factory and build something even larger than what he had in front of him. *S Club* had been cast through traditional means—talent scouts, open calls, and the like—with the finalists flown to Italy to perform before Fuller. But as these auditions took place, a whole new dimension was just opening up in the brand-new space known as the World Wide Web.

"This was sort of when everything was the Internet," Fuller recalls. "It was the boom years and so all my thoughts at this time were about talent, finding talent online and creating an experience born out of *S Club*. . . . The next phase I was imagining was that if I had this huge audition where people online registered to be in my next project, I could choose talent and then work with them in different ways. So the original idea was an online talent search but it was for singers, dancers, and actors. I thought that I'd do *S Club Mach II* and it'll be a talent search and when you win the competition, you win a part in this online reality show. But all these ideas are all linked. It's so bizarre."

In 2010, when *American Idol* announced it would open up its auditions to online submissions, the world didn't bat an eye. But when

Fuller conceived his online reality show in 1997, the concepts "reality TV" or "online show" barely existed. The Internet was still very much in its infancy. Yahoo! was all of three years old. It would be another year before two nerds at Stanford would invent Google in their dorm rooms. In 1997, a mere ten million people on planet Earth had e-mail accounts.

Not surprisingly, Fuller's pitch to create the show of the future on a medium not yet in general use found few takers. Through 1999, he pitched the talent competition he now called *Fame Search* to, among others, the United Kingdom's ITV, eventual home of *Pop Idol*. They summarily rejected the proposal. Fuller moved on to other projects, including a Eurythmics reunion tour, but the *Fame Search* concept, the idea of a massive audition and talent hunt utilizing interactive technology, wouldn't leave his head.

In February 2000, Fuller took another run at it, pitching *Fame Search*, now renamed *Your Idol*, to Nigel Lythgoe, a flamboyant television executive Fuller was friendly with. Lythgoe, as it turned out, had just committed to producing another talent competition that would soon be coming to the airwaves—a show called *Popstars*. Like the *Fame Search* concept, Lythgoe's show also featured a talent hunt through the ranks of unknown singers and musicians, casting a new band, to be then launched on the commercial market.

THERE ARE MANY streams that fed into the great river that was to become *Idol,* but one of the most significant started its journey in a remote corner of the world, with a little singing contest/reality TV hybrid that appeared on the airwaves of New Zealand in 1999. *Popstars* was a huge hit in its first New Zealand season; the band it created, a girl group called TrueBliss, debuted their first album at number one on the Kiwi charts. Ironically, considering Fuller's coming role, the band was widely derided by the New Zealand critics as being a Spice Girls rip-off.

From New Zealand, the show's success quickly fueled a replica of the format for Australian television. And from there, where it also caught fire, it was discovered by Lythgoe, then a U.K. network executive whose son was a member of the show's crew and who saw the show while visiting him on vacation.

Lythgoe recalls, "He said, 'Dad, you've got to see the program I'm working on. I think you'll really like it.' So we stayed in. We were on our holiday and so you can imagine that my wife, Bonnie, really didn't want to stay in on our holiday to watch television but it was so good and so interesting that we made a point of staying in the following week to watch it again. What thrilled me was the actual audition process, watching people judge honestly this talent, this raw talent. . . . I'd never seen that on television before, to be frank. I don't remember any show that ever did that. I found it inspiring and immediately contacted the producers."

Lythgoe made a deal to bring the show to the United Kingdom and serve as its executive producer and showrunner. Like Simon Fuller, Lythgoe, the man who was to become a critical figure in the growth of *American Idol*, began his road to the pinnacle of entertainment from the unlikeliest of starting places. A real-life Billy Elliot, the son of a Northern England dockworker, Lythgoe developed an interest in dance at ten years old. After attending classical conservatory, in the 1960s he joined a modern dance troupe called the Young Generation, which performed televised shows on the BBC. By 1970, he moved behind the cameras and became the group's choreographer, eventually working his way up to the producer's chair, and from there, to the network front office, becoming head of entertainment and comedy for London Weekend Television. But by 1999, after a decade behind a desk, Lythgoe longed to get back on the set again. So when *Popstars* appeared in his life, driven by its musical elements, it seemed the perfect excuse to return to the stage.

As preparations began for *Popstars* U.K., the production ran into another breeze floating through the entertainment skies in those days: the mean host phenomenon.

Since the debut of *Weakest Link* on the British airwaves in mid-2000, the show's deadpan dominatrix of a host, Anne Robinson, had become the United Kingdom's most talked about new star, her acid tongue cutting its way through the clutter of the still soft world of television programming. Robinson's direct and unforgiving demeanor projected to the public something refreshingly direct, something authentic. Years later, Simon Cowell would dismiss Robinson's influence as calculated and contrived, calling her "this awful woman dressed in black like a ghastly, sadistic schoolteacher."

But Robinson's debut had made the world safe for truth telling on prime-time television. Her hard-edged persona hit the marketplace at just the right moment. After the decade of Clinton and Blair had played itself out, the era had come to be seen as synonymous with the sort of weasely evasion exemplified by Clinton's famous statement "It depends upon what the meaning of the word *is* is." The stage was set for the ascent of a certain self-styled straight shooter in American politics, and in entertainment it would be reflected in the rise of a generation of no-nonsense personalities who *tell it like it is.*

Suddenly, every show premiering in England needed its own meanie, and *Popstars* would be no exception. When Simon Fuller approached Lythgoe about *Fame Search*, Lythgoe informed him he was about to leave the front office to produce a talent competition. However, he quickly turned the tables and pitched Fuller to become a judge on the show. The publicity-shy Fuller declined. "I thought about it and I thought, *I don't want to be on television. That's not what I want to do but I'll help you with the record deal. I'll help you put it together.*"

Which left Lythgoe with a slot to fill.

His next choice—he would later say, his *favorite* choice—to fill what would become for a generation of TV shows the mean music critic slot, was an eccentric, bombastic figure named Jonathan King. Britain's consummate impresario, King was widely known in the United Kingdom as a singer, songwriter, producer, talk show host, newspaper columnist, and novelty act. Most recently prior to the *Popstars* launch, he had released a cover of "Who Let the Dogs Out" under the pseudonym Fat Jakk and his Pack of Pets.

A massive presence with giant glasses and a triple chin, exploding with hyperbolic personality from every pore, King seemed the perfect star presence to anchor the *Popstars* judging panel. His fearless truth-telling bona fides had been well established a decade earlier when he went public as perhaps the only person in the Western world to criticize Live Aid. England was at the height of beatific hysteria about the project when King lambasted the charity concert, as well as its organizer and candidate for sainthood, Bob Geldof, for seeking fame rather than simply good works. To Lythgoe, such a history of brash iconoclasm seemed the answer to *Popstars'* prayers. King's bold, unapologetic style seemed the perfect attitude to capture the reality of what it is to audition in the real world. He had the rare ability, it seemed, to speak unvarnished, to deliver a truth to people that would cut through an entitled generation's sense that life should be handed to them on a platter.

Unfortunately, as the show was in its planning stages, King's role came unmoored in the most dramatic and horrifying way. In November 2000, Jonathan King was arrested and charged with sexually molesting five boys between the ages of fourteen and sixteen. The alleged events had occurred over a decade earlier, and questions of the authorities' handling of the events persist to this day. Nevertheless, King was tried and ultimately sentenced to seven years in prison. He was released after serving half that time and continues to protest his innocence. At the time, however, there could be little question of King judging *Popstars*.

Lythgoe then turned to the man he thought closest to King—the friend who had in fact put up the bail when King was arrested—a little-known record label executive named Simon Cowell. Cowell, by Lythgoe's account, was eager to jump into the role, but was prevented from doing so because the band that the show would produce would be committed to a company other than Cowell's. "He said yes originally and then we did the record deal with somebody else. At the time we did the deal with Universal and he was with BMG and he was told that he couldn't be a judge on the show."

Cowell remembers it differently: "[W]hen I thought it through, I felt uncomfortable being on a show that would show people how the process actually works. I didn't feel comfortable with that. I always thought it was something which should have a certain mystique about it, and I didn't really like the idea of being on TV either, so I took a step back and said I'm not interested."

It was a decision he would soon regret, but one which, in the long run, would prove fortuitous beyond his imagination.

With the clock ticking, Lythgoe decided that the judge he was looking for was, in fact, he himself. Nasty Nigel was born.

The panel was filled out with manager Nicki Chapman (suggested by Fuller) and Paul Adam, the director of A&R at Polydor Records.

The show debuted at number one for its time slot, pulling in a very significant—by U.K. standards—7.6 million viewers in its first week. Its advertising campaign put the new judge front and center with a series of billboards featuring young singers crying out, "Pick me, Nigel!" The early audition episodes immediately struck a chord as the public watched judges Lythgoe, Nicki Chapman, and Paul Adam bestow in unambiguous terms showbiz life or death on the 3,000 variously talented young people who came out for the first series. "Have you seen *Popstars*?" wrote the *Independent*. "It's hugely exploitative and artistically bankrupt and horribly contrived and all that, and I'd most certainly boycott it, if only it wasn't so gripping and fabulous and I wasn't so spectacularly addicted already."

The thrill of those early episodes sprang from seeing the extravagantly untalented have their illusions stripped away by the barbed tongue of "Nasty Nigel," as he was quickly dubbed by the British press. Adapting the Robinson formula of sharp comic put-downs delivered in an unapologetically direct manner, Lythgoe restaged the tension of the showbiz tryout as dramatic spectacle. His zingers such as "I'm sure there's a tune in there somewhere," or, when one singer asked if he could pick up a song from the bridge: "You can take it from the bridge or you can take it from the hold, but I can tell you now the ship still sinks in the end" became water cooler fodder across Britain. "He had asked a number of people to do it," Simon Fuller recalls, "and the irony is that in the end Nigel did it himself. He was fantastic at it. He created the bad guy character."

More to the point, by speaking the truth in the setting of an entertainment audition, Lythgoe did not merely cut through the clutter of smarm that had, so the sentiment went, poisoned civic life; he was, in a sense, standing up to the mediocrity of entertainment that had been foisted down the public's throat in recent years. "After a lifetime of climbing the entertainment ladder, Nigel Lythgoe has now achieved cult status," wrote the *Guardian*.

Those who knew Nigel understood that the "Nasty" role was very much an act. In fact, having been a performer himself, he knew all too well the pain of flubbed auditions. Years later, when he took the judge's chair in a show much closer to his heart, *So You Think You Can Dance*, he would eschew the put-down for constructive criticisms. But at this moment, he sensed a vacuum in the culture and stepped in to fill the void. And the public instantly responded.

HIT THOUGH *POPSTARS* might have been, Simon Fuller watched and thought, "I could do this much much better. I saw certain similarities in what *Popstars* was to what I wanted to do with *Fame Search*. It

was singing as opposed to mine, which was singing, dancing, and acting, but it was the same mechanism, if you like . . . what I always intended for *Fame Search*. That was to make it a real-time experience but
just focus it on singing because it's easier to make it into a TV show.
That was really where *Pop Idol* began."

Pop Idol, as he now called it, would build on the audition element
that made the first section of *Popstars* such a success, but in addition to
casting off the slower training *Making the Band*–type documentary of
the second half, it would add the element that had excited Fuller about
the Internet concept in the first place: putting the decisions in the hands
of the audience. Essentially, *Pop Idol* planned to take the power away
from the record executives and let the people play label bigwig by letting them decide who got the recording contract. The revamped pitch
brought that element into a TV show, adding audience voting to make
the people at home the ultimate arbiters and create a very quick verdict
for the tryouts.

Within a month of *Popstars'* launch, on February 7, Fuller was pitching *Pop Idol* again in a meeting with Richard Eyre, an executive with
the British TV giant Pearson (now Thames TV, a division of the multi-
national FremantleMedia entertainment conglomerate). This time
around, with *Popstars* riding high, the fish were biting. The project
moved forward.

But one other element needed to be brought in. As in *Popstars*, Fuller
saw the need to have an immediate on-air response to the performances.
"If you're going to do it live, you need real-time feedback."

The first thought to anchor the panel was, in fact, Nasty Nigel himself, the man who had created the role. Soon after *Popstars* launched,
Fuller approached him about jumping ship and coming aboard the re-
jiggered *Pop Idol*. Fuller offered Lythgoe a full partnership in the newly
created 19 TV.

Lured by the promise of ownership in *Idol*—on *Popstars* he had
been a mere salaried executive—Nigel finally signed on, abandoning
Popstars and the exploding notoriety it was bringing him. "Fuller is
hoping that Lythgoe is the secret ingredient that will make *Pop Idol* a
hit and thus establish 19 TV as a major entertainment player," wrote
one press report after the announcement.

There were, however, complications. Showtime, the Australian company that owned the international license to *Popstars*, threatened suit

against 19 for copyright infringement. In the protracted settlement, Showtime agreed not to press a case on the grounds of format, and agreed to look the other way on the matter of poaching Lythgoe the producer but not on the matter of poaching Lythgoe the star. Another British singing competition starring Nasty Nigel was just too much. So racing to move forward, wanting to strike while the iron was hot, Fuller and company began searching for a new judge to preside over the show, someone who could fill the shoes of Nasty Nigel.

They turned to a man Fuller had known around the music business for years, a record company executive named Simon Cowell.

Chapter 3

ENTER THE DRAGON

When set designer Andy Walmsley reported for his first meeting about the new project called *Pop Idol*, he recalls being told about the record executive who would occupy the "mean judge" chair: "His name is Simon Cowell and he has more money than anyone in this room will ever see in their lifetime."

It was a typical description of the man who would remake television, if only because so little was known about him. For decades, Cowell had skirted amidst celebrity, shaped it, known it, dated it, and profited from it, but he had only made rare appearances on the margins of the British tabloid culture.

The year before Cowell stepped on the *Idol* stage, the freewheeling gossip column of the *Sun* tabloid ran a blind item reporting that an un-named executive was spending time with a pop star named Naima from the band Honeyz. A few days after the blind item appeared, the column published a follow-up: "WASN'T going to name the RCA exec 'tending the garden' of NAIMA from Honeyz for the good reason nobody—including me—has heard of him. However, bloke in question has spent the past 48 hours pestering colleagues demanding to know how I rumbled him. And frankly, he's becoming a nuisance. So step forward SIMON COWELL who, when not podgering Naima, acts as WEST-LIFE's chief backside kisser."

Outside the music industry, it may have looked like backside kisser was Simon Cowell's complete job description, but those who had worked with him—and those who had tangled with him—had come to learn that belittling Cowell was a loser's game. For over a decade prior to *Idol,* Cowell had stood as the United Kingdom's record industry's most ardent proponent of shameless commercialism, pushing a string of companies into the realm of novelty recordings and unabashed pop that gave chills to those who thought themselves the arbiters of cool. Since the beginning of his career, the raw populism of Cowell's artistic vision had elicited jeers and catcalls from his fellows in the industry, but although he had had more than a few embarrassing flops, by the late 1990s his record of smash hits was such that no colleague would dare mock him again.

Some ten years after signing on to the little singing contest, Simon Cowell is, by the account of one poll, the most famous British person on Earth, his renown surpassing that of the Queen. The summer after departing *Idol,* sitting in his grand but subdued corner office suite at the headquarters of Sony Music UK, Simon Cowell pauses somewhere between trying to sign a new recording act and cutting an episode of *The X Factor* for a rare moment of reflection, remembering the time just before *Idol.*

"I was very happy just being behind the scenes and had absolutely zero desire to be in front of the camera. I never had that desire," he recalls, sipping ginger tea and dragging on Kool cigarettes, lit candles flickering gently around the sitting room. While he might not have been motivated by fame, Simon Cowell, like his comrade-to-be Simon Fuller, was driven by an unquenchable desire to build. Ten years later, having exited at last from *Idol,* his brain clearly buzzes with ideas, and his eyes still light up with enthusiasm, even after an all-night editing session, about the challenge to keep making something bigger and better. And if enormous, unprecedented fame for an executive was to be the price of that, so be it.

On a very surface level, the two Simons appeared to be sides of the same coin. Over time, their similarities would fuel countless profiles, magazine pieces, and brothers-in-arms comparisons. Indeed, Simon Fuller and Simon Cowell are a year apart in age, have similar rigorous flattop haircuts, and worked on the poppiest edge of the U.K. music business. Both had bold visions for success and weren't shy about ruffling feathers to achieve them. And of course there are the names. Beyond those superficial resemblances, however, the two men who would reshape entertainment in their respective images are, in fact, as different as men can be. Where Simon Fuller is shy, gracious, soft-spoken, and wary of the limelight, the on-screen Simon Cowell is famously caustic, abrasive, and, once he got a taste for it, a creature who revels in being the center of attention. Where Fuller was the quintessential outsider who made his own way through the recording industry, Cowell was the high-achieving company man who rose through the ranks of industry giants.

The future partners began in opposite corners of the world. Fuller was raised at a remote distance from the entertainment industry, while for Cowell, the entertainment industry was the background music of his childhood, a seat at its table just a father's phone call away. Cowell grew up in Elstree, Britain's Hollywood-east and home to two of the nation's major film studios, where he developed an early taste for the high life. His parents have been described as exceptionally attractive, rather dashing figures. His father, Eric, was a noted presence speeding around town behind the wheel of a white Jaguar; his mother, Julie, was a former dancer. "The stars soon became our friends and neighbors," he wrote in his autobiography, *I Don't Mean to Be Rude, But . . .* , "and whenever they were in town, I got to rub shoulders with the cream of Hollywood, as long as I could squeeze my way past my mum." Childhood memories include sitting on the knee of Bette Davis and visiting Roger Moore on the set of *The Saint*.

The adorable child on Bette Davis's knee soon became, by his own self-described legend, the mischievous scamp talking back to adults at fancy parties, prompting roars of delight for his precocity. At four years old, Cowell recalls looking up at a furry hat his mother was wearing and telling her, "You look like a poodle." And no doubt, getting away with it.

Cowell's reminiscences alternate between tales of coming of age on the sidelines of showbiz and reveling in his rascally back-talking nature, a trait that a succession of outraged schoolmasters saw as the nerve of an overprivileged brat, but that would eventually resolve itself into the "fearless truth telling" that would reshape entertainment.

Cowell also found music. With his two older brothers, he fell in love with the Beatles and the Stones, and grew to despise what he saw as the simpering banality of his parents' music: Perry Como, Shirley Bassey, and the like. On these artists, he let forth his first known expressions of disdain, begging his mother to "turn that rubbish off." But whereas many others, Fuller included for a time, were to follow a path that was increasingly daring and iconoclastic—from the Beatles to the Stones to the Who to the Sex Pistols and the Clash—Cowell got off the boat when it veered away from mainstream pop. To this day, he declares that he "doesn't get" punk.

At age seventeen, Cowell left school with no clear plan for the future other than a vague desire to go into show business. "All I did know was that I wanted to make money," he wrote. "Real money. I credit my parents with this. From an early age they made us earn our own pocket money. But pocket money wasn't enough. I soon became obsessed with getting rich."

It was an obsession that would stay with him. After leaving school, Cowell drifted into a series of odd jobs.

While floating from ill-suited job to ill-suited job, young Simon longed to break into the music industry. Eventually, his parents acknowledged their son's dreams, and after his mother wrote a letter to an acquaintance at the EMI label, Simon won a job in their mailroom.

The bloom on the rose came off quickly for Cowell. After a year delivering mail, despairing of ever moving up the ladder, he returned home and asked for a job in the real estate business. But it didn't last, and after a few mind-numbing weeks, Cowell raced back to the music business, his father securing him a job through a contact at EMI Publishing. That job required Cowell to shop songs from the company's catalogue to recording artists. Soon he enjoyed his first success, getting an unusually high number of songs recorded. He had, by his account, a knack for finding the right material and matching it with the right artist, and a knack for persuading artists to take a look at the songs he was bringing in. Most of all, he had a knack for getting people to take him seriously.

Like Simon Fuller, Cowell used his first blush of success to break out on his own, setting up his own company after just a year in publishing. But whereas Fuller's plan, at least in retrospect, seemed a sensible step built on the progress he had made after a long apprenticeship, Cowell's move smacks more of dilettantism, flitting from one easily won slot to another, fleeing at the first signs of boredom, his ambitions getting ahead of his actual place in the industry.

Ellis Rich, his immediate superior at EMI, suggested that he and Cowell walk away from the day job to set up their own publishing company. Cowell writes, "Within a day of moving into our new offices in

Soho, London, I realized I had made a big mistake. We didn't have the funding to do it properly: We couldn't get the business off the ground, and many of the fundamentals of running an independent company were foreign to us." Cowell raced back to EMI and pleaded for his old job back, but he was shown the door.

E & S publishing weathered a year of solvency problems before Cowell finally broke it off with Rich and threw in the towel. "He wasn't pleased but understood that I wanted to get out of music publishing," is how Cowell describes the breakup. Believing that actually making records was the proper path to riches, Cowell joined forces with Iain Burton, a former dancer/manager who was looking to start a label. With Burton's financial backing, the duo started Fanfare Records. The label scored a quick hit that was emblematic of Cowell's success in the next phase of his career in the novelty end of the pop world. The record was a fitness instruction video hosted by *Strictly Come Dancing* star Arlene Phillips. *The Keep in Shape System (KISS)* featured Phillips, her overflowing brown mane held in place by a white headband, leg warmers in place, cheerfully leading a class of Lycra-suited aerobics enthusiasts through a routine guaranteed to help viewers "Get in shape in just ten minutes a day with Britain's number one exercise and dance teacher." The video was an instant success, selling half a million copies and putting the fledgling company on stable footing.

Soon after, Cowell met an eighteen-year-old singer named Sinitta in a nightclub and began pursuing her, by his own telling, both as a potential recording star and as a potential date. He won her over on both counts. Sinitta's first song, a ditty entitled "So Macho," became Cowell's first true hit, selling a million copies. The two became a much spotted pair around the London night scene, but Sinitta later denied the relationship was anything more than just friendly.

In the years that followed, Cowell took the mechanics of the music business more seriously. He began appearing—uninvited—at the studios of Pete Waterman, one of the United Kingdom's most successful songwriter/producers, and shadowed him through his days. At the same time, with the first taste of success, he raced to acquire the trappings of 1980s music biz success, complete with Porsche, house, and high-flying partying lifestyle. "I thought I was Jack the lad," he would later tell Oprah. "I had the Porsche, the lifestyle, the credit cards, everything." But the party was financed largely on debt and it all came crashing down, sending the thirty-year-old Cowell back home to his parents with little more than cab fare in his pocket.

Years later, in 2010, he still seemed visibly shaken by the impact of this period. "I had to live with my mum and dad," Cowell said in his *Oprah* interview. "And I had to sell the house, the Porsche. I had literally nothing. I had about a half-a-million-dollar loan I had to pay. It was a pretty awful time. Everything was based on hype, not substance. Then it became reality that I literally had to start again with nothing. It took about three or four years to pay everything off."

This brush with financial doom must have been particularly harrowing to a man whose goal in life had been, in his own words, to get extremely rich. Whatever the effect on his psyche, the practical effect was to send Cowell back to the shelter of big business, a refuge he would never leave.

In the coming years, Cowell would often find himself a fish out of water, like Fuller, looking for commercial success in an industry that seemed more concerned with protecting its aura of cool than with selling records. Reacting against what he saw as preciousness, he would push his companies to the pop extremes with songs like "So Macho" and Eurosong-friendly acts such as Ultimate Kaos and a Spice Girls rip-off called Five. But Cowell's alleged crassness also placed his finger on something unseen by his colleagues: the value of television as the launch pad and promotional vehicle for a recording artist. Instinctively, Cowell understood the challenges of an increasingly crowded media world. Over the next years, he would meet those challenges by championing a record version of *WrestleMania*, a *Teletubbies* album, and a *Mighty Morphin Power Rangers* album, all massive hits. Cowell wrote of the period, "Most of my colleagues were obsessed with signing the next coolest rock or alternative band, and I was considered by many to be a laughingstock—a freak."

Cowell's memoirs of this period fairly bristle with these memories; the very specific insults still are clearly alive in vivid Technicolor for him in lines like "those imbeciles at Arista, most of whom are out of the business today." The moment when he slammed the door on the faces of the fools and their inevitable comeuppance clearly thrill even after all the success to come.

His mega-breakthrough wouldn't come until 1995, however, just as the Spice Girls were hitting the market. While Simon Fuller was turning his firm, 19, into an empire, Cowell was struggling to get to the top of the corporate pyramid. "I was doing well financially, but not as well as others in the business. I was making a small fortune, but not a large one. I wanted to be the top dog within RCA and wasn't happy that other A&R men were having bigger hits than I was," he wrote. His chance to break out came via another television tie-in. *Soldier Soldier* was one of the most popular shows in the United Kingdom, a drama about the lives of the members of a fictional British army regiment during the military downsizing years of the 1990s. During an episode in the show's fifth season, its stars, Robson Green and Jerome Flynn, had broken into song, performing a version of the Righteous Brothers classic, "Unchained Melody." When Cowell's office was flooded the next day with calls about the song, he was determined to make an album of it, despite the stars' reluctance. For weeks, he hounded the pair until he finally got them into the studios. The resulting single was the United Kingdom's best seller of that year and started a run that sent two albums to the number one slot. In the years that followed, Cowell signed the boy band Westlife, which became the first group in U.K. history to have their first seven singles hit the number one slot, certifying Cowell's position as a hit-maker on a massive scale, while his work on the extreme pop side of the table caused the BBC's Radio One to label him "the Antichrist."

But by the end of the 1990s, he had begun to knock up against the ceiling for an A&R man. Whether he sensed it or not, he had reached the summit of a recording industry that itself was standing on a precipice. In the coming years, those who did not embrace new formulas to reach the public, who held on to the traditional models and the traditional record execs' need for "cool" over commercialism, were about to be pushed off this cliff, a fall from which few would survive.

Simon Fuller wasn't the only one watching *Popstars* and seeing its immense success and the huge possibilities this hinted at. Cowell, with his history of marrying television and music, also sat watching, pondering the possibilities.

Ironically, turning down the offer to become a judge on *Popstars* would be the deciding factor that changed everything for him. "I started to regret it about three or four weeks later because I just had a feeling that this show sounded like it had all the makings of a hit. And then, when I came back from holiday, I saw one episode and I remember my stomach dropping when I watched it because I thought, this is great TV and whoever ends up as the group, they are going to sell a ton of records, which is exactly what happened. And that was the motivation to say, 'I can't just sit there and allow this to happen.'"

As it turned out, this new world was about to come calling for Simon Cowell.

"SIMON HAS BEEN a friend of mine forever," recalls Simon Fuller of the decision to offer the Lythgoe seat to Cowell. "We both love music. We're both entrepreneurs. So when it came to me finessing this show, there were two things I needed. One was a record company, because I was a management company, to offer the prize and to drive the show. Then also a kind of partner in crime, someone who could work with me, who knew artists, who could be on the panel." The panel, as Fuller saw it, would reconstruct the forces behind an artist's career, including a manager and a record exec. As he had when the subject came up earlier, Fuller declined to appear on camera himself, so he selected one Nicki Chapman, an employee from his firm named to fill the manager's chair. Cowell, he imagined, could fill the record executive's slot. Furthermore, from the first he saw the on-air executive character as the person who would actually oversee the winners' careers.

"So I called Simon up and I said, 'Look, I've got this idea. I need a partner in crime here. I think you could be amazing,' because he's charismatic. He's funny. He had all the things that I imagined."

Cowell was receptive. "'Yes. I want to do the exact same kind of show. I've got my vision.' So he was on the same page. We were very much two peas in a pod. It was the perfect combination. Simon could provide the record company. He worked with BMG at the time. He'd be on the panel and my idea would come to fruition and we'd go conquer the world. Nigel, who produced and started *Popstars*, now worked for me and spearheaded the production. It worked better than a dream. It was like bang and off we went."

To that end, Fuller and Cowell agreed that the *Pop Idol* winners would be managed by 19, while Cowell and BMG would put out their albums. Cowell's motivation was simple. "My real interest at that point was having the acts on my label," he said. "It was nothing more than that. It wasn't thinking, *Great I'm going to be on TV now.* It was, *I will at least have some artists on my record label.*"

On February 13, 2001, the two now partners in crime went back to meet with Pearson, the U.K. production arm of FremantleMedia. Having limited experience in TV production, Fuller felt he needed a team with more experience putting the show together, expertise for which FremantleMedia received a one-third ownership stake in the Goliath-to-be, a deal that Fuller now calls "the biggest Christmas present they'll ever have, ever, ever, ever."

"Gone with the Wind" is how the Fremantle executive headed his notes from that pitch meeting, since printed in the *Guardian*. The epic scope of an *Idol* season might have come as a shock to viewers, but to the partners in crime, off and running, this was already to be no normal talent hunt. "Never before have 50,000 people auditioned," the notes continue. "Prize money. A huge life." The notes show the basic elements that became *Idol* all in place from this early meeting: the multidisciplinary judging panel, the connections with an active media covering the competition (going as far as to suggest a *Sun* editor serve on the panel), and the role of public voting.

FremantleMedia wasted little time buying into the concept. They quickly got on board, fleshed it out, and pitched the show to both the BBC and ITV (the United Kingdom's two major networks), ultimately finding a home on the latter. "I've never pitched a TV show in my life. But I thought God, this is easy. Literally two minutes in [Claudia Rosencrantz] bought it." Within seven months of that meeting, *Pop Idol* would make its debut on the British airwaves.

"*Popstars* was a big hit," Fuller remembers. "It was a big hit show. So everyone in the music space was like, 'Shit. These shows work.' I was so fast on the mark because I'd already had it worked out and so the whole industry was thinking. . . . It's not so rare that I was ahead of the curve, but I was ready to go."

Chapter 4

POP GOES THE IDOL

In the fall of 2001, as the United Kingdom mourned the attacks on New York and Washington, and braced itself for the fallout to come, the television viewers of Great Britain began to embrace a new form of diversion. Angry, belligerent, fearless—the star of the newly debuted *Pop Idol* was being heralded as the nation's much needed truth-teller. He is "brutally frank in the show, which could eclipse the success of *Popstars*," wrote the *Daily Record*.

Pete Waterman—the sixty-something songwriter/recorder producer dubbed "Slaughterman" by the media—instantly became the breakout star of *Pop Idol*. Singled out as the worthy successor of Nasty Nigel, Waterman gave brutally honest rebukes to the untalented which were winning him legions of fans. "I'm not being rude," he told one, "but you have the worst voice I've ever heard in my life." "So what part of 'You ain't got no talent' would you like explaining any more of that?" he asked another dumbfounded contestant in his garbled syntax.

"Pete was always there to be the bad guy," recalls Cowell. "Pete was my mentor. . . . And he's got a big mouth. And I thought, *This is great. He can soak up everything and I'll just sit beside him.*"

Despite the interest sparked by Waterman's barbs, the show was far from a hit. While the truth-telling bit caught the public eye, *Pop Idol*'s mix of frothy production, over-the-top singing contest, and reality TV seemed out of step with the somber spirit of the moment. More than one reviewer predicted its early disappearance, writing it off as just another one of entertainment's many victims of bad timing. "*Pop Idol* has failed to capture the nation's imagination," wrote a critic in the *Guardian*. "ITV executives will probably blame September 11 for what has— or rather, has not—happened, and claim that water cooler conversation is distracted by more serious affairs. It's a pity such a handy excuse is available, as it may obscure an interesting discovery. Contrary to all TV's calculations, it appears that there is, after all, a limit to how much nastiness we can take."

A decade later it's a limit we're still seeking.

LAUNCHING *POP IDOL* was a gigantic task. For one, there was a need to demonstrate that the show was different from its predecessor of just six months, that—in the word that seemed to come up frequently at the time—it was epic. At *Pop Idol*'s very core was the idea that to find a true superstar would require a search on a massive scale.

Set designer Andy Walmsley recalls crafting a stage that went beyond the normal cheesy setting for a television contest. "I wanted the set to resemble the rock-and-roll touring sets typically seen at Rolling Stones or U2 concerts. That style was very commonplace in an arena setting but not on network TV, so I used a lot of aluminum scaffolding with a dozen or so towers connected together via gantries that were more reminiscent of an oil rig than a glitzy talent competition."

Walmsley's *Pop Idol* design was also the first to "extensively use video walls which were haphazardly scattered all over the set. Now, of course, the use of video screens on sets is in fact overdone, but at the time the sheer volume of screens I used was completely new and it made the set stand out as something different. It worked for the show because we were trying to be a very young contemporary pop show, not a *Star Search*–type, safe, middle-of-the-road show."

For Cowell, the preparations for *Pop Idol* were also an introduction to a whole new world of television production. "When we first started, we spent I think ten, eleven weeks sitting in five-hour development meetings going through this show. Really working on this format. I loved it. That was my favorite part. The whole time, the ideas. It was a really exciting time."

A comedy duo called Ant and Dec (short for Anthony "Ant" McPartlin and Declan "Dec" Donnelly) was hired as the show's hosts, a glib pair who had been performing as a stand-up comedy duo since they were fourteen. Filling out the panel with Cowell and Waterman were Nicki Chapman and Neil "Dr." Fox, a radio DJ.

Pop Idol premiered on October 13, 2001, with an audition episode featuring the now familiar mix of diamonds in the rough and the painfully misguided. Apart from the titters set off by Waterman's first cruel dismissals, the buzz around *Idol*'s early weeks focused on a character made famous on another show. When he had appeared months earlier on *Pop Stars*, Scottish singer Darius Danesh had become the nation's favorite contestant you love to hate. With a smarmy goatee, ponytail, and a stratospheric level of self-confidence, Darius had become the United Kingdom's leading subject of water cooler conversation when he performed a jaw-dropping version of Britney Spears's "Hit Me, Baby, One More Time." His reputation only continued to grow when he publicly expressed outrage and contempt for his dismissal that followed. The return of Darius to the airwaves to audition for *Pop Idol* gave his new home an initial burst of publicity. "He's back—and he is still as cringeworthy," proclaimed the Scottish *Daily Record*.

While the early audiences were merely average by British standards, the groundswell was quietly beginning. Beyond the Darius spectacle, another singer caught the public's eye in that first audition episode, one Gareth Gates. The fantastically cute seventeen-year-old suffered from a lifelong stammer, rendering him barely able to squeak out his name. When he sang, however, breaking into Westlife's "Flying Without Wings," the stammer magically vanished. "You sing brilliantly," Waterman gushed. Sensing the power of a storyline in this medium, even Cowell congratulated him: "What you've done today is unbelievably brave." The draw of Gates's teenage good looks, his obstacle-beating backstory, and the discovery of a raw, unknown preternatural talent took hold almost immediately. Gareth fan clubs sprang up around the nation and stutterers support groups announced their backing of the young singer.

What would become *Idol*'s showcase moment, when the hopefuls submit themselves to the judgment of the professionals, took a bit of working out. Cowell recalls of the first audition shoot, "We hadn't really thought about how the audition process was going to work and we sat down and I asked Nigel, 'How do you want to do it?' Initially he wanted the contestants to sing, leave the room, and we'd deliberate and then they'd be invited back into the room. I think I remember saying to Pete Waterman, 'This isn't a real audition. You've got to tell them, as you would in any audition.' I've auditioned kids all my life and this felt wrong and we changed it to what it famously became, which is you sing in the room and you get a comment."

Despite these blips of interest, the ratings remained mediocre. It was not until the format turned to the semifinals that the first stirrings of the sleeping giant were seen. A staggering 1.3 million people cast votes on who would make it through to the next stage, 62 percent of them voting for Gareth Gates.

But Gates wasn't the only star. On November 11, just one month after the series debut, the first article about Simon Cowell appeared. "Women Fans Fall for Mr. Nasty" declared *Sunday People*. "The record boss is being chased by besotted women wanting to get to know him better—despite his sarcastic comments and cutting remarks to young wannabes on the hit ITV talent show. Single Simon admitted last night: 'It's certainly come as a surprise. I thought that by being outspoken it would create a lot of animosity but it has had the opposite effect.'"

While it was Waterman's zingers that attracted the greatest notice, the public was noticing that beside him on the panel was a man whose put-downs were delivered with conviction like nothing ever before seen in the public space, a man without an ounce of self-doubt whose very being radiated certitude. Nasty Nigel's zingers had felt more playful than deadly, coming as they did from an older, more established figure whose attitude to talent was not, in fact, terribly nasty. ("It was a performance," he says today. "Nasty Nigel was a character more than me as a person.") Waterman's taunts had wafted with traces of wobbliness, touches of that most beloved of British stereotypes, the aging eccentric. But Cowell's barbs were precision guided missiles, delivered without mercy and packing the explosive force of a thousand nuclear blasts.

Lythgoe tells of Cowell's finding his way into the role: "Peter Waterman was outrageous. He was fun. He was sharp. Simon had to learn certain things. I think that Simon was very nervous to start with and was a little lost with what was going on. We had words about it and I said, 'You've got to take control of this show. Be the judge.' Simon learned very quickly. He learned how to handle people and how to direct them. In the early stages, he needed inspiring. I've heard people say that I fed him lines but he would fight lines. If you gave him a line he would fight it or find a way of putting it into his own words. He was never going to take words."

"I wasn't trying to be mean. It was just a hilarious audition," Cowell said. "Just like I'd been doing all my life. It was like seeing my day job on TV. I thought it was hysterical."

Coming as they did in a time of anxiety and uncertainty, after a feckless decade that had come to a crashing halt with 9/11 and the end of the boom market, it was a voice the public longed to hear.

By the end of *Pop Idol*'s second month on the air, the spotlight had shifted. "Simon Cowell is the new pantomime villain of the music industry," wrote the *Daily Telegraph*. "As the most outspoken judge in ITV's *Pop Idol* program, Sarcastic Simon is the dasher of dreams, reducing young hopefuls to tears with his blunt assessments of their talents. 'Are you serious? You can't sing, you can't dance,' he witheringly informs teenage wannabes who have just put on the performance of a lifetime.

"The forty-two-year-old's credentials for deciding who has got what it takes are based on past successes with such musical talents as the Teletubbies, Mighty Morphin Power Rangers, Zig & Zag, Robson and Jerome, and boy bands Five and Westlife. While none of his signings are likely to collect the Mercury Prize for their artistic contribution to music, over ten years Cowell has achieved sales above 25 million albums and scored more than seventy Top 30 records, including fifteen number one singles. 'I'm paid based purely on the profits I make,' Cowell candidly admits."

Mr. Nasty had become a star who, for the first time in his career, had a public image to consider. And consider it he would. Cowell claimed that he had gone on the show just to secure talent for his label; nevertheless, once he stepped onto that center stage, he never looked back.

If ever a person could be prepared for fame and all that came with it, it was Simon Cowell. Perhaps unique among the world's mega-stars, he has not shown one moment of regret since becoming an internationally known figure. Having made stars, dated them, lived with them, and grown up around them, he was intimately aware of all that came with celebrity. For twenty years, Simon Cowell had been involved in every aspect of the shadowy business of creating stars, from spotting the talent, to finding the right material, to selecting the moment to hit the marketplace, to overseeing careers. He had seen how the magical alchemy could transform people into stars, and he had seen how it could go wrong.

In the modern media age, no single person has stepped from the role of star maker into the role of star on anything close to this scale. No entertainment executive has ever become as renowned a star as Simon Cowell would. Cowell gave all signs of enjoying the role change. Asked by the *Guardian* whether he was surprised by all the attention he was receiving, Cowell answered, " 'Not in the slightest.' He runs a loving hand through his hair. 'When you're hot, you're hot.' "

AS HIS PUBLIC profile increased, Cowell took action to make sure that the story the public would hear would be the one *he* wanted told. In January, Cowell engaged the services of one Max Clifford, a publicist and image consultant known for defending the good names of some of the United Kingdom's most controversial figures, including Mohamed Fayed, David Copperfield, and internationally reviled *Big Brother* star Jade Goody. An article in *PR Week* announcing the hiring noted that "Clifford's first job after being contacted by Cowell was to quash untrue allegations in the tabloids about Cowell's links with a certain fallen pop promoter and sex offender," a clear reference to Cowell's friend and mentor Jonathan King, at the time serving the first year of his prison sentence. Asked in another interview with the *Guardian* why he hired Clifford, Cowell responded, "One simple word: 'protection.' "

Which begs the question, protection from what?

Where the rumors began is hard to determine from this distance. Having passed the forty-year-old mark when *Idol* began, Cowell had had a handful of semipublic romantic relationships with singers and model types, including his first star, Sinitta, and a former Miss Nude UK named Jackie St. Clair. However, his lack of permanent commitment paired with a certain campy mise-en-scène—heavy on the famed skintight T-shirts and high-waisted pants—certainly seems to have raised the question as to Cowell's sexuality.

In the months after Cowell signed on with Max Clifford, British TV personality Louis Theroux profiled the publicist in an episode of his BBC series *When Louis Met. . . .* In the episode, Clifford attempted to demonstrate his work on Cowell's behalf, showing the host newspaper articles in which Cowell's alleged exes discuss their relationships with him. Theroux cut off Clifford with a direct question:

Theroux: *I had always thought Simon was gay and you're talking about kiss and tells with women. Is he gay?*
Clifford: *No.*
Theroux : *Would you tell me if he were?*
Clifford: *No, I wouldn't if it was something that we were going to keep quiet.*

Among the controversial assignments Clifford has undertaken, it has been alleged that he has manufactured false relationships for clients who wished to cover up their sexuality. In the interview, Clifford discussed the practice in a theoretical way:

Theroux: *If a TV performer were gay and you wanted to defray that or put a stop to it, then what would you . . .*
Clifford: *The most effective way would be for me to create a relationship.*
Theroux: *(Theroux opens a newspaper to a story featuring the confessions of another alleged Cowell ex.) Like . . . for example . . . this one?*
Clifford: *No, not like this one, it would have to be a long-term one.*
Theroux: *Really? (reads newspaper headline): "Naughty Simon was my sex idol in bed."*
Clifford: *He's the one who really scored.*

Later in the episode, Cowell himself strolled in as the conversation continued.

Clifford: *He's asking me if you're gay.*
Theroux: *I asked him. It's the word on the street*
Cowell: *The word on the street, what does that mean?*
Theroux: *I can't remember where I heard it but I always assumed you were gay.*
Cowell *(miffed): I love that . . . the word on the street. . . .*
Theroux: *Then you deny it.*
Cowell: *(looks at the camera) I deny it.*

Still later in the interview, Clifford pointed to a story that had just appeared in the *Express* about a fling Cowell was having with Georgina Law, an exotic dancer from the Spearmint Rhino gentlemen's club. Theroux interrupted, pointing out that Spearmint Rhino is in fact also a client of Clifford's—a convenient coincidence.

The article quotes Cowell's brazen assertion of heterosexuality. "She [Georgina] was a magnet for me—that's why I spend a lot of time in [lap dancing club] Spearmint Rhino. But now I get my own dances in the privacy of my own home. I'm a lucky boy and we get on extremely well."

Whatever the truth about Cowell—Jonathan King wrote, "He's not [gay] but he's the campest straight person I know"—the stories and the speculation about the United Kingdom's newest sex symbol were only serving to fuel the *Pop Idol* fires, which, as 2001 ended, were flaring out of control.

By the time the show transitioned to the final rounds, the press was jumping all over the storylines offered by the final eleven who made it onto Andy Walmsley's arena-like stage. There was still the mass appeal of Gareth Gates, which only continued to grow in these middle weeks as he remained the odds-on favorite to win, not to mention the obvious favorite of Judge Cowell himself. But there were also the continuing antics of perpetual antihero Darius Danesh, an Irish girl next door, a plus-sized singer who it was reported had dumped his fiancée due to an entanglement with another contestant, a handful of bombshells, and a coolly charismatic singer named Will Young who had quietly begun rising in the odds-makers rankings.

Young had, in fact, leaped out of the pack, like Gareth Gates, thanks to Simon Cowell. But it wasn't the judge's support that propelled Young, it was his scorn. On a late November episode, Cowell dismissed Young's rendition of "Light My Fire" as "distinctly average." After a female contestant had been driven to tears early in the show by the judges' put-downs, Young sensed that the time was perhaps right to fight back. Staring down Mr. Nasty, he fired, "I think it's nice that you have given an opinion on this show. In previous shows you haven't, you've just projected insults. It's your opinion. I don't agree with it. I don't think it was average. I don't think you could ever call it average."

Young became a folk hero overnight. "Dark horse William, seemingly a no hoper until he stood up to bullyboy judge Simon Cowell, blossomed live onstage" wrote This Is Lancashire. The tension between Young and Cowell simmered through the season. Young pledged if he won "not to wear my trousers at an unacceptable waist height," a reference to the fashion statement that was bringing Cowell unwanted renown—his habit of wearing pants pulled up practically to his chin.

The Cowell-centric subplots continued to grow. Offscreen, he fought with Jay Kay, the lead singer of Jamiraquai, who called the *Idol* judges "money-grabbing twits." Cowell fired back: "It sickens me to hear champagne socialists like Jay Kay sitting in his big mansion patronizing people. I challenge him to take six months out from his life to help someone become a star. Then he can criticize." He insulted the United Kingdom's reigning rocker in chief Bono after the U2 star criticized the rise of television-driven talents. "He says 'I think it is harming the music industry—this is all cheating.' Fine, he's got millions in the bank—why doesn't he give somebody an opportunity. All these people want to do is take. It's staggering—so hypocritical." He fought with the manager of pop star Robbie Williams, who worried that *Idol*'s singers were being "humiliated" and that the show was "destroying them with really nasty comments that are, in my view, quite unnecessary." Cowell brushed the critique aside with an offhanded, "Having a tough time for two minutes on camera—so what? If you don't want that, go to another talent show." He became a one-man militia against self-indulgent and spoiled celebrities who had lost touch with the public.

As the season progressed, Cowell's on-air battles with his former mentor Waterman became so intense that executive producer Lythgoe felt compelled to issue a tongue-in-cheek rebuke. "I reminded them that the talent was appearing in front of them and they should not hijack the show with their own petty quarrels. . . . The pair of them acted like a slightly senile bickering old couple who had never had enough courage to get divorced twenty years ago."

By the time *Idol* returned from Christmas break and entered its final months, the press, which had given the show only moderate attention when it debuted, now provided blanket coverage to every highlight and lowlight, offstage rumor and onstage controversy. The shape of this reporting, driven by the cutthroat world of British tabloids, would soon become the template to reshape coverage for American media consumers, who were still used to more genteel reporting of its television shows.

The media covered every outbreak of Gareth's stutter with heart-warming dispatches on his attempts to overcome the handicap. They covered the complaints of an eliminated contestant who claimed he had only lost because he had been outed as gay to *Idol* voters. A newspaper in Northern England wrote an editorial and began a crusade, demanding justice for an eliminated local girl, saying she had lost due to problems with the phone lines. From backstage, the press reported the contestants were "cracking up" under the strain. They covered the tension between the families of Gareth and Will, the former's complaints that the latter didn't applaud for singers other than their own son. They reported that from behind bars, Jonathan King was watching and had begun his own prison *Idol* competition with his fellow inmates. They dutifully wrote that Will Young had thrown "sex parties" while in college. They covered rumors of romance between Gareth and a female contestant, studying their body language for signs of intimacy. It was a circus that extended far beyond the show's on-screen episodes, spilling over to become a daily soap opera played out in the tabloids.

And the ratings, which began on a mediocre footing three months before, took off. By the end of January, ten million people tuned in to *Pop Idol*, a massive 48-percent share of the TV audience. The epic that Simon Fuller had promised had actually, to the surprise of all but perhaps him, come to pass.

As they approached the finale, a showdown between sentimental favorite Gareth Gates and the cool lion slayer Will Young, Cowell made no secret of who he thought should win, saying in interviews that he felt Gates deserved the prize. In the final week, the pair toured the nation, each in his own campaign-style "battle bus," shaking hands with the public and spreading word of their candidacies. Preparing for the big day, Fuller announced an unprecedented move for a TV show: He had booked London's massive 90,000-seat Wembley Stadium, the second-largest arena in all Europe, a venue typically reserved for only the most proven of musical acts.

Tickets sold out in two days.

The finale was seen by nineteen million viewers, a breathtaking 59 percent of the TV audience. In the end, Will Young squeaked to victory after his dazzling repeat performance of the Doors' "Light My Fire," earning 4.6 million votes to Gates's 4.1 million. The volume of calls was so massive that it caused phone outages in thirty sections of Britain, with emergency services forced to fall back on CB radios to communicate.

Immediately after the victory Will Young was whisked off to Havana to shoot the video for his victory song, to be rushed to the marketplace with all due haste. Despite the audience's verdict, Cowell groused in postshow interviews, "The final vote has been irrelevant—Gareth Gates is *the* major pop star to have come out of this show." This was, as it turned out, something of a self-serving assessment. After crossing swords with Mr. Nasty all season, Young had refused to sign on to Cowell's BMG label, defeating what had initially been the point of the exercise for Cowell. A contract was hastily arranged for Young with RCA, where he would become one of Britain's major solo stars of the past decade. Gates also had an enormous launch on the pop charts, his debut album going double platinum. His second album, however, failed to catch fire and he was ultimately dropped by BMG, going on to a career in musical theater on the West End.

Reflecting on Gates's defeat today, Cowell says, "I always took the view that if I'm going to judge the show, I'm allowed to have a favorite if I want. I can't pretend to be neutral, because you're not. You always prefer one person to somebody else and not like another as much. And I liked him from day one and rooted for him and was frustrated when he lost.

"Will Young was a good singer and people liked him. It was just one of those situations where it was like a really good election battle. It was really, really close and you had two opposing sides. But in a weird way that's what made the show so successful year one . . . people passionately cared about both contestants. They were like me, genuinely upset or thrilled when the results came through. No one was indifferent about it. But we couldn't have designed it better if we tried. We just got lucky big-time on that first show."

In the hangover after the show, Cowell made a statement suggesting he was ready to move on from *Idol* and didn't necessarily see himself returning. "A few years ago, I got a couple of big awards for my work, but I went home depressed. It means nothing to me when things are based on something that has happened. I am only interested in the future and what I am going to get."

For the moment, however, no one was taking such talk seriously.

Fuller, Cowell, Lythgoe, and Thames TV had just launched the biggest thing anyone had seen since, well, since the Spice Girls, and the idea that anyone would walk away was ludicrous. There were records to put out, a book and video tie-in to get to market. The Wembley concert was expanded into a national tour.

Then on February 18, eleven days after the finale, an announcement appeared in the papers. *Idol* was heading to America.

Chapter 5

THE CROSSING

There's a legend about *Idol*'s journey to America that has been told so often it has come to be accepted as fact. It goes something like this: Simon Fuller had pitched *Pop Idol* to television networks in America and every last one of them slammed the door in his face. It seemed as if the chances for a U.S. version were finished until, as Anderson Cooper told it on a *60 Minutes* segment in 2007, "the daughter of Rupert Murdoch, CEO and chairman of News Corporation, Fox's parent company, loved the English version of *Idol* and convinced her dad to buy the show."

It's a fantastic story, a heroic tale of a pop culture phenomenon snatched from the jaws of oblivion by a visionary young woman who just happened to be a media mogul's daughter. Truth rarely fits so neatly into a nice little package, however, and the story of *American Idol*'s journey is far more complicated than the myth suggests.

When *Idol* crossed the Atlantic in early 2002 it chose a particularly perilous moment for the trip. In the years leading up to the new millennium, network ratings had been going in one direction, straight down. Throughout the 1990s, the major networks had been hit by a series of seemingly fatal plagues. TIVO allowed viewers to fast-forward over commercials, decimating the major networks' financial base. Cable channels were proliferating, taking audience share away from the once untouchable three-way monopoly enjoyed by ABC, NBC, and CBS. Worse still, those cable networks, once the home of bargain basement offerings barely above public access programming, were now stealing the thunder, with shows like HBO's *The Sopranos* and *Sex and the City* winning the critics' praise, not to mention the Emmy Awards that were once the big three's sole property.

Although you can't pay the rent with awards or critical praise, and ratings for HBO were minuscule compared to those for the major networks, the landscape was changing—*fast*—and it was becoming harder and harder for new shows to break through the increasingly cluttered media noise to establish themselves. Suddenly cable networks were able to deliver niche programming that could go outside the traditional lines of the networks' broad audiences and formulas while the big three were still using playbooks that had barely been updated since the 1950s.

By the end of the decade, the networks' ratings were dominated largely by a handful of old-fashioned properties that were long past their prime. Shows like *Friends*, *ER*, *The West Wing*, and *Everybody Loves Raymond* still chugged along, as did the *Law & Order* franchises. But in the face of competition from cable, these shows felt tame and predictable. Each new season since the mid-1990s had come to resemble a World War I charge out of the trenches into a line of machine guns; the bulk of the shows were mercilessly mowed down and quickly replaced with fresh cannon fodder.

In *Desperate Networks*, *New York Times* reporter Bill Carter's account of the era, he writes that the industry was coming to believe that the networks' slumping fortunes were no longer just the natural ups and downs of the programming cycle, but an irreversible slide to doom; the fate of the Soviet Union was all that lay ahead for the once powerful major networks. He wrote that one network's struggles were taken as "the proof" that television had changed irrevocably, that a network really on the skids could no longer turn around its fortunes, that a network could simply fail again and again until it ceased to matter as a competitive entity.

Then there was reality or, as it was known in the industry, "unscripted programming."

From the dawn of television, three basic formats had dominated programming: comedy, drama, and variety, the latter dating back to 1948 and Ted Mack's amateur hour. Since the late 1970s, though, variety had all but disappeared from prime time. In television's early years, giant variety spectacles like *The Ed Sullivan Show* dominated the cultural conversation and prime-time game shows were a viewing staple. In the 1970s, variety shows remained an integral part of the network formula, with shows like *Donny & Marie*, *The Sonny & Cher Show*, and *The Carol Burnett Show* drawing huge audiences. By the late 1970s, however, the format had descended into camp, most infamously demonstrated by the *Pink Lady and Jeff* show, hosted by a comedian and a giggling language-challenged pair of Japanese pop singers. As the 1980s came around, music and variety had all but vanished from prime time.

One major exception to the rule was *Star Search*, which debuted in 1983. A gaudy competition hosted by a tuxedoed Ed McMahon, the show pitted actors, singers, dancers, comedians, and "spokesmodels" against each other in a search for the world's greatest talent. Aired in syndication, the show retained enough of a following to stay alive for twelve years, launching the careers of a handful of midlevel stars, including singers Sam Harris and Tiffany. For most, however, the cheesy *Star Search* remained a dubious guilty pleasure. By the time it went off the air in 1995, it seemed to have poisoned the well for one of TV's oldest formats.

Throughout the 1990s, as the networks' stalwarts calcified, new forms of programming dubbed "reality" found their way into American homes. The phrase was a bit of a catchall, describing everything from game shows to competitions to documentary-style shows such as *The Real World*. But its increasing use showed that programming outside the traditional comedies and dramas was gaining foothold. Shows such as *America's Funniest Home Videos* and *COPS* had found their way onto network slates. On CBS, a documentary-style battle of wits called *Survivor* had become a certified hit.

For the fledging Fox network, reality had proven the key to breaking through the media landscape and attracting new viewers. Mike Darnell, Fox's impish head of alternative entertainment, a determined iconoclast given to dressing like a bejeweled marching band, pioneered the rule-breaking brazen new style of television. A former child actor who had appeared in his youth on 1970s staples such as *Welcome Back, Kotter* and *Kojak,* the young man dreamed of following in the footsteps of NBC's legendary chief Brandon Tartikoff. He found his way through the production door working on the news team for Fox's local L.A. affiliate, and shot up the ranks when he put together a segment of *TV Stars: Where Are They Now?*, featuring *Batman*'s former leading men. That piece caught the eye of Barry Diller, then head of the Fox network. Eventually, Darnell became director of specials for the young network, which did not yet have a full-blown reality division. He had his first hit with *Alien Autopsy: (Fact or Fiction?)*, a quasi-documentary that debated the veracity of a bootlegged video purporting to show an extraterrestrial corpse being dissected by earthling scientists.

Throughout the 1990s, with shows like *Temptation Island* and *Who Wants to Marry a Millionaire?*, Darnell and Fox found that by continually reaching outside of the public's expectations, by pushing the staid boundaries of network programming, they stampeded their way into the center of America's cultural dialogue with love-them or hate-them programs you had to watch. By the end of the 1990s, these programs had helped put Fox on the map, adding a fourth network to the ranks of the big three for the first time since the dawn of television.

But reality had a downside. It was one thing to create waves, to shock an audience into viewing. Keeping them shocked—getting them to return week after week once the outlandish became familiar—was quite another.

"The first time you view it," explained Preston Beckman, Fox TV's head of scheduling, "nobody knows what the fuck it is. You know, like with *Survivor* now everybody knows, Oh, here's how you play the game. So, it's a phenomenally well-to-do show but there's nothing like that first time. I think that's what happened with *Joe Millionaire* and that's what happened with *Temptation Island*."

In the years before *Idol*, ABC had learned this rule in an especially harrowing manner. In 1998, the network had scored a monster hit with the prime-time quiz show *Who Wants to Be a Millionaire*. Seemingly drunk on the show's success, the following season they practically turned over their entire schedule to the quiz show, running *Millionaire* a shocking five nights a week. The audience quickly overdosed on the novelty and turned away as fast as they had come, leaving ABC, which had cancelled and halted development on a slew of shows to make room for it, with barely a heartbeat.

Likewise, by 2001, Fox looked back on a decade of hits and found that after many successes, the cupboard was nearly bare. The network's attempts to market itself to male viewers with edgier, darker programming seemed to have run its course. Its once buzzed-about new show, *24*, was receiving good press, but had yet to find a major audience.

Then came September 11. If that day changed much for the nation, it changed everything for network programming. The attacks on New York and Washington ignited a bomb under the nation's already tenuous economy, sending the ad market reeling, decimating the funding base for new programming.

At the same time, the boom in the shock value–centric brand of reality suddenly evaporated in favor of comfort programming. Wrote Cox News service at the time, "Sure, millions of folks still tune in to *Survivor* to check on the contestants in Africa, but the once-deafening buzz has faded to near silence. *Who Wants to Be a Millionaire* has sunk like a stone, and *Temptation Island 2* arrived to a hurricane of indifference."

"After September 11, there was speculation of massive changes in popular tastes," said Tim Brooks, a vice president of research for Lifetime cable network in an interview. "Instead, we've just moved to the familiar and safe. People now seem to prefer plots and performers they know and are comfortable with. . . . We're in for a long period of shows that are reassuring."

And at this moment, a little singing competition called *Idol* arrived.

GAIL BERMAN, THEN vice president of Fox Programming, later to become president, tells the story this way: "We were proposing in the press that we were going to offer year-round programming. Year-round programming was our mantra." This meant stocking the summer months with fresh content, not just filling it with reruns as networks had traditionally done. "The problem was that we didn't have any money to pay for year-round programming."

Idol had been around the block in U.S. programming. In this much the legend is correct. Even before *Pop Idol* had launched in the United Kingdom, Fuller, Cowell, and ludicrously, a third Simon—a Fremantle-Media executive named Simon Jones—traveled to Los Angeles to pitch the show for the American airwaves. Every major network slammed the door in their faces.

Cowell remembers, "We genuinely believed we had a hit format and the first person we walked into was going to buy it. And of course it didn't work out that way. We had some awful meetings. They were so bad they were actually laughable. I remember saying to Simon Jones after one meeting, 'It cannot get worse than this.' "

As it turns out, what had helped them in the United Kingdom was hurting them in America. Whereas the success of *Popstars* had opened the doors for *Pop Idol* in the United Kingdom, its relative failure in the United States had done just the opposite. In 2001, *Pop Stars* had debuted on the WB Network, where it failed to catch fire. The show attracted a modest following, and the band it produced—Eden's Crush—went on to put out a decent-selling record, but by and large, the show's reception did little to fuel the idea that there was much public appetite for a TV singing contest. Another music-oriented reality show, *Making the Band*, likewise had met with mediocre results.

Contrary to legend, the executives at Fox were not blind to the success of *Pop Idol*, but it had hit the U.S. market at an inopportune moment. "There had been a lot of shows in this area in the marketplace and they hadn't performed particularly well," says Gail Berman, ". . . so there wasn't any real reason why anyone would go crazy on the concept." But Fox was still seeking a summer show that could come fully paid for, and with the Coca-Cola connection kept the conversations with *Idol* alive, if on life support.

Meanwhile, *Idol*'s producers, unwilling to give up, were scrambling to raise the money to make the show happen in the United States. Cecile Frot-Coutaz, the Belgian native who was head of FremantleMedia's North American production arm and who would oversee *American Idol,* and become the keeper at the brand in the years ahead, remembers traveling to New York with others from the company to persuade advertisers to come aboard. "I went to see this lady who represented an auto maker. She said, 'Well, do you think you can feature cars in this?' We answered, 'Oh, of course we can feature cars.' At that point we would have done anything to get it off the ground and anything to get the money. We were just throwing out ideas on how we could get the cars into the singing competition. When we left, we looked at each other, we're like, 'Boy . . .' We were very aware of what we had just done, which is just promise something that we weren't sure we were going to be able to deliver just to get the money."

They brought aboard Sony as their partner on the record side, persuading them to invest money up front to cover the show's production costs. It was a risky move for the label; *Pop Idol*'s first season was still playing out, so the idea that people would buy records based on a TV talent contest was untested.

It was at this moment, while the *Idol* team was pulling together its funding, that Elisabeth and Rupert Murdoch had their legendary call. Murdoch would later say he was also told of *Idol* by one of his editors in London when he called to check in on what was hot over there. Shortly after, Rupert Murdoch got in touch with the network—not to tell them about this great new show his daughter had tipped him off to, but to find out what they were doing about it. Something had changed, people at Fox noted, and at that moment, signing *Idol* became a major priority for Murdoch, and hence for Fox. Murdoch called Fox Entertainment Chairman Peter Chernin who, in turn, called Gail Berman. "What are we doing with that show?" Berman recalls Chernin asking. "And I reminded him that we were waiting to find out whether Coca-Cola is in or out. As a full sponsor of the show." After hearing her response later that day, even though the network still didn't have an advertiser-supported situation, Chernin instructed Berman to close the deal with or without Coke.

Frot-Coutaz remembers getting the call. "All right, there's a change coming from the top. We're buying eleven episodes and we're paying for them. That was a complete change overnight. So, all the initial conversations with the auto maker went out the window. Fox had a relationship with Ford, so Ford came in."

Fox, however, decided they wanted more than just the show. They wanted its star. "We had seen footage and of course we knew for sure that Simon Cowell had to be there. Period," Darnell says. The sensation he caused was "immediate. From like the moment we saw footage we knew that he had to be part of the show."

Cowell's brutal behavior called to mind that of many Hollywood moguls. To Fox TV President (Berman's then boss) Sandy Grushow, in particular, the resemblance in tone between Cowell and legendary manager/producer Sandy Gallin was uncanny—so much so that Gallin was summoned for a conversation about coming aboard as a judge himself. Not yet ready to make the leap to stardom, Gallin declined and the show went forward with his British alter ego.

But Cowell got a case of cold feet. After signing on, he worried that he didn't know the American recording world and that his persona would not translate to the more politically correct U.S. airwaves. One week before *Idol* was to start shooting, Cowell announced to all that he would not be making the trip after all. Cowell recalls, "I kind of went along with everything and then it finally hit me one day. . . . I remember being at a meeting about my record label. And I had so much to do outside of being on a TV show. I remember calling my lawyer and I said, 'I don't want to do it. I haven't signed the contract. Get me out of it.' . . .

"Then a friend of mine, a girl named Nicola, called me and she said, 'I think you're making a big mistake because if it's a hit you'll wish you were on it and if it's not a hit, you'll think you could have made it a hit. So my advice is, take a deep breath and do it.'

"And then Ken Warwick, the same evening, called me. And I'd gotten on real well with Ken on the first show. And he asked me what I was nervous about and I said, 'In America, do we have to dilute the whole controversy? Do we have to go by their rules? Because if we do, I genuinely don't want to do this. I want to make sure that if we do this we do the show we want and not what an American network would want.'

"But he said, 'Simon, I absolutely one hundred percent guarantee after the meeting I had with the network, you can do whatever you want. You have free rein. Nobody's going to tell you what to do and I'm there to look after you.' So I thought about it there and said, 'Okay, let's give it a go.' "

Recalls Gail Berman, "We never thought that it was going to change the entire fate of the network. There wasn't a single person who went into it thinking that."

THERE'S A RICH history of foreign shows getting lost in translation on the journey to America, their rough edges being so smoothed over that their entire allure was glossed away. That had largely been the story of *Popstars'* translation. The style and aesthetic of British and European TV was more brassy and brazen: hosts with pompadour hairstyles and brightly colored silk suits, sets decorated with dripping chandeliers. The effect to American eyes could be something like Liberace by way of David Lynch. And then there was the matter of tone. Compared to the reassuring, polished scripts in the States—worked on by a team of writers and subject to round after round of executive notes and revision—British shows could feel alarmingly ramshackle and laissez-faire. *Pop Idol*, while marking a step forward production-wise, certainly arose out of this tradition. So in thinking about how to make *Idol* palatable to an American audience, the Fox team got busy planning what changes would need to be made.

However, since making the decision to import *Idol*, Rupert Murdoch would continue to exert an influence on the show, the consequences of which would reverberate for years. In a meeting with the Fox executive team, Darnell began to lay out tweaks and changes, many of them, one participant remembered, pushing the show in the traditional Darnell/Fox reality direction of shock value and sensationalism. In the middle of his pitch, Murdoch suddenly slammed his fist down on the desk—never a good sign from the mercurial mogul—and blared, "You Americans, you think you've got to change everything! The show was perfectly good! You don't change a thing!"

The man had spoken.

The U.S. version of *Pop Idol* was to be *Pop Idol* in look, feel, format, theme song—even opening credit sequence. If the show was to remain the same, the first thing that would have to be boxed up and brought across the seas was the production team led by Nigel Lythgoe. American television production was traditionally an extremely closed circle. To have someone run a network show who had not worked their way up the network ladder, who didn't understand "the way we do things here," who didn't have ancient relationships with the network executives, was almost unheard of. Yet dancer/choreographer/iconic personality Nigel Lythgoe was about to be given the keys to the U.S. prime-time airwaves. He was joined at the helm by yet another British dancer, Ken Warwick, a friend from dance school, whose background included the U.K. *Gladiators* series and who had served as the producer of *Pop Idol*. Not entirely able to set their minds at ease about the British invasion, however, Fox insisted that a third showrunner be added, Brian Gadinsky, a veteran U.S. TV hand who had overseen the athletic competition show *American Gladiators*.

Unfortunately for Murdoch, he was forced to swallow one very basic change right off the bat: the name. As part of the settlement with the *Popstars* owners, the word "Pop" was not to be used in any of *Idol*'s overseas incarnations. Debating various versions, one executive had pushed to title the show *America's Idol*, but Darnell retorted, "That sounds like a fireman or a policeman or a hero. That's not what the show is. . . . This is more about becoming an idol *in* America." Darnell hit upon *American Idol* as the proper alchemy that would capture the show's ambitions. "I don't believe it was ultra patriotic at the time. I really don't. I think it was just a good idea," Darnell said.

Mr. Murdoch, however, was not thrilled. "Rupert was very unhappy with the fact that we couldn't call it *Pop Idol*," one executive recalls. "He thought the name *American Idol* was ridiculous." While many among the Brits looked on the idea of nationalist branding as jingoist—*Pop Idol* had come from the more internationalist Europop tradition—American culture has no such timidity about waving the flag, particularly in those days after 9/11.

Slapping *American* on the door of the U.S. incarnation in many ways sealed its fate. In the coming years, *Idol* would become not just our national epic, at a time when the nation needed a feel-good national epic and a full-scale variety show celebration of America. The annual audition road trip to the heartland would itself focus on every aspect of the American musical tradition, from Motown to country rock to Miami Latin rhythms. *American Idol* would be very much American.

One element of the show definitely did *not* change, and for very good reason. When the show's logo was first designed for *Pop Idol*, the blue oval with old-fashioned cursive lettering in white evoked something of an old-time jukebox look. But the resemblance would prove highly fortuitous between that design and the logo of a certain American auto maker. For years since, the *Idol* logo has sat atop the set, ostentatiously evoking the banner of one of its signature sponsors, the Ford Motor Company. Curiously, the resemblance is almost never noticed or commented on until, at the occasional Ford-sponsored *Idol* event, a backdrop will display the ovals side by side and the almost subliminal reference will, like the subject of a Magic Eye painting, suddenly leap to the surface.

Soon after signing the deal, another change fell upon the *Idol* crew. But once again, it was a forced change that, in years to come, the team would thank God for. The problem was in revealing the voting results. In the United Kingdom, after each episode of *Pop Idol* aired, the audience was given a couple of hours to cast its votes, at which point the show would pop back on the ITV airwaves to reveal the verdict. There was no way to do this in a country spread out over four time zones. The West Coast couldn't possibly vote in time to reveal the results while the East Coast was still awake.

Beckman remembers receiving the alarm bell call from Darnell. "'Look, we've got a problem.' So I went down to Darnell's office. They couldn't figure out how to announce the results. If we announce the results at the end of the evening that would be excluding the entire West

Coast and Hawaii and Alaska. I do remember someone saying, 'Well, maybe we just don't let the West Coast vote.' I said they were out of their minds. Then I pitched the idea of a second night.

"I called it a results show. I said, 'Add a show that you do the results. Do a half hour.' We even talked about doing like five minutes or something." Ultimately, they accepted the need to shoot an entire second night every week.

IT WAS MID-FEBRUARY by the time the deal was signed, which gave the team a mere two months to put the show together if they were to make it to air by summer. With a million details to be sorted out, the first major order of business would be filling out the judging panel. With the edict not to change a thing from the British version, that meant finding three new judges to share the panel with Cowell.

Knowing that they had a very potent force in Cowell, one likely to be shocking to U.S. audiences, the team sought to soften the blow as much as possible with the rest of the panel. The idea was to cushion Cowell's nuclear blasts in as much sweetness and light as they could get their hands on. "Non-threatening" is how Lythgoe remembers his job description for the other judges. Berman recalls as well, "We wanted believability in the music business. We wanted authenticity. We knew that we wanted only people who had professional credibility. We wanted different personality types."

A casting call was put out and faces from the music industry began to troop through the production offices. Among those who came in was a former bassist currently working as a record producer—Randy Jackson. "No one knew Randy," says Berman. The then portly figure sat with Lythgoe, Warwick, Darnell, and Berman for a get-acquainted meeting. "We talked about the music business. We didn't have them do trial judging. It was just like 'Could you talk to somebody, tell a young person—' and a lot of people felt that they couldn't do that and some people felt that they would be too harsh. Randy had a really nice way about him when he came in. He was a bass player and had done some producing and talked about Mariah and talked about Whitney and some people that he had worked with. He had a really nice way about him."

A consensus quickly formed that the affable Jackson would make an "unthreatening" yet knowledgeable counterweight to Cowell, and the second seat was filled. Cowell recalled meeting him over lunch shortly after arriving for shooting: "It was one of those rare occasions in life when, within seconds, you find yourself totally at ease with another human being. The first thing that struck me about him was his personality. 'Sunny' didn't begin to describe him—he could light up a room—any room, no matter what the size—without being irritating."

Then there was Paula.

Abdul had spent almost twenty years in the public eye before *Idol*. After a youth spent largely in dance studios, she auditioned to become one of the legendary Laker Girls during her freshman year at Cal State Northridge. Winning a slot on the team, she ascended to the head cheerleader role—the squad's chief choreographer—within three months and promptly dropped out of school. A couple of years later, Abdul was spotted by members of the Jackson family entourage, cheering at a game. She was recruited to work with the family as a choreographer, an association that ultimately culminated in her arranging the dance moves on Janet Jackson's videos for her *Control* album.

By the late 1980s, Abdul took a shot in front of the camera and dipped into her savings to record a demo of herself singing. Her exuberant manner and dance prowess proved to be a potent combination in the still early days of MTV. Still, her debut album, *Forever Your Girl*, got off to a slow start. At sixty-two weeks, it was, in fact, the record holder for slowest climb to the top of any LP in history. Eventually, driven by Abdul's energetic videos, the album became a massive hit. It sold twelve million copies in the U.S. and produced four number one singles, the second most of any album in history. With her even bigger follow-up, Abdul was certified as one of the strongest forces in music.

From here, however, her tale took a stumble. For Abdul, the 1990s saw two failed marriages (one to actor Emilio Estevez, another to clothing manufacturer Brad Beckerman), a public struggle with and treatment for bulimia, struggles with prescription meds, and after four years off the charts, a comeback attempt that saw only middling sales.

Paula was clearly "open to offers."

Berman tells of Paula's appearance in the *Idol* world. "I knew Paula and had talked to her about projects in years past. She came in and she met with us. She represented a lot of categories. She had a lot of credibility. She had been a pop star. She was looking for other avenues for herself. She was looking to produce certain things. She had an interest in doing other things, but I will say that they just seemed like a good pairing of three people."

Ten years later, it's difficult to recall that when *Idol* began, Abdul was the show's real star. Paula Abdul was the only person on the screen— from the judging panel, to the hosts, to the contestants—who anyone had heard of. It was Paula Abdul who supplied the curiosity factor to the show. But for Abdul, used to the coddled, highly choreographed world of American entertainment, this leap into a very different kind of enterprise, pulling her back from the road to entertainment oblivion, was to come as a huge shock to her system.

With three seats filled, there remained the question of the fourth judge. In the United Kingdom, that fourth seat had been filled by a DJ, Neil Fox, and the crew attempted to complete a similar mix here. They settled on a flamboyant and edgy young DJ from LA's KROQ station, known as Stryker, to be the fourth judge. The deal was ready to go, but at the last minute, Stryker pulled out, citing what he would later term "image concerns" over appearing on what he no doubt considered a cheesy singing contest that might damage his rock creds.

Murdoch's edict "don't change anything" was still in effect, but Stryker's turnabout had left them with no time to fill that final chair. In the end, in another twist of fate, no decision was ever made *not* to have a fourth judge. The clock simply ran out before a suitable partner for Simon, Paula, and Randy was found.

THE FINAL ELEMENT was the hosts. Here the "change nothing" edict would be untouchable. Because *Pop Idol* had had two hosts, so must *American Idol*. But the United Kingdom's front men, Ant and Dec, were not just two smiling faces tossed together. They were a comedy duo who had worked together, developing complementary characters and rhythms, since they were fourteen. But that point seems to have been lost under the operating edict, and with just a few weeks to go before auditions began, a broad casting call was put out to find not one, but two front men.

Dozens came through to audition, appearing before the producers individually and in pairs, improvising hypothetical situations that might come. Producers scrambled to find two people who not only had the charm and wit to front the show, but who also had chemistry with each other. In the end, they chose Brian Dunkleman, an L.A. comic actor who was on the brink of breaking out, having a strong run of guest slots on network sitcoms. An understated, sardonic presence, Dunkleman seemed a natural counterweight to a more frenetic host. For that role, producers settled on an ambitious twenty-seven-year-old, then famed as a local radio DJ in Los Angeles and the host of such shows as *Radical Outdoor Challenge* and *Gladiators 2000*, Ryan Seacrest.

The negotiation with Seacrest, however, came down to the wire, with Ryan's father, acting as his representative, haggling over terms and threatening to pull him out. This went on until they were just hours away from shooting, until finally, at the last moment, Seacrest signed on the dotted line.

The new hosting team was sent to a get-acquainted breakfast at Nate 'n Al's deli to try and find their chemistry. From London, Simon Cowell flew in and met his fellow panelists. Symbolizing perhaps the cultural divide, as he flew over to begin shooting, Nigel Lythgoe arrived shortly thereafter, after being arrested on the plane for sneaking into the restroom to smoke.

Five years after Simon Fuller had first dreamed of his interactive talent search empire, it was curtain time for *American Idol*.

Chapter 6

SHOWTIME

What if they gave a talent competition and nobody came? That was the *Idol* team's fear as they prepped the first audition tour. "We were freaking out," Beckman remembers, "because we didn't know if anybody would show up for the auditions. I remember when it was in Los Angeles I actually brought home flyers and gave them to my daughter. I think she was starting high school that year. I said, 'Will you please pass these around the school?' Literally, we had no idea."

Meanwhile, across the plains, twenty-year-old Cumming, Georgia, native RJ Helton believed he had just walked away from his singing career after having spent nine months in Nashville trying to break in with a Christian boy band. "We were all poor, working at Applebee's and living in a small apartment, the five of us. It just wasn't working out and I had moved back home to Atlanta with my family," he recalls. "That's where I saw the auditions for *Idol*. They were advertising it on TV and the advertisement said, 'Do you want to be the next big superstar?' I definitely had some apprehensions just because all of the other music reality shows had kind of failed. They weren't very successful and people took them as a joke but I figured, 'What the hell. I have nothing better going on. . . .'"

In Philadelphia, twenty-three-year-old Justin Guarini was singing with a party band at weddings and bar mitzvahs while commuting to New York for Broadway auditions. "My mother was upstairs and she saw this advertisement on TV. . . . She said, 'Check this out. Go to this

Web site.' I go to the Web site and it's just this basic Web site. Many of the links didn't work because they had just literally thrown this thing up. I went there and I checked it out. They had a contract that you were supposed to print out and I looked over it. It was standard fare for any sort of basic production and you more or less are signing your life away, as you would with any other production. I printed it out and I saw that they were having the audition on whatever date it was at the Millennium Hotel in New York City." Guarini was accustomed to showing up to open calls. *American Idol* was just one more.

For Nikki McKibbin, in Grand Prairie, Texas, *Idol* was not her first encounter either with reality television or singing competitions. The straight-shootin', orange-haired, pierced-tongue barroom rocker had won a slot on the U.S. version of *Pop Stars*, making it a few weeks into the competition. Once the show ended, however, she had returned home to her suburban community outside of Fort Worth, where she parlayed brief notoriety and a little money into the seeds for a karaoke company, hosting evenings at local bars. When she saw the ad for *Idol*, she decided to give it a try. "I got up the next morning and went to my friend Eric's house and was like, 'Hey, let's go audition for this show.'"

The turnout was extremely hit-and-miss. An extra stop in Miami was hastily added at the last minute to try and bring out a few more contenders. All told, just over ten thousand people showed up for the seven-city tour—about fifteen hundred per stop. It was nothing like the vast armies that would turn up in seasons to come, but enough to avoid embarrassment—enough to get the show on the air.

For the *Idol* team, that first tour is still remembered with a bit of a halo hanging over it, a time of pure goodwill and fun, a road trip with little sense of how it would change the lives of those aboard for the ride.

Brian Dunkleman remembers, a decade later, "One of my fondest memories is that in Miami we all went out to a club one night and we're all dancing and Paula and I, I don't know how we ended up there, but we ended up squaring off, having a dance off and I just had to take a second and think, *You're in a fucking dance off with Paula Abdul. How insane is that?*"

For those auditioning, the thrill that still stands out a decade later was singing before Paula Abdul *herself*, the one true star in the room.

"I just remember being really nervous, very, very nervous," RJ Helton recalls of his Atlanta tryout. "I think the first audition for me was just in front of a producer and then they sent me on to the second round. I guess there were about four rounds that we went through before we even saw the judges. I think there were two auditions that day and then I went back, I guess two weeks later, to audition a few more times and right before we saw the judges. So I think there was two times again and then I went and saw the judges. I had no clue who Simon was. I had no clue who Randy was. . . . I remember that I sang straight to Paula."

At the end of his audition, Helton was told he was "going to Hollywood." He still didn't know what lay ahead or what this show was, but those words were enough. "It was a pretty exciting thing, especially when you got in front of the judges and they said that you were going to Hollywood. That was a big deal and especially for a lot of the Georgia folks because we're all kind of Southern, country-type of people."

ON TELEVISION, THE contestants are seen jumping straight from the enormous lines to standing before the judges. In truth, the appearance before the judges comes only after several other levels of screening take place. After lining up, the contestants first must survive a mass culling where they stand three at a time before tables of screeners. The vast majority of contestants are dispatched instantly. Those who survive that round are called back for one or two more appearances before the show's producers. It's those survivors who are allowed to step before the judges. In the seasons to come, this process would be organized into a gigantic machine, but for this first season it was a relatively informal affair.

As the competitors advanced past the first rounds, the culling process became not just about looking for the best (or the worst), but also seeking out a range of stories to showcase. That first year featured both the high temper of Tamika, "pronounced ta-ME-ka," as she repeatedly reminded the judges, and the tale of Jim Verraros, who learned to sing for his two deaf parents, signing the songs for them. The former blazed the trail for a long line of alternately talented hopefuls right down to "General" Larry Platt, season 9's breakout author of "Pants on the Ground." Verraros, for his part, was the first in a long line of heartbreaking tales that would parade past the audition table, turning each year's opening weeks into a compilation of real-life tearjerkers worthy of a dozen Lifetime network specials.

The auditions were also America's first introduction to Mr. Nasty. Brian Dunkleman admits to being having been extremely freaked out by the experience. "It's one thing to watch it on television, but then you spend time with these kids and you have to look at them right in the eyes and then their mother is looking at you, like, 'What just happened?' That was kind of the first day. It was just off. 'You're telling me that I suck? That I should never sing again?'"

Justin Guarini recalled waiting for his audition outside the judges' room. "It was soundproof. You couldn't hear anything. We're waiting and all of a sudden the doors grind open. The camera crew rushes to meet this person who's just coming out and it was this girl and she was bawling. She was bawling her eyes out. She was so upset. It was shocking for us because we think we're going in to see the judges and here this girl is bawling. I felt like I was about to go in and face a firing squad or something."

In the diplomatic or, as our British guests would describe it, "politically correct" culture of American television, such raw honesty bordered on vicious. The United Kingdom had an entire culture of freewheeling sharp-elbowed tabloid speak. But America had nothing like that and it came as a big surprise. America had its political screamers heard on talk radio, and shock jocks like Howard Stern, but by and large they were relegated to margins of the culture, written off as cranks and clowns.

"When Simon first spoke," stage manager Debbie Williams remembers of her first day on the set, "suddenly it was terra firma. I still didn't know what the hook of this show was, all these kids come out and sing, until he spoke, and then I said, 'Okay. I get it now. That's the hook.'"

Cowell's value was instantly clear. And as Fox prepared for launch, it became the centerpiece. "When we were getting ready to promote it on the air," Darnell remembers, "there was a lot of debate about whether Simon should be the focus . . . literally someone was arguing with me that little girls are going to be in the audience for the show and they're going to be scared of him. I'm like, 'You guys are crazy . . . the only thing that's separating this show, at the moment, from *Pop Stars* and *Making the Band* is Simon and the sort of entertainment value he brings.' So I fought for it really hard and won. That ended up being the thing that did get people. But there was some outrage at first. I think at first even Simon was a little nervous that maybe the American public wouldn't accept him in that persona."

"The footage we gave the press," recalls Preston Beckman, "was predominantly Cowell eviscerating people. At that point, nobody knew who Simon Cowell was. And he was making them cry and making them miserable. So it was kind of like nasty . . . the way we were selling it."

But it occurred to some that there was another story here, perhaps not as instantly sensational but no less potent.

Beckman continues, "Then at some point, Mike must have given me a copy of the auditions. I went home and I showed it to my wife and my son and my daughter and we loved it. It was very emotional. I called up Sandy [Grushow] and I said, 'There's kids here who you want to root for. I honestly don't think we're selling it right. We're selling it as a Fox show. We just sell nasty, edgy.' So Sandy looked at it and we kind of changed the promos a bit to make them a bit more aspirational, a bit more female friendly."

In the end, it was the combination of these seemingly polar opposites that created *Idol*'s appeal: the dream of coming to Hollywood from middle America and facing the ogre that awaited. For tens of millions, *American Idol* would create our national hero's journey, overcoming the most fearsome of terrors—the fear of being mocked before the eyes of a nation—in the hopes of realizing that most precious goal: fame. Ironically, it took a flock of Brits to make this come true. "We brought coals back to Newcastle. We brought the American dream back to America," says Lythgoe.

IT DIDN'T SEEM to matter what Fox was selling. The media wasn't buying. Despite Simon, Paula, Randy, Mike Darnell, Nigel Lythgoe, and half the Fox executive suite sitting for interviews, only a handful of newspapers and magazines covered the show's launch, and those with the most perfunctory of articles. The pre-debut press played up the *Star Search* comparison and quoted some of Simon's choice barbs from the advance clips tape. "Televised talent contests have been around nearly as long as the medium itself," wrote the *Indianapolis Star*, "dating from the January 18, 1948, broadcast of *Ted Mack's Original Amateur Hour* and continuing from the long-running *Star Search* into the 2002–03 season with the Fox show *30 Seconds to Fame*. For a couple of recent seasons, too, we had *Pop Stars*, a show that auditioned young singers and assembled them into groups, and *Making the Band*, which took viewers through the creation of the boy band O-Town. So Fox's summertime series *American Idol: The Search for a Superstar* is nothing new."

"This twice-weekly *Star Search* variation does in fact offer someone the chance to have his or her dream of stardom realized through a nationwide popularity contest. But, this being Fox, it's also very much about crushing the delusions of the dozens of also-rans who might have thought they had talent but apparently were dead wrong" was the *Chicago Sun-Times*'s dismissal.

The Anne Robinson comparison was universally mentioned, to Cowell's annoyance, and he hit back: "She is rehearsed and it is an act. I've been doing auditions like these for twenty-five years."

On June 11, *American Idol* debuted with a ninety-minute episode, taking the air after a rerun of *That '70s Show*. The first episode whipped through all seven of the audition cities in a single night and paused constantly to explain itself to viewers, with frequent references to "as in the British version." *American Idol* began with the two hosts, Ryan and Brian, standing on a dark Kodak Theatre stage, where they promised the journey would end several months hence. "This show was created in the United Kingdom and it is hoped that the winner will be as big as the British winner who went on to make a million dollars," Seacrest announced. They then introduced the judges, who attempted to explain the foundations of the cruelty that lay ahead.

"We are going to do something that I think is going to shock people," Simon Cowell told America's viewers. "We are going to tell people who can't sing and have no talent that they have no talent, going to show the audition process as it really is. Warning you now, you are about to enter the audition from hell."

That first episode of the show that would change the world established the basic plotline that would be repeated for years to come. First came a hilariously bad rendition of a cover song—in this case, "My Girl" sung by seventeen-year-old Steven Ware—followed by Simon Cowell's first rebuke: "That was terrible, seriously terrible." Then a handful of sob stories, and two "star is born" instant sensations in Justin Guarini and an R&B singer from Maryland named Tamyra Gray.

The show did not feature one Kelly Clarkson. Her audition wasn't shown.

Simon's barbs were the most noticeable element of this first episode, but so was the unmistakable love/hate chemistry between Simon and Paula as they argued, flirted, and blustered their way into a classic good cop/bad cop routine.

The charity was more charged behind the scenes. "Paula got very upset at some of the first things Simon said," Darnell recalls. "She wasn't ready for it and she cried." Others remember her being so thrown off balance by Cowell that she threatened to quit. In the end, the threats proved more an early example of Paula's propensity toward drama, a tendency that would haunt the show offscreen and on for years, than a true ultimatum. After being taken aside for a stern heart-to-heart with Lythgoe, Paula returned to her seat and shelved her threats. Forced to swallow Cowell's role, however, Paula instinctively saw her place on the set as a counterbalance to his brutality, as his antagonist and the people's defender. She warmed to the role and one of the most famous buddy acts in history was born.

Cowell recalls, "When I look back on the first show, no question about it, Paula was a huge reason why the show was a hit. We had this instant incredible chemistry which was real. We liked each other and then we would argue. I mean, I've never met anybody like her in my life, but I loved working with her because she was unpredictable and genuine. It wasn't for the cameras."

THE CRITICS WERE not impressed. To say that they slammed *American Idol* would imply that they gave the show some thought. The majority of publications continued to ignore Fox's latest summer reality offering.

But those who did tune in came with a huge chip on their shoulders against the whole "unscripted" genre. "Ugly Reality Shows Will Provide Viewers with a Sleazy Summer" read the headline of the *Cleveland Plain Dealer*. The story continued: "As the temperature climbs, the medium's IQ falls. And, sorry, that means another wave of reality programming. Rarely idle in the bad-taste department, Fox will unveil *American Idol: The Search for a Superstar* with a ninety-minute episode."

"*American Idol*," wrote the *Chicago Tribune*, "copied from a British hit called *Pop Idol*, operates under the flawed assumption that this nation wants or needs another treacly pop star. Don't the producers know that Celine Dion is back from exile and only one of the 'N Sync boys is planning to go to space? The entirely typical moment is ill mannered and cruel. What might have been 'kind,' delivered in private, becomes brutal on such a public stage. What did this young man do to deserve such humiliation except exercise his apparently genetically mediocre vocal cords?"

Perhaps the only kind words *Idol* received were a throwaway comment from Diane Sawyer. Chatting with her colleagues on *Good Morning America,* Sawyer admitted to turning on the new show the night before. "I watched a little of it, I got hooked. It's a little bit *Star Search,* a little bit *Gong Show.* But a lot of people come on to sing and hope for the chance to go to Hollywood and do it."

In the end, the only vote that mattered was that of the viewers. *Pop Idol* had taken some weeks to take hold and catch fire, so Fox executives, with their expectations downsized to virtually nil, braced for the underwhelming initial response. And so it came that after being panned by the critics, ignored by the media, airing in the dead of summer, built around a format that was a proven loser in America—starring a foreign record executive no one had ever heard of—the first night of *American Idol* was watched by 9.9 million people. It was the biggest audience Fox had scored in seven months in the critical 18- to 49-year-old demographic. It added 3 million viewers onto its lead-in from *That '70s Show.* Fox won the night for the first time in years.

"If it had stayed at 11 or 12 share we would have been thrilled," says Darnell. "It launched at 15, which is still a shock. I think I was in disbelief."

Cowell remembers having returned home from shooting the audition episodes. "I went back to the U.K. and genuinely forgot when the show was going to air. And I got this call out of the blue. It was either a producer or an agent screaming into the phone. 'It's a hit!' 'What's a hit?' '*Idol*!' I had no idea the show was airing that night."

More stunning still, the numbers only improved on the second night as the show brought its singers to Hollywood. The Wednesday night episode grew to 11 million viewers, despite going head-to-head against the final game of the NBA championship. The growth indicated that after Tuesday night's show, people had started buzzing about the new program, which had the goal of placing *Idol* in the midweek Tuesday and Wednesday slots. "Here's one thing I knew," scheduling guru Preston Beckman recalled, "that reality shows work best if you could put them on during the week where people could talk about them the day before and the day after. I think that one of the secrets of reality shows is people like to talk about them."

And people *were* talking. Following the single night of auditions, *Idol* brought the 100-some singers who had won their golden tickets to Hollywood for what they referred to then as "hell week."

The episode continued to build on the themes developed the night before: a tear-jerking segment featuring Chicagoan Jim Verraros performing in sign language to his deaf parents; Simon telling an overweight singer she "doesn't look right"; a hopeful dressed as Zorro. Compared to Hollywood Weeks of years to come, the tone was modest and low-key. Shot at the Pasadena Civic Center, the episode had the look of tryouts for a high school play, complete with the kids being summoned to gather around the piano for a little sing-along.

As they shot the episode, however, a concern began to develop on the set. After witnessing the contestants all together—gauging their stage presence, their confidence and comfort level, their basic skills and maturity—the producers worried that one competitor was so far above the rest that the contest would be over before it began. Justin Guarini, it was felt, was so strong that no one else stood a chance. Guarini himself credits his work entertaining at parties with teaching him to get comfortable before a crowd and how to get their attention whatever the situation. It certainly worked with Paula Abdul; Guarini oozed a sex appeal that sent her into vapors.

"He was what we call our *banker*," Cowell says of Guarini. "Once I'd seen him I was confident that we had a genuinely good singer for the final. He was charismatic. Good-looking, confident. Girls loved him. And that was enough for me to go all right, we've got enough for me. Kelly Clarkson wasn't even mentioned."

The front-runner might have been in a different league from the rest. But he almost hadn't made it. A week before he left for Hollywood, Justin was offered a part in the chorus of *The Lion King*'s theatrical run. After trying to break in on Broadway for years, this was the foot in the door he had dreamed of. However, he managed to stall for a few days while he flew out west to see what might come of this little game show.

He remembers arriving in Pasadena for the taping. "They sat us down and Nigel Lythgoe gets up and gives us a whole spiel about, 'This is a television show. It's designed to set you off, to put you off your guard. Just concentrate and focus and be aware of what you're doing. We are going to film you.' There were no punches pulled. With reality television nowadays it seems as though there is a sort of pull-the-wool-over-your-eyes mentality for the producers, like, 'We won't tell the talent that we're going to be filming them 24/7 and we're going to edit it together to make them look however we want them to look.' *American Idol* was very, very open about that. They said, 'Look, you do something stupid we're going to catch it and we're going to use it, FYI.' Some people heeded that warning and some people didn't. It was a very open system and I think that's something I definitely respect about *Idol* because they've always been that way."

After the disclaimer, Cowell braced the group for what was to come, telling the assembled singers that half of them would be gone by the following night. In short order, the singers stepped forward, and the numbers were whittled down from over a hundred to just thirty. Though the contestants still weren't clear what it was they were auditioning for, having come this far they each now wanted the journey to continue, wherever it was going.

Guarini might have been the front-runner in the back-office buzz, but he had little sense of that. "I just remember thinking, *Man, I have to go out and get some clothes.* I went to Armani Exchange in Pasadena and ended up getting this blue sort of—it wasn't jean but something like that—with a white shirt. I still have it. I remember going out and singing by myself on the very same stage where years and years earlier Michael Jackson had done the moonwalk for the first time. . . . I just remember going out and doing my thing, feeling good about it, and the audience went crazy. All my peers were happy, clapping for me at the end. The judges were clapping. Paula was touched. It was just such a defining moment that I'll never forget because it was the first time that I thought, *I might have a shot at this thing. I don't know what this thing is but I may have a shot at whatever the heck this thing is.*"

For viewers who weeks later would watch these defining moments, there was little doubt of Guarini's place on the totem pole. The first breakout star, he seemed to get as much screen time as the rest combined, being placed in every shot, at the center of every group picture, the focal point of all the action on the set.

While Guarini was searching for a decent outfit, Nikki McKibbin was on the prowl for something else. The Texas girl had brought with her a sizable case of stage fright, as well as a burgeoning drinking problem. She remembers Hollywood Week as a time of searching for neighborhood sushi bars where she could throw back a few shots before her next number. Nikki's issues with liquor would rage much further out of control in the years to come. But in her time on *Idol*, it was the hidden bottles and quickly tossed-back shots before airtime that would sustain her through the terrors of the show. She also recalls the nervousness at the hotel that first year: "I was like one of the only people that smoked in front of the cameras but everybody is coming to my hotel room, everybody, all hours of the night, 'Can I have a cigarette,' right? Then I was the only person smart enough to make the hotel clean out my refrigerator—the minibar stuff out of my refrigerator—and go grocery shopping and put groceries in that little refrigerator. I felt so bad for some of the kids who the only meal they would have all day because they didn't have any money was a bag of chips and a peanut butter sandwich that they would come get from my room before they went to bed.

"It's different now, but back then they didn't know how big the show was going to be and they just didn't know what they were doing yet. So they weren't thinking, *The kids are starving. We've got them sequestered and we haven't fed them.* There was nothing malicious but it was new and those are details you don't think of."

For many of them, coming out to this first Hollywood Week required a ticket on a very uncertain lottery. For Nikki, who won the money to make the trip in a bingo game, taking the time away from her karaoke company sent her finances dangerously close to the brink. While she was gone, her landlord locked her apartment for nonpayment of rent. "I wasn't making any money. I had to leave my job, my company that I had just started. I left all this stuff behind, which seemed silly at the time, to go and try to do this television show, to win a talent show."

RJ Helton recalls the time as the most stressful week of his life. "I remember screwing up a few times and I think that I ran out of one of the auditions. My mother was staying at a hotel nearby and I was like, 'Mom, I just can't do this. There's just no way that I'm going to make it through to this next round. I screwed up and forgot my words,' and most of the people that day did forget the words when we were doing the group numbers. I ran out of the hotel, down to my mother's hotel, and she said, 'Come with me.' I went with her and she took me to the bar and she got me a shot of whiskey to calm me down and then I went back and I ended up making it through to the next round. It was a stressful week. I think that was the first time that I was called dreadful and terrible and all of those things. I think that each of us at one point was called something pretty negative."

Despite being totally in the dark, these thirty young people suddenly had a lot riding on *American Idol*. Whether the producers were aware of it at the time or not, Hollywood Week tapped into the most potent myth in American culture, even more potent than the legend that any boy can grow up to be president. *Idol* breathed new life into the fantasies of millions who dreamed of going to Hollywood and being a star.

The audition episode had set it up, taking the show out into the country, cameras visiting the small towns, seeing the people in their homes. While other shows had brought people to Hollywood, none before had scoured the country in search of them, allowing the audience to meet them in their homes. And no other show on television actually visits the nation so completely, deepening the sense that this is America's show.

As *Idol*'s director Bruce Gowers said about these establishing moments on the show, "Every time I see a shot of that water tower in the small town with the name painted on it, that is America. That's Middle America. And I think everybody identifies with it. Totally. And so the backstory's really so important. And sometimes obviously we plan it. Sometimes there's a tragedy, there's emotion, there's whatever."

Cecile Frot-Coutaz, the FremantleMedia North America chieftain overseeing *Idol*, said succinctly, "The auditions establish the whole point of the show. If you just met these kids on a stage in Hollywood, it would make no sense."

And somehow, despite the fly-by-night, slapped-together-at-the-last-minute, no-one-was-quite-sure-what-it-was production, it all came through on the screen. The heartbreaks, the cheesiness of the group numbers matched with the desperation to get them right, the instant lights quality shining out of Hollywood Week's two breakout players, Justin Guarini and Tamyra Gray. After two brief episodes, America was on board. By the end of the second week, even the media had heard the news, and suddenly stories about the new show were everywhere.

However, there was an element that still had yet to come online, one part of the *Idol* myth that hadn't even been glimpsed yet. The auditions had aired, thirty had survived hell week and made it through to *American Idol*'s semifinals. But as yet, America still had not heard a single note from the mouth of Miss Kelly Clarkson, and a greater myth than anyone could yet imagine was still to be born.

Chapter 7

ONCE UPON A TIME

F airy tales can come true, it can happen to you. Newspaper stories don't begin this way. But Kelly Clarkson's made-for-TV trip toward a glass slipper so far is a feel-good fable in the making," the *Dallas Morning News* summed it up. The girl next door, the waitress turned superstar, the diamond in the rough finally breaking through and winning over the mean goblin to become the greatest star of them all—this version of the Kelly Clarkson story has been so often repeated that it's hard to recall that she was never meant to win.

Kelly Clarkson's journey invented the mythos that has guided the stories of almost every *Idol* champion from the Velvet Teddy Bear (Ruben Studdard) to abuse survivor Fantasia to paint salesman Lee DeWyze. In fact, Kelly Clarkson shaped the image of *American Idol* as much as *Idol* shaped her. And if the story about how it all went down wasn't exactly true, well, it was close enough. Kelly Clarkson's voice, her exuberance, her story, gave America something to believe in during those post-9/11 days.

CLARKSON WAS THE quintessential Texas tomboy, youngest of three, growing up in the Fort Worth suburb of Burleson. Young Kelly found her voice singing in high school musicals, where she won starring roles in *Brigadoon* and *Annie Get Your Gun*. Whether consciously or unconsciously, playing Annie Oakley seems to have rubbed off on her.

By the time she auditioned for *Idol*, the down-home, "anything you can do I can do better," rootin'-tootin' spirit of the Old West legend inhabited the small-town girl with the infectious spirit that could bring a smile even to the face of Simon Cowell.

The official legend told during her *Idol* rise had it that Clarkson came out to Hollywood straight from high school, but after having door after door slammed in her face, a fire burned down her apartment, leaving her homeless and on the streets. Alone and shut out of show business, the country girl decided to pack it all in and go home. She crawled back to the bosom of Burleson, and was just beginning to take stock when she heard about the local auditions for this new show called *American Idol*.

The tale is true in spirit even if many of its particulars have been fudged . . . just a little. Kelly's Hollywood roommate would later recant a piece of it, claiming the fire was elsewhere in the building, that Kelly was not homeless, and that her return to Texas was unconnected with the fire. It would also come out that, far from having doors slammed in her face, Kelly had made some impressive headway in Hollywood, recording demos and working toward an album with respected producers.

A few laps around the Hollywood track though she might have had, when Kelly Clarkson stepped into the *Idol* auditions, the expectations for her couldn't have been lower. While the more polished, professional, poised duo of Justin and Tamyra were lapping up the attention, little Kelly from Texas didn't even make it on-screen. The only shots the audience sees of her during Hollywood Week are of her standing in groups, her voice unheard.

"We just did not see her coming," Debbie Williams recalls. "I mean, Justin was so fabulous he knew where every camera was. When Bruce [Gowers] would cut to a camera, this kid was looking at it. It was like, what does he have? *Sonar* in his head. So we thought he had it locked up, and we didn't notice Kelly because Kelly, think about it, was a very unassuming little thing."

When Kelly sang to America in the semifinal rounds, she stepped out with no fanfare and zero expectations from either the *Idol* team or the television audience. The semifinals' little stage that was the way station between Hollywood Week and the top twelve big stage was, at that point, a tiny postage stamp with no live audience. It was a setting that mimicked the hostile environment of a music industry audition. There was no applause or theme music to welcome them, no band. The other contestants and their families were banished to the Coca-Cola–themed Red Room off to the side. The contestants walked out to a cold, quiet room, said an uncomfortable "Hi" to the judges, and broke into song to the accompaniment of a lone piano. The early episodes were pretaped rather than live so the contestants felt a little bit of comfort knowing that if disaster struck, in theory there was a net. They had had a bit of guidance beforehand, with voice coach Debra Byrd coming on board right before the semifinal episodes as the sole coach for thirty contestants, giving them some basic exercises and trying to remedy a problem that had been running riot with the contestants during Hollywood Week—forgetting the lyrics.

The semifinals marked the first time America met Kelly. The 5'3" singer stepped onto the stage clad in a black shoulderless Liza suit and her soon-to-be-trademark pigtails teased out, and busted out a show-stopping powerful rendition of "Respect." The judges, expecting nothing, struggled for words. "I don't know what to say," babbled Simon. "You have a good voice but I honestly couldn't remember you from the previous rounds."

Cowell recalls of the night, "Genuinely, I had no idea. I didn't remember that first audition. Looking back on it you could tell that all of us had gotten to that point in the day we were bored. She did enough to get through but nobody commented on her. There was no buzz on her. It was the first live show when she really made her mark. The first live show I turned around to Paula and said, 'Where did this come from? This girl is incredible.' And that's when it all changed."

As the semifinals began, Cowell's verbal assaults ratcheted up to a new level. Those viewers who had invested in the dream narrative of the show's first few weeks now saw their favorites stand before the judges on that cold, empty stage. If the audience expected Cowell to offer the singers a pat on the back for having come so far, they were about to receive the shock of a lifetime.

In many ways, Cowell's put-downs came as straight talk to a frivolous national culture that was itself ready for a reality check. "We were moving into the age of the celebrity," Lythgoe says of the context for

Cowell's lash. "The 1960s going into the 1970s showed that ordinary people could become stars like the Beatles. You got to understand their foibles. You got to know where they came from, the mistakes that they made. 'If that lad from round the corner in Liverpool can be a star so can you, my son.' That came through. The star system of Hollywood was breaking down. We were starting to create celebrities and not stars. Consequently, that led into 'I don't have to have talent.'

"We also had technological inventions that harmonized your voice . . . you didn't have to be a great singer. Everyone thought that you just go in, sing into a microphone, and you could be pitch perfect. And as this whole thing grew, as reality shows grew, so did this feeling of young people, that they were owed something and that they could achieve it through television, through technology. 'I'm willing to work hard.' 'Well, yes. Good. But you need a modicum of talent and you haven't got it,' was sort of my reply. There was a real sense of 'the world owes me.'"

To that indulged and indulgent culture, Simon Cowell would be the first to say, "No."

THAT FIRST SEMIFINALS episode began on a high note. Tamyra Gray rocketed to the front of the pack with her rendition of "You're Gonna Love Me." On the next number, nineteen-year-old Jim Verraros, the son of two deaf parents and the subject of perhaps the most heart-warming of the heartwarming audition clips, took the stage. Still high from Tamyra's performance, the other contestants and their families gave enthusiastic whoops for the sentimental favorite. So it fell like a ton of bricks when Cowell weighed in: "I don't think it was good enough because you have just followed a star. I thought you looked ordinary up there and I think if you win this competition, we will have failed."

The tiny stage was filled with gasps; shots flashed of the other contestants, their reactions ranging from disbelief to outrage. Verraros walked back to the Red Room and was greeted by stunned silence, his comrades looking like they had just realized that the kindly old man who had invited them into his castle was in fact an ogre who planned to eat them for dinner.

As the night wore on and more and more fell to Cowell's sword, the shock turned to outrage, with screams of "NO!" and shrieks of disgust coming from the Red Room.

The wounds were still raw the following night when seven of the ten were due to be eliminated on the first results show. Given the chance to put questions to the judges, seventeen-year-old contestant Natalie Burge asked Cowell directly, "Do you feel bad? Did you sleep last night?"

There were indications, however, that the public, at this early date, was not quite ready to fall in line behind its new cultural arbiter. As the results were announced, Cowell's first victim, the grievously wounded Verraros, advanced to the finals, earning a seat on the big stage along with Tamyra Gray and the midriff-baring Ryan Starr.

But this was not, in fact, the night's original verdict. When the *Idol* team shot that first results episode, doubts still lingered about turning the wheels of this thing entirely over to the audience. Execs decided that to goose the tension, a twist was needed. So at the end of the episode, after the results had been revealed, the show had thrown in a judges' cut, allowing the jurists to send one more person packing. That *one more person?* Audience favorite Jim Verraros. After the show ended, Cowell walked up to the Red Room, where those who had made it through sat celebrating their victories, and abruptly told Verraros that audience verdict be damned, he was cut anyway. A stunned Verraros and his fellow contestants burst into tears.

Cowell, however, was very happy. "I loved it," he said. "Soon as he [Darnell] came in and said the word 'twist' I thought, 'You and I are going to get on great because you're breaking the rules here.' Because I hate rules, I absolutely despise them. And that's what I loved about Mike, that he could feel that things were getting a little too safe and boring and he dropped a bomb on everything."

With that feel-bad ending waiting to be aired, however, Lythgoe had second thoughts. He called Frot-Coutaz and told her he thought this was taking the power out of the hands of the people, that it was contrary to the show's whole premise. Frot-Coutaz agreed and brought all parties on board. The episode was recut and the news was broken to Verraros that he was suddenly *un*eliminated.

ELSEWHERE, THE EPISODE struggled with half an hour to fill and not much to fill it with. The unveiling of the results, which in later years would become Lythgoe's artfully choreographed masterpiece, was a bit of a three-footed square dance, with the news given out almost offhandedly. Seacrest wasn't yet skilled at the pregnant pauses that would become his signature, and the half hour was fluffed out with outtakes, awkward banter between Seacrest and Dunkleman, and perhaps the strangest Ford ad they would ever record, featuring the contestants driving around Los Angeles while talking aloud to themselves about their dreams.

Whatever the production values, the media swarmed to take notice. "Fox's Reality Show Search for a Superstar Is the Talk of the Summer Season," declared the *South Florida Sun-Sentinel*. "America's Newest Guilty Pleasure" was the headline on the *St. Louis Post-Dispatch*. The *Today Show* and *Good Morning America* both ran segments about a show on a competitor network. On *GMA*, Cowell defended his barbs, saying of his trashing of one overweight contestant, "It was brutal but . . . I don't make the rules up. The record-buying audience tends to make the rules up. And I don't think if Aretha Franklin, looking as she looks now, if she walked into this competition, would have got through, no, because I don't think she would have been voted through by the people who were going to vote for the winner."

The following week marked the debut of Kelly Clarkson, who, despite her surprising version of "Respect," remained in the shadow of Justin Guarini riding high from his much-lauded version of Stevie Wonder's "Ribbon in the Sky." Guarini recalls the following night's results show, when he, Kelly, and a young singer named AJ Gil—who had also been trashed by Cowell—made it through. "I'll never forget the three of us being backstage after the show was done. That's when it truly hit me. I was like, 'I'm in the top ten. All the pressure, all the stress, everything that had built up and led me to that point all came out. I was just hugging people, so thankful. It's funny because I'm not usually one for that kind of emotional outburst. AJ and I were bawling it up and Kelly, who *is* an emotional person, as well in that moment was just like, 'Okay. This is cool.' She'd had some experience in the industry before. She was like, 'I'm not going to count my chickens.'"

The ratings held up.

The *Hollywood Reporter* noted, "*Idol* helped Fox become the only major network to post a year-to-year hike in the demo last week, with a glamorous 18 percent increase," while *Variety* pointed out, "It's the first time since August 1990 that Fox series have held down a week's top two spots in adults 18–49." Still, while the reviewers continued to sneer ("Think of *American Idol* as *Star Search* goes to hell," wrote *Time*), an emerging class of *Idol* pundits noticed another trend. "Are voters defy-ing Simon's will?" the *Chicago Sun-Times* wondered. "Superstar fans seem set on softening the blow for the most abused of these competi-tors. Twice in two weeks now, they have advanced sensitive, slightly nerdy, nice-guy teenage men to the next level of the contest after Cowell has roughed them up."

As the public dove ever more deeply into Cowell-watching, feelings on the set remained unsettled, with Paula struggling to maintain her compo-sure next to the toxic import. But nobody could have guessed that when the eruption finally came, it would not be Paula who bubbled over but the affable anchor at the other end of the table, Randy Jackson.

On week three of the semifinals, after RJ Helton led off the night with a rendition of the Jackson 5's "I'll Be There," Cowell lit into him with a more annoyed than usual slam, throwing a temper tantrum at the performance. He ranted, "In the last two weeks, two losers went through because of sympathy votes. I'm fed up with it because I don't believe that's good enough." From the end of the table, Jackson, who had praised Helton's performance, argued back.

Jackson: *You know what I disagree with: Week after week you've been insulting people. You can't call people losers.*
Cowell: *I can call people whatever I like.*
Jackson: *I have a problem. We need to talk about this later. This is America. You don't do that to people. You don't insult them like that.*
Cowell: *Can we discuss this later?*
Jackson: *But you don't have to call them losers.*
Abdul: *America is about celebrating effort.*
Cowell: *Can we drop it, Paula! I'm here to give an opinion.*

Onstage, Helton shifted nervously, fighting back tears as the argument raged past the bounds of vigorous debate into territory that had become very personal. The spat was capped off when Jackson rose to his feet and extended his arms to call out Cowell, demanding, "You want to take this outside! Come on!"

It made for fantastic television and *Idol* would of course make the most of it. But the truth behind the fight was not exactly what the viewers saw. Helton himself explains: "What Simon's comment was originally—we had to retape because of what he said. He called me a monkey. I guess that some people thought that could've been a racist type of comment. So they went back and retaped it and he called me a loser instead. It ended up that it wasn't about me so much as it was about the two of them and whatever their beef was with each other. It was just uncomfortable. I didn't know what was going on and I just stood there making very odd facial expressions."

The original fight had been very real, sparked as Helton said by Cowell's use of the *m* word. Even though Helton himself is white, the racially charged term pushed an already annoyed Jackson over the edge, sparking the altercation. Once they cooled down, however, and the misunderstanding over the term—a benign pejorative in the United Kingdom, where it has none of the racial overtones—was explained, the producers were left with a quandary. The fight had been great drama and to let a dramatic moment like that go to waste would have torn the heart right out of the chest of a showman like Nigel Lythgoe. However, as suggested by Jackson's reaction, the use of the word *monkey* was unthinkable. There were taboos you could break and taboos you couldn't, and using a racially loaded term fell into the latter category. It was an overreach that could have turned Cowell from a lovable villain to a national disgrace, never able to show his face on American airwaves again.

So they regrouped. They filmed the scene again, restaging the fight with *loser* subbed for *monkey* and taking the best shots from the two takes. Indeed, at one moment in the tape you can almost make out the word *monkey* even though *loser* was dubbed in over the original tape. The overlay doesn't *quite* fit.

The episode revealed how different this show was from all that had come before it. Until now, network shows had been self-serious, packaged projects that never referred to their own missteps and internal drama, never gave any hint of the life offscreen. All of a sudden, here was this renegade show, *American Idol*, that was celebrating its backstory, playing up its frictions, and openly acknowledging its missteps. Every tabloid brouhaha would be played up on the *Idol* stage rather than being shoved under the carpet. It was completely unprecedented in American programming.

The following night, *Idol* reveled in the altercation; the show was all but turned over to repeating the clips of the fight. This time, for whatever reason, the crowd did not stand by Cowell's victim and Helton failed to advance to the finals. He looked on as Nikki McKibbin, EJay Day, and Christina Christian moved forward.

THE FIRST SEASON was a time of trial and error, as the show stumbled into what became the U.S. formula. The judges summoned the abused Helton back for the Wild Card round, in which ten contestants were to compete for one last slot. Helton remembers that in those early days of *Idol*, the judges mingled more freely with the contestants on the set, even offering advice. Despite his earlier bashing, in private Cowell had been shockingly supportive. "He said, 'I believe in you but come back and wow me.' It was behind the scenes that he talked to me, which was much different than on camera. On camera he said, 'You were average,' and then behind the scenes he was like, 'You're really an exceptional singer but you need to pick ballads or things that can really showcase your voice.' That's one thing about Simon that I was surprised about. He is pretty cocky and arrogant but he knows it and he has this really great personality and even behind the scenes, while he knows he's an ass, he can still be very, very kind." This was a dichotomy many contestants would note in the years ahead.

Fortunately for Helton, that kindness continued on-screen, and he found himself chosen as the Wild Card pick to join that year's top ten on the big stage.

For Nikki McKibbin, however, the backstage mingling led to what she remembers as a very different kind of encounter, one that would have a big impact on her *Idol* career. In her semifinals appearance, she had wowed the judges with her take on "Total Eclipse of the Heart," a performance that led Cowell to call her "one of the strongest singers in this competition. And I hope you do really well in this competition."

Sometime in the weeks that followed, Cowell chatted with Nikki backstage. She offers the following description of their encounter: "He told me that my eyes were beautiful and he wanted to take my eyeballs out of my head and put them on his nightstand so that he could look at them every night before he went to bed and I pretty much in a nutshell told him that I thought he was a perv and kind of creepy. He was never nice to me after that."

However Cowell meant the statement, one can imagine the gale force winds that blew over him when the cussin' and cursin' Texas girl

McKibbin lashed back. Whatever the reality of that encounter, as they entered the big stage, Nikki found herself recast as the judges' whipping post from that day forward.

Ten years later, Cowell protests that he doesn't recall the incident and claims no ill will toward Nikki. "I genuinely don't remember it. Look, I get it a lot. After a live show, you bump into someone afterwards and they might not be very happy, but I don't remember it being anything unusual or over the top. Normally you just get glared at. I actually liked her. I thought she was feisty. I quite like it when they argue with me afterwards. I think they wind themselves up over a period of time. They like to think that somebody else is the reason for it not working out. I'm a decent person to blame for that."

With the naming of the top ten, the media coverage continued to grow. The handicappers at *Entertainment Weekly* named Guarini the heavy favorite, giving him 3 to 2 odds of winning. Clarkson sat near the back of the pack at 10 to 1.

THE JOURNEY TO the big stage also brought the singers into a new home, the Idol Mansion, a house far up in the Hollywood Hills, which the show played up as a bit of a fantasy element.

"We were so thrilled about this house because we had never seen anything like it," recalls Guarini.

The mansion was intended to add a bit of *The Real World* drama to the show. "We had them living in a house at that point and people always sort of loathed that because it was nothing to do with what we were doing," Lythgoe recalls. "We weren't out to make a group. We weren't out to be nice to each other. I wanted a much more cutthroat environment. It was, 'I'm really sorry to see you go but thank goodness you're going because a place is open for me now.' It wasn't *Big Brother*. I wanted us to be a leader and not a follower."

Another problem with shooting in the house was that the goal of stirring up backstage drama was fundamentally at odds with the goal of a fair competition. "The things that they wanted to shoot at the house, it was the clash between the kids," Bruce Gowers recalls. "But it was incredibly negative. If you could see somebody who seems rude to one of the other kids or seems nasty to one of the other kids, when that kid got on the show to sing, people would say, 'Ah, I'm not going to vote for that one. That was the one who had the fight with so and so.' So, that was dropped almost immediately . . . it was really a nonstarter." In the end, the mansion's onscreen appearances would be limited to the setting for the Ford commercials and video packages of the top ten getting makeovers and the like.

THE FIRST NIGHT on the top ten stage, dedicated to Motown songs, seemed to confirm all everyone had hoped for: the grandeur of the big stage, the excitement of seeing these ten kids, plucked from the haystacks a month before, elevated by the spectacle, with a surging audience behind it. It confirmed everything Fox had hoped for too: The top ten episode saw the show's highest ratings yet, with 10.3 million tuning in.

The first night also confirmed the public's early selections of Guarini as the runaway front-runner, with Tamyra Gray stepping into her role as the leading challenger. Guarini thrilled the crowd with an exuberant "For Once in My Life," which left the girls in the audience shrieking and Cowell cooing, "All I'd say is, Timberlake, watch out for you." After the show, a *USA Today* online survey confirmed Guarini's status at the head of the pack, with 30 percent selecting him as their favorite to 21 percent for Gray, and the rest in single digits.

Guarini recalls of that first night on the big stage, "It was the culmination of everything that I had done up to that point. I go back and I look at it and I listen to it now and I cringe at the performance, but at the time people really enjoyed it. I certainly enjoyed it. . . . That night was really special to me because it was just the first time that I had ever been live on television in front of millions and millions and millions of people under my own terms."

On the following night, the show eliminated Jim Verraros and EJay Day. After they wrapped, however, the set was hit by a bit of unplanned backstage drama as an accident sent RJ Helton to the hospital, coming extremely close to paralyzing him for life. "We were doing a bunch of interviews onstage, all of us, with like *Entertainment Tonight* and *Access Hollywood*, and I ended up losing my balance and I fell off the stage onto my back and knocked myself out. I was rushed to the hospital for a few days. The next show I got out of the hospital to do I was on pain

(2004) Built around a foreign record executive, a long-faded pop singer, and a former eighties backup musician, there was little to indicate the massive stardom that awaited *Idol*'s original panel. *(KEVIN WINTER)*

(SEASON 1, 2002) Rupert Murdoch's order that nothing be changed from the British formula led to season 1's greatest misfire, the hosting duo of Seacrest and Dunkleman, a pair that was awkward onscreen and openly hostile off. *(KEVIN WINTER)*

(SEASON 1, 2002) The first Top Three: Kelly Clarkson, Nikki McKibbin, and Justin Guarini. Of all season 1's surprises, none was more shocking than the rise of the singing waitress from Texas. *(KEVIN WINTER)*

(SEASON 1, 2002) Along with the *Idol* format, Fox picked up its UK producers Ken Warwick and Nigel Lythgoe, who would bring a British sensibility to the American airwaves. *(MATTHEW IMAGING)*

(SEASON 2, 2003) With a jaw-dropping rendition of "She Bangs," William Hung blundered his way into a career that most singers would kill for. *(PETER KRAMER)*

(SEASON 3, 2004) A functionally illiterate high school dropout from a background of abuse, Fantasia Barrino personified *Idol's* rags-to-riches dream. *(RAY MICKSHAW)*

(SEASON 2, 2003) Two years after being disqualified from the show, Corey Clark's allegations of a romantic relationship with Paula would cause her lowest moment. (JUSTIN KAHN)

(SEASON 3, 2004) In the bubble. While on the show, *Idol* stars are kept so busy they rarely get more than a fleeting glance at the hysteria outside the show. A rare moment of quiet during season 3 for Jennifer Hudson, John Stevens, and Diana DeGarmo. (DAVID STRICK)

(SEASON 3, 2004) Part of the *Idol* experience for the contestants is a boot camp on stardom. LaToya London receives vocal instruction from singing coach Debra Byrd. (DAVID STRICK)

(SEASON 4, 2005) Simon Cowell was dumbstruck by the first appearance of *Idol*'s Golden Girl, Carrie Underwood. Her fellow contestants, however, often found her remote and aloof. (KEVIN WINTER)

(SEASON 5, 2006) "I really was there looking for fans. Not friends." Taylor Hicks was *Idol*'s most unlikely champion, but his down-home demeanor masked a razor-sharp sense of how to succeed in modern reality, and a ruthlessness that rubbed many the wrong way. *(VINCE BUCCI)*

(SEASON 5, 2006) Chris Daughtry brought a contemporary rock sou[nd] onto the *Idol* stage and changed [the] face of the competition forever. *(VINCE BUCCI)*

(SEASON 6, 2007) With his ponyhawk aloft, Sanjaya Malakar became *American Idol*'s greatest anti-hero. *(FRANK MICELOTTA/ AMERICAN IDOL)* meds and was in a wheelchair onstage and I don't even remember doing the show but somehow I was there."

"That was so emotional," recalls Debra Byrd. "It was so devastating. I had to do his song choice from the hospital on the phone. We had to sing in the phone because he couldn't come to the show. . . . They thought he may never walk again."

As they prepped for the following week's show, ratings continued to climb. Fox announced it would be bringing back *Idol* for a second season. A mere two months before, no one in the media or in network television had given the show a second glance. Now it was being quickly re-upped in the middle of its run. At the annual Television Critics Association meeting that convened that week in Pasadena, *American Idol* was on everyone's lips. The gathering was treated to a group number from the top eight contestants, singing "California Dreamin'." The trip would be the first and last time they would come to visit the press. After that first season, *Idol* didn't come to the press, the press came to them.

The bulk of the questions, however, were directed not toward the contestants but to the series' one already certified phenomenon, Judge Cowell. Canada's *National Post* wrote, "The great irony of *American Idol* is that the show actually discovered its superstar in its first episode: He is Simon Cowell, the frank, villainous Brit who serves as one of the judges and without whom the series would most likely have been on a voyage to the bottom of the Nielsens. Last week, Cowell was compelled to return to London on business, and the show missed him the way Andrew Ridgeley misses George Michael."

AS THE COMPETITION got serious, a new element was about to be unleashed in earnest: the power of Kelly Clarkson. Despite her strong semifinals showing, Kelly continued to coast at the back of the pack. Now audience and judges alike were about to see what they had overlooked.

What Kelly Clarkson at last related to *Idol* viewers was that beneath the nonchalant demeanor there was a voice that had the power to take leaps few singers could contemplate. Byrd recalls rehearsing that week with Kelly: "Her voice was getting tired, and I would lower the key a little bit. Every other week I'd lower the key. We were at Capitol

Records and she pulled me in a little room. She said, 'You know, this key is so low.' Because she is a real soprano and, at that time, she could not sing below middle C. She said, 'The key is too low. If it's going to stay in this key, would you do this?' And then she hit a Mariah Carey/ Minnie Riperton note."

Stunned, Byrd told her, "I would do that in a heartbeat; I would sing that note."

Byrd was to find, however, as would many in the industry, that in this little overlooked girl at the back of the pack there was an amazing sense of where she wanted to go, a vision that took her well beyond the next week on *American Idol*. To Byrd, she demurred about using her "big note." "I said, 'Why are you doubting it?' She said, 'I don't want to be compared to Mariah Carey.' Who was huge at that time. I told her, 'Well, Mariah Carey's not in this competition. I'd like to make a suggestion . . .' because I can only make a suggestion. I said, 'I'd like to suggest you do it and then move on.' So, we practiced it. She had this whole flourish up there. I said, 'Hit one note. That way you won't be compared to Mariah because she lives up there. So, sing a song, hit the note, and then move on.' We practiced it, she dug it, but she was still on the fence about doing it. Kelly told me she spoke with her mom about this conversation. Her mom said, 'Well, are you going to do it?' Kelly said, 'Mom, I really don't know. I'll do it in the moment if I do it. If you see me do it, you know Byrd's got a gun to my head.'"

Like some comic book character struggling about revealing her superpower, Kelly grappled with the question of whether to use her "big note" right up to airtime. But she did it.

That night Kelly Clarkson sang what was probably the most career-making single note ever unleashed. With 10 million watching the show that had become America's leading conversation topic, Clarkson, clad in a black fedora, a white-collared shirt, and black tie, at the end of her run through a strong but not earth-shattering rendition of "(You Make Me Feel Like) A Natural Woman" for five seconds held the note that suddenly made her a star. As the crowd roared, Randy Jackson shook his head and said, "I didn't know you had all of that."

"Yeah, I thought I'd show my range this time," Kelly panted, struggling for breath.

"America," ruled Judge Cowell, "is not known for nice singers. It is known for great singers. And you are one of them."

Having given the world a glimpse of her superpowers, having gotten their attention, it would be the last time that Kelly Clarkson would sing her "Mariah" note.

"She was always fun, but she was Creek Girl," Lythgoe recalls. "We always saw her in a little creek somewhere down in Texas and didn't think too much about it. Then of course, when she started singing, I remember she did an octave jump in one of her songs, it was like, 'Wow. Where did that come from?' I still thought Tamyra was going to win. But it put us all on notice that here was a real talent. Then she did some stuff like that there, a big band number, a Bette Midler big band number and her personality shined. She was one of those girls, not particularly pretty, not a particularly gorgeous body or anything. Just talented. You suddenly realized the young girls associated with this. She wasn't outrageously beautiful. She wasn't on a pedestal anywhere. This was another girl like the girl next door who's going to come on and everyone starts going, 'She's a really good singer.'"

Until recently, it had been the job of record labels to search the nation for these unknown talents and bring them to a wider audience. But as hip-hop, grunge, and heavily produced pop had overtaken the industry, the labels had walked away from that role. *American Idol* stepped into the void, and it was only there that a diamond in the Texas rough like Kelly could suddenly become a star.

The following night, sixteen-year-old AJ Gil was eliminated, and *American Idol* edged past CBS's *Big Brother* in the ratings for the first time to win the week.

IF THE TOP eight week marked the beginning of Kelly's rise, it also showed the first chink in the front-runner's armor. For the first time, receiving poor reviews for his take on "Sunny," Justin appeared to argue with, even talk back to Cowell, responding to his criticism by saying, "I'd like to hear what they [the public] have to say."

In the United Kingdom, talking back to Cowell had fueled Will Young's rise, but Guarini would find no such support. The next day he found himself labeled "cocky" by the media, which a week before had called him unbeatable. "Cocky, look who thinks his fan base is bigger than it is!" wrote the heretofore Justin partisans at *Entertainment Weekly*. The next night on the results show, Justin found himself in the bottom three for the first time. Ultimately on that night, it was the controversial midriff-baring Ryan Starr who saw her time come to an end. But for Guarini, the brush with death was harrowing enough that he felt compelled to offer an apology to Cowell—and to the audience—for his seeming back talk the night before.

A decade later, the memory of that night still packs a punch. "It was rough. I went out and I did a song, a good song, a decent song. But unfortunately it just wasn't one that people knew. The song was great. My performance of the song was okay. I go out there and I was angry at myself. I got a negative critique and it was hard to hear. It was one of those things where, again, you grow up in front of the camera and you learn one way or another to think before you open your mouth. So when Simon finished his critique I said, 'Okay, great. I hear that but I want to know what the audience thinks.' It was not meant as a slight to Simon or the judging panel but it certainly came off that way. . . . So there I was having my entire existence on *American Idol*, everything that I had worked for for twenty-three years, threatened by my own doing. I just didn't think before I opened my mouth." It was to mark one distinct feature of the U.S. version: Throughout the years, American audiences would demand their stars be respectful and well mannered. Insolent brooding rockers need not apply.

After that brush with death, Guarini would never again find himself in the bottom tier. Nevertheless, what had seemed a closed contest was now wide open.

For Nikki McKibbin, the week marked her permanent move to Cowell's black list. Whatever had happened in their private encounter, and whether or not that had influenced him, a month after he had told her, "You're exactly what this competition needs," he was now saying, after her rendition of "Heartbreaker," "It was not good enough. And you will not win this show." Nikki found herself in the bottom three the next day, a position she would occupy every week until she was ultimately eliminated; she herself began to refer to the bottom three as the "McKibbin Zone."

AS THE COWELL juggernaut grew, he settled into America, renting, as the *Los Angeles Times* reported, a $25,000-a-month five-bedroom, seven-bath home equipped with guest house, pool, and waterfall. And on-screen, Cowell was finding his public image evolving in quite an unexpected way. In the United Kingdom Cowell remained the man you love to hate, but in the United States he was becoming the man you love to love. As Guarini demonstrated, while Cowell's early slams had generated sympathy votes, a month later the audience followed his lead close to the letter.

When the season began, Lythgoe had told Brian Dunkleman that he would eventually become Cowell's foil. "'Simon's the mean guy and there's going to be one episode where you're going to stand up for those kids,'" Dunkleman recalls. "'The whole country is going to be behind you and cheering.' But then the season went on, it was like, everybody loved Simon. How was I going to be the foil for this guy? They loved him."

That left Paula as sole counterweight to Cowell, which so strengthened the chemistry between the two that their buddy act became the linchpin around which the entire show revolved. However, the sheer potency of Cowell's barbs allowed the show itself to play nice guy. Throughout the first season, *Idol* featured segments where Seacrest mocked not just Cowell's ego, but his fashion choices. The effect was magical. Cowell may have served the yearning for unvarnished truth-telling, providing a sensational, attention-getting element, but the show itself managed to float above his brutal edge. While Cowell was seen as lovable, if vicious, the audience came to see the show itself as supportive, nurturing, and protective of its young stars—a sentiment that would prove crucial as *Idol* busted beyond the niche audience of reality shows to become an all-American pastime.

The show became a national sensation by providing an element that had all but vanished from the air—family viewing. In the increasingly divided, niche-marketed world of network television, *Idol* became the one show that families across generations would watch. Nevertheless, in this first year, it struggled to find its footing. The first season's episodes featured the singers going for photo shoots, building a house for Habitat for Humanity, and getting image advice from the editors of *YM* magazine, and the first attempts at group numbers featured them singing around a campfire. Stage manager Debbie Williams remembers, "We had no choreographer, we just did a number. I said to the kids, 'Just have fun. Run around the stage. Have a good time, you know.' They were very inventive, but it was mayhem."

Helton recalls of those early shoots, and the campfire sing-along in particular, "We were home that night and we were all in pajamas, just hanging out and we had to do that and from what I remember it was a pretty quick shoot. We just sang through it a few times and it was done . . . and when we went back and watched it on TV we would laugh so hard at ourselves because it was just that cheesy.'"

The results episodes, in particular, became so thin that the *Dallas Morning News* suspected they were padded with extra commercials and set their timers to see how much actual programming was in the half-hour show. The entertainment content clocked in at eighteen minutes, three to four minutes fewer than the average for a network show of that length. Fox president Sandy Grushaw conceded to the paper, "It ain't easy, and there is a little bit of treading water."

Great discussion developed around how to treat the exiting contestants. Darnell tells, "Either after the first or second one, I came up with this idea of having the kids sing out in the end. Everybody said, 'That's going to be cruel.' It seems so normal now. But at the time, there was a big debate, wasn't it mean to have them have to sing after they just found out they're gone. I said, 'Well, maybe it's a little mean.' Which I'm not opposed to. But if I'm right, it'll be a big emotional send-off. You're giving them their last shot to sing off. They may be emotional during the song, and it's their last moment in the sun."

With the ratings now surpassing twelve million viewers, plans for building up the *Idol* brand sprang up from every corner. Poland and South Africa had already launched their own versions of *Idol*. Germany and France announced plans to jump in the game with talks under way in dozens of other markets. With *Idol* on its way to becoming an international phenomenon, Simon Fuller announced plans for a *World Idol* show, pitting the winners from various nations against each other. A movie featuring the stars was being shopped around Hollywood. As in the United Kingdom, a nationwide concert tour was planned, a Vegas reunion special, and a Christmas show. T-shirts sold online. In every network suite, a host of *Idol* imitators were planned, including, in the ultimate irony, *Star Search*, which CBS announced would return to the airwaves, starring Arsenio Hall in the Ed McMahon slot.

While much of the media had swooped down to cover the *Idol* phenomenon, the contempt of America's critics had only hardened as its popularity grew. *The Washington Post*'s influential Tom Shales wrote, "One might argue that Chuck Barris's inspired romp *The Gong Show* trafficked in humiliation of amateurs too, but it was good-natured, harmless stuff. It was, in that time-honored phrase, all in good fun. *American Idol* is all in mean spirit." The Web site Slate harrumphed, "As an English import, the show is jubilantly indecent: Coke-sponsored, footlight-flooded, presided over by a graphic, androgynous idol that flaunts disturbing protean anatomy. I wonder if the universally pious Christian contestants (they all seem to pray constantly; one is even named Christina Christian, straight up) have any problem with the show's crass look, a monument to the cut-rate exploitative sensibility of the post–Spice Girls London pop music scene."

But *Idol* had become almost the definition of a criticproof show. By turning its controls over to the public, it wasn't Fox's picks that the critics were sniffing at: These weren't Simon Fuller's singers or Rupert Murdoch's, they were the singers America itself had chosen, and if the critics had a bone to pick, it was with the public itself.

APPROACHING THE FINAL stretch of the season, the remaining stars were near the brink of exhaustion. The performers were working around the clock. Their voices were giving out, and the signs of strain and stress were beginning to show. Finally, on the top six week, singer Christina Christian collapsed and was rushed to the hospital.

"All of them were tiny because they weren't eating properly," recalls one crew member. "Christina had gotten so thin . . . you know that expression you turn sideways and I can't see you? I swear to you, she turned sideways and I was looking at her and I couldn't see her. I was like, how did her organs get in there?"

The following night, in what still stands as the most awkward results show in *Idol* history, Christina was eliminated in absentia. Seacrest and Dunkleman read the results and looked into the camera, informing the singer in her hospital bed that her journey had ended.

Christian's elimination came to the audience as something of a surprise, as she had been an early favorite, and given that Cowell's punching bag, Nikki, remained, the decision sparked the show's very first flurry of conspiracy talk. In American history, the conspiracy mind-set has lurked beneath the discussion of all our great turning points; the American mind has been constantly on the lookout for the shadowy forces silently manipulating events. And so would it be with the discussion of *American Idol*, for which every season has produced a new conspiracy legend of vote fraud and dastardly doings.

The theories tied to Christian's ouster were hazy and unfocused, but many alleged that the combination of the hospitalization and the surprise verdict were somehow too much to be believed. The *Seattle Post-Intelligencer* wrote, "Conspiracy theories abounded last week when judge fave Christina Christian was the latest contestant booted from *American Idol*. Add to the mystery that Christian wasn't even present to receive the news, cited as being ill and in the hospital" and *Entertainment Weekly* fumed, "Something is rotten in the state of Hollywood. How gullible do the producers of *American Idol* think we really are? Does anyone really believe the sultry Christina Christian got booted off? Yeah, right, like she got fewer votes than Nikki or RJ. I don't think so. Sorry."

The chatter gained legs a week later when the Associated Press wrote a story about the potential for "power dialers" using automated devices to, in effect, stuff the ballot box. They wrote, "With fast Internet connections and powerful computer autodialing software, about 100 'phone phreaks' are casting thousands of votes with the touch of a button, producers acknowledged this week in response to questions from the Associated Press. 'They're all over the country and they tend to be slamming the system at all ends,' said Michael Eaton, vice president of home entertainment for FremantleMedia, the show's London-based producer. So far, these calls have had a 'statistically insignificant' impact on the outcome, Eaton said, but he wouldn't release any data on individual contestants and their vote totals." While no evidence was to surface that the power dialers had any significant effect on the voting—and to this day, *Idol* producers assert they did not and have not—the revelation of their existence was salacious enough to keep the story afloat until the end of the season, picked up and duplicated by nearly every major publication in America, discussed on network news shows, and referenced on magazine covers.

The conspiracy theories had, however, the effect of keeping *Idol* at the center of the national conversation even when the show hit slow patches. The chatter ultimately convinced few that a fraud was afoot, but ironically it kept the *Idol* ball in the air, one of many ways in the coming years that the show would prove incredibly adept at turning even its negative attention to its benefit. In the end, rival shows would kill for such conspiracy theories.

Elsewhere, tensions began to show. One obvious flashpoint was the hastily paired cohosts. Thrown together moments before air, it was becoming obvious that the two had never found a chemistry. At best, they took turns reciting scripted lines; at worst, they appeared visibly uncomfortable with each other. Having struck up a friendship with the star judge on-screen, the frenetic Seacrest felt comfortable diving in and ribbing Cowell, exchanging insults in what would become their trademark banter. Hanging back, Dunkleman was often left looking like the odd man out at the dinner party. His discomfort with the format, particularly with the cruelty of it, also peeked through.

"Things would upset him," remembers Debbie Williams. "He would sometimes change things on the air to mess with Ryan. He did that a few times and Ryan would look at me after we stopped doing whatever that intro was, and he'd look at me and he'd go, 'What was that about?' Ryan always handled it. He always handled it and it was tough at times. I think as Dunkleman became more unsure and it was so comfortable for Ryan, I think that bothered him."

Elsewhere, the already fraught relationship between McKibbin and Cowell boiled over. One day during dress rehearsal in top five week, Nikki stood onstage while a taped segment showing the contestants going to get makeovers ran. A dozen feet away, Cowell sat at the judges' desk watching. "I had blue eye shadow on and red lipstick, and they showed that clip and I hear him say, 'Oh, my God,' when they showed my face. So when it was my turn, instead of coming out singing, I came out bitching, 'What did you mean, oh, my God?' because at this point I'm just fed up and I didn't care anymore. He said, 'What are you talking about?' I said, 'I heard you say "Oh, my God" when my face came up there. What did you mean, oh, my God?' He goes, 'Let me tell you something, the world doesn't revolve around you, you little bitch.'

"I was mad as hell. I was thinking to myself, *Shut up, Nikki,* but before I could shut up a foot popped out of my mouth and I yelled, 'I'll fucking show you a bitch,' and that was it. We did not get along ever after that." The audience, Nikki recalls, was frozen in mute horror.

That week also marked the end of the road for RJ Helton, sent home after his rendition of "Arthur's Theme (Best That You Can Do)" on love songs of Burt Bacharach week. Helton recalls of his experience, "I knew that I was not going to be the winner by any means. I either thought that it was going to be that week or the week after. I tried to mentally and emotionally prepare myself for the worst but when I woke up the morning of the results show, I don't know what it was, something came over me and I just knew that it was my time. I knew that I was leaving that night.

"Normally there's an assistant producer, one that I was very close with, and she always came up to me and said good morning and we'd hang out and have coffee or whatever and she didn't come up to me that morning and a lot of the staff kind of stayed away from me. People weren't coming up to me and being friendly. I was like, 'Well, shit. Two plus two equals four.' I knew that was my final night. I tried to cry and get it all out before the show. Nothing I guess prepares you for that."

As the top four week beckoned, Kelly's surge continued. In the Vegas oddmakers' charts, Tamyra was now reckoned to be the favorite, with her odds to win at 2 to 1, but just below, tied at 3 to 1, Kelly now shared the challenger's berth with Justin. "We all thought Tamyra was going to win," says Lythgoe of the competition at that point.

While the contest turned into a three-way race in the public mind, there were also hints that it had turned into a three-way something else in the background. Initially, the rules separating the male and female sections of the mansion had been strictly enforced, but in the waning days of the season, as schedules grew more harried and as the contestants were rarely all in the house at the same time, it became easier to come and go freely, a fact, it was said by some, that was taken advantage of by the lone male now living in the house. Apparently Justin Guarini had very quietly become close with the new front-runner, Tamyra.

Later, the rumor would fly around the set that Justin had been getting close with another front-runner, Kelly Clarkson. It would not be hard to believe that among young, attractive people, living and working together in a very intense situation with the eyes of the world upon them, their relationships could spill over into something more than just work. Whether they did or not in this case is hard to know for sure; ten years later, the subjects aren't talking. But one hint, and a sense of how the participants may have felt about this triangle, appears on Kelly's first album. On that first effort, there is one song, "You Thought Wrong," cowritten and sung in a duet by Kelly and Tamyra, that lurks in plain sight as a possible insight to an experience they shared. The lyrics told the story of two women who realize they are being played by the same man. The potential meaning of the song, whose one line declares "Boy, your cover's blown," went over the heads of the album's critics.

As top four night approached, the pundits assumed that the bells would now, at last, toll for Nikki, who had dodged fate while falling into the "McKibbin Zone" week after week. Before the show, however, *Idol* had to face its first sex scandal, another ritual that was to become an annual tradition. The morning before the performances the *National Enquirer* published an issue with the cover story "Idol Cutie's Shocking Life as a Stripper," detailing Nikki's stint dancing at the Heartbreakers club in Texas. While she and the show shrugged off the story, it added to the popular sentiment that, with a clear top three chosen by the pundit community—voters be damned—it was time for McKibbin to go. *USA Today* wrote, "Nikki McKibbin fans won't want to miss tonight's *American Idol* as even the most rabid among them have to figure that this is her last stand on the show. Then again, few *Idol* experts thought Nikki would last this long, so you never know."

As it turned out, on what was supposed to be her swan song, Nikki had one of her best nights of the year. Her rendition of "I'm the Only One" even inspired kindness in Cowell, who likely thought he was delivering her eulogy, and reversed his recent verdicts: "You've absolutely proven to yourself and to everybody else that you belong here in this competition." Tamyra, for her part, after a string of stellar nights and relentless praise from the judges, had a just okay night.

Coming down to the wire, fifteen million people tuned in for the top four week. Better still, proving the intensity of the viewers, a full fifteen million votes were cast by phone.

In the end, when the votes were cast, it was Tamyra who was sent packing.

It was, and remains, arguably the most shocking ouster in *Idol* history. Seven years later, Cowell would say he felt that it was the greatest disappointment the voters had ever delivered. Looking back, Guarini says, "I really, truly believe that Tamyra would've gone to the finals if she had not been voted off shockingly that night. I believe that she and Kelly would've probably gone to the finals."

In the studio, the audience seemed on the brink of rioting: Actual screams of horror could be heard, boos sounding from every corner. The judges looked as though they were about to be sick. "I'm in a total state of shock. It's like I'm seeing Muhammad Ali get knocked down for the first time," a shaken Paula said. Standing awkwardly beside the toppled favorite, Nikki smiled as best she could as the wave of *boos* washed over her, breaking down in tears as Tamyra said her farewells and as the judges assured her superstardom awaited on the other side of *Idol*'s threshold. Although the jeers may have been for the elimination in the abstract, for Nikki they felt very personal. Coming after weeks of abuse, it was all getting hard to take. "Week after week they just degrade her and degrade her," Nikki's grandmother told a Texas interviewer.

It was about to get worse.

"New Idol Boot a Shocker" screamed the headline in the *New York Post*. The next day they followed up with a story asking their readers to weigh in on "Should Nikki Just Quit?" The *Toronto Star* wrote, "The official Fox message boards immediately lit up with thousands of posts, most containing intricate conspiracies, grave pronouncements about racial inequality in America . . . or outraged cries for vengeful boycotts and petitions."

"The list of finalists gets more depressing," wrote the *Washington Post*'s Lisa de Moraes. "It's now down to a tone-deaf hottie mom, an all-American type with a great voice, and a narcissistic wedding singer who talks to his hair. . . ."

In retrospect, Tamyra's ouster can probably be attributed to a factor that would plague many a contestant to come. Tamyra Gray was poised, professional, and unflappable, the very qualities *Idol* audiences do *not* want. Part of the *Idol* myth is the story of unprofessionalism, the diamond in the rough, the amateur. *Idol* audiences want to see their princesses squeal with excitement when they make the big stage. Again and again, they have shown they want to see their champions stumble, overcome with emotion and so blown away they can't believe their good fortune. Again and again, singers to whom it all seemed too easy would find themselves at odds with the reigning mythos.

The following week, Nikki's agonies finally came to an end, but not before one last twist of the knife from Simon. "America will have got it right if Kelly and Justin are on the Kodak stage next week," he said, just in case anyone had missed his point the night before. Nikki recalls of the moment: "Those are the instances that a lot of people capture on their pictures to print out for their camera, that split second where you can tell how really pissed off I am. That's the picture that they print up. My grandmother has them all over her house. It's just the picture where you glimpse just how pissed off I was. I think the top three, I always kept smiling but when we got to me and Kelly and Justin and Simon said that, when they panned back up to my face, too, I'm livid, like . . . 'You're a fucking asshole . . . I don't give a shit. Whatever.' "

The end did finally come that night. Nikki was eliminated and the historic matchup of Justin and Kelly for *American Idol*'s first crown was confirmed.

IN THE MINDS of everyone involved, it could still go either way. Kelly had been ahead in the previous week's voting but not by so much that a great night for Justin couldn't tip it, and there was no telling which way Nikki McKibbin's supporters might turn.

What uncertainty remained evaporated for most when they heard the "winner's songs," the two original pieces that both contestants would sing for their final showdown. Both "Before Your Love" and "A Moment Like This" seemed tailor-made for Kelly Clarkson's voice, the latter particularly falling right into her range. Lythgoe recalls that the debate about the song became fairly heated. "There were a few arguments on that because they recorded a song that was really too high for Justin Guarini. There was a bit of a falling out over that."

Byrd remembers at the finale, "Justin said to me, when it became song choices, he knew, 'That song's not for me. It's for her.' "

Nikki McKibbin, who returned to participate in the finale, remembers doing the math and saying to Kelly backstage, "I told Kelly, 'You won the show.' She said, 'Shut up, Nikki.' I said, 'A million bucks if you didn't win this show, seriously.' "

Guarini himself remembers telling her after their performances the first night, "I said, 'Honey, I tried but you know you're going to win this, right?' And it was with a happy heart because I just knew that song was perfect for her and she nailed it and it just was right. Everything was right. I remember being off to the side of the stage with Nigel

Lythgoe when she was performing 'A Moment Like This.' I remember saying to him, 'If I win this you're going to need to hire some extra security,' and this is while she's singing it. He said, 'Why is that?' I said, 'Because there's going to be a riot if I win. Do you hear this?'"

In the first *American Idol* finale, 15.8 million votes were cast and 22.8 million people watched the spectacle. Kelly's coronation became a national moment. The *Idol* fairy tale of the girl from nowhere transformed into a star was born.

Justin himself created another tradition, and if that night is strewn with stardust in people's memory, his behavior would have much to do with it. Justin Guarini, without missing a single beat, joined in a gracious celebration for Kelly that set the standard forever, allowing the winners to step forward with no mixed feelings. Justin remembers, "I was up there and the possibility, of course a part of me wanted to win but a part of me really knew what the score was. When it happened I was like, 'Yes! Yeah, babe, you did it.' We were very close by that point. You can't go through something like that with someone and not be close to them. It just was what it was and I was very joyous and still am to this day."

Gail Berman recalls, "The chemistry of the whole thing was absolutely special. Not only were we on to something in terms of a successful ratings winner, but it was just a thrilling night. It somehow had captured a wave and made people feel good about homegrown talent and possibilities. It just was a moment in time."

Chapter 8

THE EXILE

Brian Dunkleman didn't want to talk.

It was hard to blame him. Since parting with the show at the end of season 1, Brian Dunkleman has had a dark cloud cast over his life. In the few interviews he's given since leaving *Idol*, he's tried to make light of it, embracing comparisons with the fifth Beatle and resurfacing on Howard Stern. Nevertheless, Brian Dunkleman is still regarded as a cautionary tale. Nine years after the fact, he is still known as The Man Who Left *American Idol*.

But after ignoring my entreaties, something happened and Dunkleman—whose existence, like Elvis, has been the subject of rumors and random sightings—was thrust back into the spotlight by no less than former partner Ryan Seacrest.

On season 9's April 13 episode, as Seacrest told audiences of the upcoming *Idol Gives Back* charity special, he noted that the show was so big that it would be held from two stages and, he added with a mischievous grin, the host from the second stage would be . . . Brian Dunkleman.

The audience tittered nervously and gasped at what seemed an ungracious reference on Seacrest's part. During the next few days the quip became a minor news item, fueling a storyline already in play about Seacrest's seeming stumbles and missteps in *Idol*'s troubled ninth season. But the incident also sparked interest in Dunkleman himself, who gave his first interview in years to *New York Magazine*'s Vulture blog and days later, having seen the need to let his side of the story be heard, gave his second to me.

It's almost impossible to recall, viewing the vast landscape of Seacrest, Inc., today, that the golden-haired boy didn't always have the stage to himself, that he had shared it with a laconic wiseacre, the buddy act that briefly guided the *Idol* show. But by season 2, for reasons that have never been entirely spelled out, Brian Dunkleman disappeared from the screen and the building of two empires began in earnest—that of *Idol* and of its now solo host.

Waiting to meet Brian Dunkleman, I'm unsure who I'll be seeing. The year before he filmed a short comedic video, a pilot for a proposed series entitled *American Dunkleman* that was posted on the Web—a pitch for a series about the foibles of a man who walked away from untold riches and success and who is seen by many as one of the biggest schmucks in entertainment history. In the video, Dunkleman sits at a bus stop absorbing catcalls from passing cars. Looming overhead is the mocking face of Ryan Seacrest advertising a "We Pay Your Bills" promotion for his radio show. The video's courage in making light of Dunkleman's misfortune causes viewers to gasp, but leaves him wondering about the man at the center of it all. After eight years, the horrors are clearly still fresh.

In person, Dunkleman shows little hint of the dark drama his name is associated with. He arrives at Barney's Beanery wearing a polo shirt and baseball cap, like any actor on his day off. He's friendly, if somewhat cautious, his northeastern accent stronger than I remember from TV. The talk is a bit awkward at first, but sitting back, looking through Barney's extensive selection of burgers, Brian's shyness evaporates and he quickly jokes about the Seacrest moment of the previous week. It's impossible to discern the slightest trace of bitterness.

"He made a joke," he says of Ryan. "No big deal. It was funny. It got me more attention than I've gotten in years. They might pick up the pilot now. I was hoping Ryan might have me on his radio show," he says, and we talk over the chances of that happening.

And then, taking a breath, we step back in time.

The road to *Idol* infamy, Brian Dunkleman tells me, began in the one-stoplight town of Ellicottville, New York, where he grew up the youngest of ten children. While attending college at the Rochester Institute of Technology, he began to perform stand-up at a local bar.

"I was always kind of the class clown," he remembers. "And so I thought, *I could probably do this*. So I said to the owners, 'Think about the next time you do a show, maybe I can emcee it.' Then, a week later, they said, 'You're on next Saturday.' . . . Everybody in town came, our family and everybody. So I actually ended up doing really well. It was a really supportive environment, and so I started getting booked by one of the guys. . . . He owned one of the clubs in Buffalo and he had me come up there and I just started getting work. I was like, 'You're actually going to pay me money to do this?' I decided that I would do the smart thing, drop out of college and start doing this."

He moved not quite to Hollywood, but closer to it, to Denver, where he had a brother in the air force academy. "I'd play a round of golf and then go straight to the comedy club and just kind of watch and meet everybody that came through. That's where I really developed."

After a few years of touring the country playing comedy clubs, Dunkleman was spotted by an agent for Disney/Touchstone, who encouraged him to come out to Los Angeles, getting him a spot at the Improv Comedy Club, where a good percent of America's comedy careers begin.

"I found a place and actually moved to Los Angeles on my twenty-fifth birthday. I spent my twenty-fifth birthday in an apartment . . . my electricity hadn't been turned on yet . . . with a boom box, batteries, and some candles, and was gently weeping, 'Why am I here right now?' That's how I started."

Dunkleman took the traditional stand-up route of performing wherever, whenever he could. "Sometimes," he said, "it was just a couple of other comics and the waitstaff cleaning the glasses, but you're onstage at the Improv." After a few years, he finally signed with a manager and an agent, won a slot at the star-making HBO Comedy Arts Festival in Aspen, and things started to click. His first acting role soon materialized, as Customer #2 on an episode of *Two Guys, a Girl and a Pizza Place*, followed by a three-episode arc as a tangential character on *Friends*. Soon enough, Brian had appeared on a dozen TV shows and was making his living as an actor and stand-up.

As was de rigueur for comics in the *Seinfeld* era, Dunkleman fleshed out the pilot for a sitcom vehicle for himself, in an eerie foreshadowing, the story of a child star who has lost everything and has to move back home. The concept won him a development deal with Castle Rock and he began pitching it around town.

"I'd always joked that I'd get a deal for my own show and the world would end. Well, I got my deal on September 9, 2001."

Forty-eight hours later, the networks had lost every bit of their appetite for new comedies. The *Seinfeld* era of scripted network television had abruptly come to an end and the pilot was dead in the water. While pitching, however, Brian had hawked his pilot to Fox. The following year he "got a call about this show, *American Idol*. They wanted me to come in and audition and it was real late in the process."

Brian was stepping into the whirlwind of a show being rushed to air; the audition process certainly reflected that chaos. "I got hooked up with another guy and they basically said, 'It's a singing competition. You're in New York City. It's one of the judges' birthdays. Just go.'"

The group was winnowed down to six or seven young men, mostly in their early twenties, mostly younger than Brian, then twenty-nine. "So they just kept pairing us up, one at a time. I went in with another guy who had already gone in and it was just one of those magical days where my first time in, there's fifteen people there with stadium seating and I got one laugh and I had them. Every time I went back in I had them. . . . Then I got a call to come in again and have breakfast at 7:00 A.M. with this guy Ryan Seacrest."

When asked how much he wanted the job, Brian explains that in order to audition and screen test he had to sign a "test deal," which included the salary he would ultimately be paid if he got the part. So, having seen the amount of money on the line, Brian wanted the job "pretty fucking bad. I mean, obviously I was an actor and I wanted to act, but being a struggling actor in Los Angeles is pretty rough."

Nerves mounting, Brian went on his arranged date with his potential partner, meeting Seacrest and season 1 producer Brian Gadinsky at Nate 'n Al's deli in Beverly Hills. "It was like, 'Where are you from,' and just very casual. He seemed like a really cool guy."

They returned again to the studio for one last team audition in front of the cameras. Before they could tape, however, Seacrest began to haggle over a sticking point in the contract, showing a bit of the cutthroat businessman that would later emerge, playing hardball before this crucial final audition. "I waited so long. I was so nervous, like, 'Please, just let it go.' I just remember people running up and down the hallways and I'm sitting there, trying to keep to myself, trying not to go nuts while he and his father—I think his father is an attorney—are haggling.

"But finally that all got squared away and so we went into the room together and it just worked."

Seacrest was an experienced host who had fronted several shows in the previous years. Dunkleman, a stand-up, had never hosted anything in his life. "The first day on the set was a little bit weird because I'd never done anything like this and it was a little intimidating, but it was actually really fun. It was just kind of figuring out how we were going to do this and so it was really just kind of like the audition."

Then the judges arrived, and with them the American debut of Simon Cowell. "That's kind of when I first saw what the show was. I just didn't have any idea of the honesty of the critiques, let's put it that way. So I was really affected that first day because you're spending all day with these kids, you're getting to know them and you're getting to know their parents. Then after a few hours they come out and . . . you know how it works. . . .

"In the second season, the kids knew that it was coming. They'd seen the show and they knew what it was about. On the original season it was just awful. 'You're telling me that I suck? That I should never sing again?' That's the thing that I think people need to sit back and try to visualize. That's why I had a hard time. And I couldn't shake it for the whole season. That said, I was the one who had a problem with it. Nobody else did."

With a director assigned to shoot segments around the Seacrest-Dunkleman duo, they ventured out in each city in search of comic bits. "The three of us really had a great time because every city was like, 'All right, let's just go around the city and find funny stuff to do.' That's my favorite thing in the world, 'Let's just go find it.' A lot of that stuff unfortunately didn't make it into the show because they just needed, 'Hey, we're in Miami. Let's check out the auditions.'"

In contrast to today's nine two-hour episodes, the first season's auditions were squeezed into a mere two one-hour episodes. Only a few of the segments ultimately made it to air. In one, Dunkleman is seen hopping into a limo and ordering it to drive away without Seacrest. In another, the pair are arrested and dragged off in handcuffs.

The general idea of the Seacrest-Dunkleman pairing was that Seacrest would take the foreground as the straightforward, information-giving host, while Dunkleman would hang back and jump in with wisecracks. "We were all trying to figure it out but we had this thing that we developed, this bickering thing I thought was funny and we played it up." But as the show evolved, the pair on the sidelines only found the occasional chance to develop their on-screen dynamic. Seacrest seized the mike at every opportunity and focused on playing off the judges, Cowell in particular, rather than sparring with his cohost.

After the auditions and Hollywood week, the live episodes began, and with them Brian's first moment helming a show that was quickly becoming a major hit. "I can't possibly convey how nervous I was. I actually thought that my head was going to come off my fucking body. Both Ryan and I . . . we're both standing there and shaking. They're counting down, 'Five! Four—,' and I'm like, 'I'm going to throw up and shit my pants at the same time.' He was the same way. We did our first thing. If you go back and watch that first moment, my voice is like an octave higher than it normally is. 'HEY, EVERYBODY, WELCOME TO—' and then we got done with our little thing. They were like, 'Okay, and out.' The graphics went up, and we were both like ahhhhh . . . and then we went to our next spot. It was an out-of-body experience I can't possibly explain to anyone who hasn't experienced it, and that was the first few live shows. By the end of it, it was like, 'All right, this is kind of cool.' It's exhilarating, but you're still scared as hell, but you almost know what you're doing. That's the part I miss the most about it, the live TV."

By this time, the show was taking off beyond all expectations. "When I really started to feel the size of it, every time I'd leave the house I would get recognized, which I wasn't used to. I went to a USC game . . . and people start recognizing me and they were rabid about this show. 'Dunkleman! Fucking Dunkleman!'"

Dunkleman's empathy for the contestants continued to tear at him, as did the difficulty finding his way alongside a highly competitive partner. "There were a few times where I had a hard time controlling my emotions about it and I look back and wish that I could've, but it was a long time ago. It was years ago. I had a lot of trouble just being upset when the kids were upset. I got a lot of, 'Your eyebrows are a little wrinkled,' because I'd really be bummed out, but that was my fault. That was my problem. I needed to be able to think, *Well, you're an actor, right? Act like you're not bummed out.*"

Despite it all, Brian realized he had been a part of something out of the ordinary, something that had changed his life forever. He recalls standing onstage during the massive finale at the Kodak Theatre and looking out into the frenzied crowd. "There was a moment when I was just standing there and I see all these people. I lean over to Justin. I said, 'Take a minute. Take this in.' That's what I did."

When the confetti settled, Brian finally had time to step back and look at what he was a part of. He thought about not only his ambivalence about *American Idol* and its format, but what it would mean to continue as a host, a role that in entertainment history has traditionally meant the end of an acting career for all who come to be known as a genial front man. But with the show having just finished its summer run and about to be raced back into production in time to make it to its new home on the spring schedule, there would be little time to weigh options.

As he begins to tell of the decision, his joviality fades. A seriousness sets in. His jaw clenches just a little. "I'll tell you what happened exactly," he says. "I went to Hawaii, my girlfriend and I, after the show had ended. It was the first time I had really just been able to breathe, sit, and take it all in. I was really conflicted and I didn't know what to do because I knew that if this show was as big as it was just that summer I wasn't going to have any chance at an acting career.

"But then I'm sitting on this amazing beach in Hawaii and I thought, *What, am I stupid?* I thought, *You know what, something will show me the way. I'll figure it out when I get back.*" When he got back, he returned to the news that almost immediately after the season ended, Fox announced that they would be bringing back first Cowell and then Seacrest.

"I started to get shredded in the press, all these leaks, like, 'He's going to get let go.'" When Brian's people called the show, they were told "no decision had been made."

What's more, with the move to the spring schedule, many had doubts whether *Idol*'s summer success would be able to be replicated. The question hung over Brian whether he would be forever mortgaging his acting career for an awkward spot atop a game show he had never quite felt comfortable with, and one with an uncertain future.

Looking for a hint, with Fox seemingly ambivalent and the press practically writing him off, Brian took these harbingers as his sign and made his fateful decision. "I can't tell you how many times I've replayed it in my head, if I'd waited another day, another week, two weeks, another month maybe it would be different. I released a statement. I just said, 'I'm grateful for the opportunity. I'm moving on.'"

Based on discussions with the *Idol* team, it's clear that a decision had been made and just not yet broken to Dunkleman. The show was not planning to bring him back. At that moment, however, and in the years since, having made the jump before he was given the word, he created a void into which a thousand what-ifs leaped every day of his life.

At this point, the conversation got more intense. I asked Brian how he felt after finally making up his mind. "Not good. I mean, obviously, I thought that I made the biggest mistake that anyone has ever made. Everything started going wrong. I actually ended up firing my manager. In reflecting on it none of it was his fault. I had to go in a different direction."

While he had been on *Idol*, Brian had talked with another manager who had expressed interest in working with him. Brian now approached that manager, who told him, "Before I can take you on, you need to sever your ties with your old manager." Brian duly cut the cord, and then checked back with his agent about making the leap to manager number two official.

"She said, 'Actually, he just called and he said now he doesn't think you're right.' I was like, 'I just fired my manager.' She said, 'There are a lot of other managers out there. Don't worry about it.' Okay. . . . So then I pitched to a pretty reputable management company. I went to the Improv to perform. They brought the whole company down to see me. Fifteen minutes and it was the best I've ever done in my life.

"Two days later, the girl at the firm, my point person, said, 'You know what, I just couldn't get everybody onboard.' I was devastated. That was the first time I realized it doesn't matter what I do. . . .

"I had called a manager who had really pursued me heavily way before *Idol*, thinking, *Well, I'm available now.* He said, 'Listen, there's not one person in this town who believes in you . . . you may get to its being between you and another guy for a pilot or a sitcom and they're not going to really believe and they're not going to know what happened and so they're going to err on the side that's safe. My advice to you is to get out of town for a while.' *Get out of town*, I thought. *Well, that's crazy talk.*"

The town, he was to discover, didn't believe he had quit *Idol* and not been fired. Or if they did believe it, that made him all the crazier. And then, after the doubts about whether *Idol* could make it in the spring lineup, season 2 debuted without Brian Dunkleman. The new season launched to 33 million viewers, an audience surpassing the Oscars and second only to the Super Bowl in annual viewing.

At that point, the bottom dropped out. Completely. If *American Idol* had suddenly become the nation's epic, there was little room left for the man who turned his back on it.

"My booking agent dropped me. I couldn't do stand-up on the road for four years. I had four or five weeks with one particular booker and he canceled on me because, in his words, *bad press.* . . .

"Nobody wanted to touch me. I don't know what happened. I don't know if I got bad-mouthed. I don't know if people were pissed off because I left. They probably were. I wish I could go back and change it but I can't. My manager actually described it as, 'You have the stink on you. You have the stink on you in this business.' "

The legend of "you'll never eat in this town again" rarely affects entertainers so immediately. When careers fade, there's typically a decline; the clubs get smaller, as do the paychecks. There is a long way down the Hollywood food chain before you hit bottom. Brian Dunkleman fell that full distance overnight.

"I WENT THROUGH such a severe period of depression I don't know how I pulled through it. The girl who's now my wife is the only reason I survived. . . . There was a period of time where I couldn't get out of bed. It was that bad.

"There was a period there—I think I went two years after that not working. Two years. Not a voice-over. Not a commercial. I try to look back and keep it in perspective but something that's so ingrained in the collective consciousness is kind of hard to shake. I think that's what happened. You've got to have an agent and a manager selling you. It's the hardest thing in the world to call yourself. That guy canceled all that work on me and that spread. I couldn't stop it once it started. Just to be in the position that I am right now and actually have people interested in me again, it kind of stumps me because I don't know how I got through it. I don't know how I survived."

The years passed, and slowly, in tiny drips and drabs, the ice began to thaw and things began to happen again. Ironically, the first break in the freeze came from *Idol* itself, when producers from FremantleMedia called as they were putting together the *Idol* retrospective show, *Idol Rewind*, and asked Brian to serve as narrator. After that, he shot a pilot for Fox, of all places, and did a couple of appearances on the Spike Feresten talk show. And finally, the reality era that *Idol* had helped begin grew far enough to call Brian back onto its shores. "I did *Celebrity Fit Club*, which at first I said, 'I'm not doing that.' And then, 'How much? All right, I'll do it.'"

Once *Idol Rewind* aired, reps appeared willing to take him on and he began to work again. "I got a new booking agent and he got me out and I was like, 'Wow, it's been so long.' You go back to the beginning and I was like, 'I don't care. I'll be so grateful to be able to do this again.' Some of the road gigs are pretty rough but I was just so excited to be able to do it again. I have a totally fresh perspective about any time I get to work because I had it taken away from me for a long time."

Soon enough, the *Howard Stern Show* came calling, finding Brian now able to make light of his experiences. Stern's producer called and sheepishly told him about a contest they were having of men in their thirties who still lived with their parents they were calling The Biggest Loser. "And he said, 'We want you to be a judge, we've got Pete Best—' I said, 'Wait a second, you've got Pete Best?!' I've been referring to myself as the Pete Best of *American Idol* this whole time. I get to meet the Brian Dunkleman of the Beatles? I'm in, man!"

His ability to make light of what he had gone through won Brian a bit of an underground following, which led to a call from a producer who had an idea for a pilot built around his traumas. The video, which would be that one active trace of him out there when Seacrest made his jab in season 9, was entitled *American Dunkleman*. It was released on the Web as a five-minute pilot presentation featuring a Charlie Brown–like star wandering the city in the shadow of his former partner, the image of a grinning, tanned Seacrest always looming nearby.

The video received a bit of attention when first posted online in 2009 and then largely sat without any bites from the networks. Until, that is, a year later, when once again, help came from the unlikeliest quarter and Seacrest's joke revived interest, garnering a flurry of calls to the producers and sending its view count soaring.

"Honestly, it feels like destiny. Honestly. I don't know why I had to go through this and there's nobody to blame but myself. That's the thing, people were like, 'You got fired.' I'm like, 'Oh, that would be so much easier to live with.' But I have to live with the fact that I did this to myself. I've got nobody to focus my anger at. I made my decision and I still think I would've even with hindsight, but I wanted to follow my dream. But if I had to do it all over again I think I probably wouldn't have done the same thing. With the benefit of hindsight, obviously I wouldn't."

It remains amazing how he seems free of bitterness toward the Goliath he left behind. Talking about it all, he displays a fragility, a sense that all this is still something very raw, something he lives with every day of his life. But it's also very clear that whatever the road he went down that got him here, through depression, anger, and every other toxic emotion that must overwhelm during such trials, he has stepped away from the worst of it and is now, just as he once was before *American Idol* came into his life, a performer, looking for a chance to entertain people.

"If by some ironic twist of fate through all of this I get to go on and do great things still, great. But my attitude is, I can go back in the corner and cry or I can suck it up and just do what I did before and keep doing that. There's something like a hundred thousand actor wannabes who move to this city every year and I think a thousand move out. It's a numbers game. I exceeded my expectations when I did *Two Guys, a Girl and a Pizza Place.* If you would've told me that this would've happened to me when I first moved out here in my two-door Cavalier I would've told you that you were nuts. I guess you could say that this experience has built character coming out of my ass, trust me. Every year gets a little easier."

Chapter 9

GOLIATH

After the euphoria of the season 1 finale, *Idol* rolled out to meet America face-to-face, heralded by an avalanche of merchandise and tie-in events beyond anything that had ever been created for a TV show. After a two-hour televised reunion special, the contestants embarked on a forty-city concert tour. The top four were signed by Fuller's 19 Entertainment and put to work on albums. There was a DVD, T-shirts, tote bags, and baseball caps. A feature film was in the works.

It was an empire like no television show had ever produced overnight.

"We were a little bit aggressive, I guess," Cecile Frot-Coutaz recalls. "We were trying to do what we normally do, which is monetize the show as quickly as possible. I remember doing a business plan for my boss at the time. We'd just finished one season. I put three more seasons in the plan. He said, 'Well, that's too bullish. Put just one more.' We weren't in that mind-set. We never imagined the show would become the phenomenon it is now."

Today, *Idol* is one of the most meticulously managed brands in the world. But there would be a long period of trial and error before that took shape. As season 1 wound down, a bigger challenge loomed before the team: the little matter of season 2.

But the sensation of that first season would not vanish without one more conspiracy to see it off.

. . . .

THREE MONTHS AFTER the finale, "A Moment Like This" still hung in the air. The winner's single had become a humongous hit, becoming the first single in over two years to sell over 200,000 copies in a week. Sam Goody sold more copies of "A Moment" in one day than they had of anything in over three years, the store told *Billboard*. "We're in uncharted territory," said the magazine's director of charts, reacting to a television show's ability to move that much music.

But with success came the inevitable downside of fame. In season 1, the tabloids had scrambled to catch up with the game, delivering one little scooplet on Nikki McKibbin's former exotic dancing life. But now they were in it to stay, and the tabloids and scandal would forevermore be a part of the *Idol* story.

After her great triumph, there was no bigger target than America's newest sweetheart, Kelly Clarkson. And now, it appeared, there was a bit more than the public had known. According to the *Star*, Kelly's amateur status was a ploy, and she had, in fact, been recording an album for three producers, including Carole King's ex-husband, before she auditioned for *Idol*.

The rest of the media wasted no time piling onto the tabloid allegation. "Idol Title in Dispute," blared the *Chicago Tribune*. "Did We Worship a False Idol?" asked the headline of the *Seattle Post-Intelligencer*. Jumping in with both feet was the *New York Post* with a story about the *Star*'s claims: "If true, that means Clarkson may have violated the show's rule about being an amateur with no prior professional singing experience."

It wouldn't be the last time the media, and the public in general, would be confused on this point. Conflating the requirements for *Idol* with the Olympics, many assume that contestants are required to certify that they have never been paid a nickel for singing before coming to *Idol*. This confusion that *Idol* demands absolute snow-white amateurism from its singers is more wishful thinking by the audience, arising out of *Idol*'s diamond-in-the-rough mythology, than an actual requirement of the competition. The *Idol* contract states simply that contestants not be under any current obligation to any management or record company. As the firestorm blared, *Idol* reps patiently explained this point. Kelly might have worked with professionals before, but she was not under any active ties and thus had broken no rules. But the explanation was lost under the cries of outrage that the fairy tale was not true.

Ultimately, whatever the truth of Kelly's past, this was a case where the story didn't match the picture. Whether she had recorded demos, worked with Hollywood pros, printed head shots, or headlined at the Roxy, Kelly Clarkson, with her pigtails, her accent, her infectious squeals, and her no-nonsense tone, felt like America, not Hollywood, and in the end that wildly appealing manner created a Teflon coating to which no dirt could or would ever stick. By Christmastime, the firestorm had blown over, and then it was gone, leaving not a trace on Kelly.

Now it was time to find a new *Idol*.

GENERATING A HIT in the summer, when the networks had little on the air but reruns and low-cost game shows, was one thing. Survival in the fall or spring would be another matter entirely. History did not bode well for the second season of reality shows. Shows such as *Temptation Island* and *Joe Millionaire* had demonstrated how quickly novelty could fade in this new era. Few would make it past their second seasons.

Would *Idol*?

There was little time to entertain such a question. The *Idol* team was occupied with getting the show to the airwaves in time for the spring schedule. It would be tough, but a January debut fit Fox's schedule perfectly. At that time, each fall was dominated by Fox's contract with Major League Baseball. The play-offs and World Series broke into the networks' September/October lineup, causing preempts and shuffles of the regularly scheduled shows, making it difficult to sustain an audience for a new show. A January premiere might have meant a clean slate for the show—and a postholiday audience ready to hunker down for some cozy and wholesome entertainment—but it also meant that the moment the curtain fell on season 1, the crew had to spring into action for season 2.

The contracts were quickly re-signed. Cowell's deal had been closed the night of the finale, one more season for one million dollars. Seacrest was the next brought back, for a reported figure just south of Cowell's million. When Randy and Paula confirmed that they too would be coming back, the team was in place.

But first just a little R & R. Clearly settling in with his new *Idol* family, Cowell traveled twice to the favored vacation spot of the British elite, the

Bahamas, once with his new BFF Ryan Seacrest, who duly reported the journey to *People* magazine, saying that he was "tanner, skinnier, younger, and faster than [Cowell] and he was very upset about that." And again with Lythgoe. "We got along fantastically well in those days," Lythgoe recalls.

Before they could launch, however, there were to be changes, or at least attempts at changes. The first was a return to the dream of that fourth judge to fill that elusive "DJ's" seat.

Idol execs settled on one Angie Martinez, a well-known New York music scenester who, the producers thought, would lend a bit of youth and urban credibility to the somewhat middle-aged, middlebrow panel. Her hiring had been announced to the media: "Hot 97 DJ to Be New *Idol* Judge," reported the *Daily News*. But inside the audition room, it was another story altogether. Martinez was largely silent during the auditions, hanging back as though too cool to dive into the fray. "It's much harder to be a judge on these shows than people think," says Cecile Frot-Coutaz. "You have to kind of criticize people who walk in and tell you they're a big fan of yours; and you have to kill their dream. It's really tough especially from an artist's perspective when you've been in their shoes." She lasted all of two cities before, by mutual agreement, it was decided that it was not working out.

The dream of a fourth judge was tabled for now, but would live to fight another day. And despite the departure of Brian Dunkleman, the show was not ready to give up on the two-host format either.

Kristin Holt had made it as far as the semifinals on season 1. To *Idol* audiences, the former cheerleader and beauty queen had been distinguished for sliding under the judges' desk when she raced to hug them after her audition. After being eliminated, Holt did some on-air work with a local TV news show, getting a taste for hosting. When she read that Dunkleman would not be returning, she called up Lythgoe and requested his slot. "Come on the road with us, cohost," he told her. "We'll see how you do."

There's some confusion, a decade later, what role Holt was signed on for, but media reports at the time make clear that she was brought aboard as the new cohost. After shooting some initial segments wearing the cohost's hat, when the audition episodes aired, Holt was relegated to the role of correspondent, filing occasional pieces on life at the *Idol* mansion.

. . . .

IN SEASON 1, *Idol* execs and staffers had desperately passed out flyers to recruit contestants. In season 2, local newspapers and TV stations ran stories announcing the circus was coming to town, covering the events like Woodstock was springing up in their backyards.

The attention, however, brought *Idol* a new problem: hordes and hordes of people wanting to get on the show. People were camping out overnight for the tryouts. There were the good, the bad, and the just plain crazy, which included a subset of people in clown suits and Uncle Sam costumes. To the shock of all involved, the auditions for *American Idol* had become regional carnivals for dreamers of every sort.

Thousands of people showed up at each location, the lines stretching off into the far distance: Miami, 6,000. Atlanta, 6,500. Fewer than ten thousand people had turned out to audition for the entire first season. By the time the season 2 tour was over, seventy thousand hopefuls had passed in review.

The avalanche had caught the *Idol* crew unprepared. There had never been anything like it in the history of television. Frot-Coutaz recalls, "I remember Cowell saying to me before we went on the road for the second season, 'Cecile, you know you're going to have a lot of people who are going to show up. Are you prepared for it?' I remember thinking, 'Of course we're prepared for it.' We sort of knew. But then we didn't expect it to the degree that it actually happened, and we weren't prepared for it. He was right."

The advance teams at the stadiums scrambled to find Porta-Potties, water supplies, and enough support workers to manage the swollen crowds, which came close to rioting at several stops. The crew was also surprised to find that not only the number but the type of people who showed up had completely changed. In that first season, whatever mythology might have developed, the people who turned out were largely those who had some sort of professional music experience and who were accustomed to going on auditions—people like Guarini, Clarkson, McKibbin, and Helton. This year, as if the myth suddenly became self-fulfilling, everyone who had been the star of their church choir or high school musical showed up to try their luck at the *Idol* dream. "We were getting good amateurs rather than bad professionals" is how Cowell described the change in his memoir.

In Nashville, Belmont University senior Kimberley Locke had just finished up her law school applications when she heard about the auditions. Locke was the quintessential candidate for the *Idol* dream. Throughout high school and college, she had become something of a local star, singing with a church choir, a girls' a cappella group, and a jazz combo comprised of some local music professors. Yet, despite constantly feeling drawn to music, Locke couldn't see how she might turn this local acclaim into a sustainable life. So she set herself on a career in the law, spending her senior year preparing for the LSATs and filling out applications.

She had watched a couple of *Idol*'s first-season episodes but hadn't given it much thought. Then, in October, "A friend of mine who had moved off and gone to college in another town calls me and says, 'I heard that *American Idol* is coming to Nashville. Have you seen it?' I said yeah, that I'd seen it. 'They're coming to Nashville and if I have to go with you to make you audition, then you're going to audition.' I thought, *Whatever*." The notion stayed with her, however, and after the urging of her boss at her day job—"What do you have to lose?" he asked her—she made her way down to Nashville's Municipal Auditorium.

Locke recalls, "I woke about five thirty, six o'clock, laying in bed. It was like a movie, staring at the ceiling, and I remember having this long dialogue in my head with God. 'Do I go? Am I going to go? What are you going to do?' I was really procrastinating in getting out of bed to do this. Finally I said, 'Okay, you're going to go.' I had seen it on the news the night before, kids were camped out. I thought, *Who does that?* I said, 'I'm not camping out.' That was my whole thing. I said, 'I'm not camping out. God, if you want me to go, I'm not camping out.'"

With not enough judges on hand, the production was forced to cut off the line. Locke was one of the last ten people given a number to audition. "I was there all day, only to have them tell me to come back the next day. I didn't even get to sing that day. I missed three or four days of work doing this whole audition process.

"Maybe it's because it was the second season and there were so many people that they were just winging it, I don't know, but it was a long time. By the time that we got ready to go they had broken us down into groups of maybe eight or ten. We all filed into this tiny little room together standing boom, boom, boom. They didn't even call us by name.

They were like, 'Number so and so, sing. Sing. Sing.' Then at the end they literally said, 'Everybody leave except for—' whatever number. In my group, I was the only one that got to stay."

Locke was advanced to another room, where she remembers Lythgoe watching her audition and giving the nod that she should be permitted to advance. Finally, on the fourth day, she stood before Randy, Paula, and Simon. "I was the last one to audition. I remember walking in and I was so nervous I thought I was going to pass out and that's all I could think about. 'Just keep it together. If you're going to pass out, pass out after your audition.'"

She received the now famed ticket to Hollywood. Unfortunately, the date she was due to begin was also the first day of law school. After gently inquiring if it was possible to miss a week and being told there was no possibility of a deferral, she'd have to apply all over again, Kimberly faced a major choice. "I wore my poor mother out. I was calling her every day, every hour. I was at her house every day on the couch. I was crying." Finally, she packed her bags for Hollywood.

THE AUDITION TOUR was followed by, in contrast to the previous season's below-the-radar launch, a full-court press build-up to rival TV's Golden Age. Magazine covers offered *American Idol* beauty tips, "How to Look Like an Idol," and ran "Where Are They Now?" features on the season 1 cast. *Twist* magazine featured love advice for girls from Justin Guarini. The *Advocate*'s cover story talked with Jim Verraros about coming out as gay. A fifty-year-old sued *Idol* for age discrimination and the entire media covered the case.

In a joint interview alongside Randy Jackson for national TV writers, Cowell played up the tension between himself and Abdul.

Question: *Simon, how do you get along with Paula these days?*
Cowell: *Well, you have your good days and your bad days, don't you? I mean, we're not having dinner tonight.*
Question: *How many good days vs. bad days?*
Cowell: *Well, there weren't any good days.*
Jackson: *Ah, come on, Simon, come on.*
Cowell: *I'm not going to lie. We don't get on particularly well. But you have to take it a day at a time. You do your job, which is to*

judge talent. And if she irritates me, which she probably will, I'll tell her to shut up.

Looking back on the first season, Cowell also regretted going too easy on the contestants. He promised no such free passes this time around. "One of the things I may have said is that I would have told Nikki McKibbin to go back to the strip club. You should say what's in your mind, and as I watched her, I thought, *You are a better stripper than you are a singer.* I know that sounds rude, but that's what I felt." Such was the state of Cowell's still-rising star that every word was lapped up as truth-telling, the antidote to all that had been squishy and dishonest in our culture.

WHEN THE AUDITIONS were done and another Hollywood Week had been shot, the team knuckled down to edit the episodes for air—a tricky process that would forever plague the show. The early episodes, with their video packages showcasing sob stories and hometown origins, are the best chance the producers have to introduce that year's contestants to the public. During these weeks, the producers make their best bets of who is going to go the distance and highlight their stories with footage shot at their homes, establishing the rags part of the rags-to-riches narrative to come, and letting the viewers develop attachments to individual singers. However, as Kelly Clarkson demonstrated, the underdog phenomenon had a perverse side effect in that the serious contenders would come out of nowhere, emerge even under the producers' radar: Every year, the *Idol* team attempts to cut these episodes together as late in the season as possible, preferably after Hollywood Week has been filmed, in order to have the best sense of who is in it to stay, but every year some are missed.

As they prepped for season 2, the crew had been working more or less nonstop since the previous spring, and they began to feel the strain. Nigel Lythgoe in particular was about to fall victim to his obsessive attention. As he describes it, one day while overseeing the cutting of the audition episodes, "I had a heart attack during the editing of Clay Aiken." Literally, that is.

"I'm lying there on the couch, going, 'I do feel terrible. I'll have a little lie down.' I lay down and then was looking up at the tapes, yelling,

'No! Don't do it like that.' Bill, the editor, said that I kept popping up now and again, going, 'No! That's terrible. Change that.' Two days, and on the third day my wife said, 'You've got to go see a doctor.' He told me, 'You're having a heart attack.'"

He agreed to stay in bed for all of eight days. "I took a week off and didn't miss any of the shows."

SEASON 2 DEBUTED on January 21, 2003, with an episode featuring the auditions in New York, Austin, and Miami. "I remember none of us slept that night," says Beckman. At 5:00 A.M., when the first numbers came in, Beckman, Darnell, and Berman were in the office, poised and waiting to learn their fate.

The ratings were beyond their wildest dreams.

Twenty-six million viewers tuned in for *Idol*'s first night, making it the highest-rated night of programming in the Fox network's history.

"I think we were stunned," Beckman said. "*This* was a game changer. I think a lot of people would be surprised about how low key we have been about the ratings of this show. With big ratings come big responsibility so we never spent a lot of time celebrating the success of *Idol*."

Sandy Grushow assembled the Fox staff that day for a champagne toast. *Variety* quoted him, "After all the hand-wringing in the press about reality TV, the simple fact is that when an aspirational show like *American Idol* can galvanize an audience of this size, it's good for broadcast television."

IN SEASON 2, a new word entered the *Idol* lexicon: *disqualification*. When the contestants enter the Hollywood Week bubble, they are put through a battery of questionnaires and examinations to learn what might be lurking in their past, hopefully to find and defuse any bombs that could detonate during the season. Kimberley Locke: "I remember getting a questionnaire of five hundred questions to answer. 'Have you ever told a lie?' Basic stuff, and you're like, 'Well, yeah, I've told a lie. What kind of lie? Is there a severity, like a white lie?' All these questions, and it was pretty scary. It was very intense for a minute because they wanted to make sure."

The show then conducts basic background checks. The problem, however, is, as it is impossible to search through the pasts of all seventy thousand who line up at the stadiums, the show is forced to wait until the field is winnowed down. But even researching the past of the fifty or so who emerge from Hollywood Week is a major undertaking, with just a few weeks to do it. Every year, every manner of nefarious past or questionable moment is unearthed in these checks. The episode that follows Hollywood Week, the "chair episode," or green mile as it's known, where one by one the contestants sit before the judges and learn their fates, is in fact most years filmed weeks after Hollywood Week has ended, time enough for preliminary checks to have been completed. In those episodes, the audience sees the judges studying Polaroid snapshots of the contestants and debating their choices. What the audience does not see, however, is the show receiving the results of the checks. When the singers take their seats before the judges and are told that they will not be advancing, little explanation is offered. But each year a few contestants have in fact been dismissed due to something that has turned up on the check.

As much as is discovered, however, it seems each season there is a salacious tidbit or two that slips by, particularly in the early seasons and particularly in season 2. Says Frot-Coutaz, "Generally speaking, as the years went by, we became more and more protective in terms of the brand. In the beginning we were doing just very minimal background checks . . . just what you would expect on a standard reality show. Then over the years, they became a lot more extensive."

She describes the discussions about what emerges from these checks: "I find it personally very, very challenging because you want to protect your brand. But by the same token, you want to be able to give kids a chance to turn their life around."

The first public disqualification in *Idol* history was a singer from Youngstown, Ohio, named Jaered Andrews. After Andrews had advanced from Hollywood Week to the semifinals, the show quietly announced it was dismissing him, saying it had learned he was under contract with a boy band back home. After he left the show, it was revealed that he was in fact under indictment regarding his involvement in a bar fight in which a man had died "as a result of blunt force trauma to the head," the police complaint read. Andrews would eventually be tried and acquitted.

The arrest, as it turned out, was revealed on The Smoking Gun Web site, which would come to play an ongoing role in *Idol* history, the very beginning of the Internet's colonization of the *Idol* story.

Another unearthed tidbit would fall just on the safe side of the line a couple of weeks later, when The Smoking Gun revealed that singer Trenyce also had been arrested for theft, but the record had been expunged for good behavior. In this case, the show ruled that her past did not endanger the show and she was allowed to continue.

While the loss of Andrews was hardly felt, the next disqualification was a bigger hit. From her first appearance, Frenchie Davis had been marked as one of the season's front-runners. A large, boisterous African American woman with closely cropped hair and an exuberant manner, Frenchie's personality and powerhouse vocals had immediately been the buzz of the set. However, something came up in her background check that was hard to brush aside. As Nikki McKibbin showed, a bit of stripping could be excused. Even a dip into the X-rated realm could be forgiven. But Frenchie had not only posed for an adult Web site, but an adult Web site of a very specific nature.

Frenchie Davis, it turned out, had been filmed performing a sexual act with a beverage container for a site called Daddy's Little Girl. For a family show, this, it was feared, was more than the brand could withstand. After some agonized deliberation, with many arguing that she deserved a chance to turn her life around, Fox decided this was a step over the line that they were not ready to take and informed Frenchie that she was being disqualified from the competition.

Predictably, the media went bonkers. The salacious tale ran in every publication, with national Save Frenchie groups springing up online and sending petitions to the show. In the end, the exposure and notoriety did not get Frenchie reinstated, but it won her a ticket to Broadway, where she was offered a part in the cast of *Rent* shortly after her dismissal. For *Idol*, once again, a controversy kept the show on the front page.

WHILE THE COWELL barbs were no longer the complete shock they had been, their sting had not been reduced. Somehow the semifinals stage was the scene for some of the harshest moments between the judge and the contestants. In the tiny room, with no mediating audiences between them, contestants seemed to well over. On the second night of the season 2 semifinals Kimberley Locke took the stage. At the conclusion of her rendition of "Over the Rainbow," Cowell told the performer, whose fashion sense still projected the somewhat nerdy look of a law-student-to-be, that while he enjoyed her singing, on personality he gave her a four.

Looking as though she had been slapped in the face with a battering ram, Locke spat back, "Well, I'd give you a zero."

A broad grin swept over Cowell's face. Enjoying the fight, he answered back that he'd raise her to a 5 1/2.

At that moment, Kimberley seemed to lose it. She charged over to the judge's desk, leaned across, and shouted in his face, "I was going to tell you you're sexy but YOU SUCK!"

Locke recalls, "That night my phone was blowing up. All the women in my church were calling me, saying, 'You should not have said that. Why did you say that? Don't be disrespectful.' But I think that particular night Simon pushed my buttons on purpose. I had been really reserved up to that point. They didn't really have a good idea about what my personality was or even if I had it in me. . . . That night I was afraid that my comments were going to backlash on me because the viewing audience is looking at your personality as well. They fall in love with the personality just as much as the performer. The last thing I wanted to do was upset my fans."

The brouhaha did neither Locke nor *Idol* any harm. The following night, *Idol* played up the fight, asking viewers to call in and vote on the following question: *Is Cowell sexy or does he suck? Suck* won 58 to 42. And Kimberley was put through to the finals, beating out another deceptively nerdy young singer who had just captured the public's eye.

WHEN HE FIRST appeared on *Idol,* Clay Aiken was the very image of the twenty-first-century nerd. The twenty-four-year-old special education instructor from Raleigh, North Carolina, also represented *Idol*'s new breed: a young man who loved singing but had never been able to take it any further than singing the national anthem at local hockey games. In his first appearances on the show, Clay was all but written off. And even though something about his earnest quality and surprising voice made him stand out from the crowd, it wasn't enough to get through his first round, even with the judges' praise.

Backstage after that show, Kimberley, Ruben, and Clay, who had become friends among the semifinalists, gathered. Kimberley recalls, "That night before we performed, Clay and I and Ruben said a prayer in the Coke room. We held hands and we prayed for Clay to come back in the Wild Card group. We'd all bonded and I think it was because we were from the South. Clay is from North Carolina, Ruben from Alabama, and I was from Tennessee. So we felt this connection, this bond. We not only said a prayer that Clay would come back but we prayed that we'd be in the top three."

The Wild Card round was urgently needed that year, but not to fulfill Kimberley's prayer. To put it bluntly, the producers worried about the distinct lack of hotties in the group. Was there enough sex appeal to keep the audience interested? Three of the four recalled and put through from the Wild Card round expressly addressed that issue; two very young blondes, Kimberly Caldwell and Carmen Rasmusen, and the sultry twenty-three-year-old Trenyce.

While Cowell griped during the semifinals rounds that the talent was failing him, viewers didn't seem to feel his pain. For the first time in its history, Fox won the February sweeps month among the 18 to 49 demographic, which determines advertising rates. *Variety* wrote, "Fox's decision to plant the hourlong edition of megahit *Idol* in Tuesday's leadoff hour has significantly affected the viewing habits of millions of Americans while shaking up the night's network leader board. In fact, not since CBS moved *Survivor* to Thursday has the balance of a night teetered so much on one show. Net was already pretty strong on Tuesday, but since *Idol* hopped aboard last month, Fox has gone from a first-place tie with ABC in adults 18 to 49 (4.2/11) to a dominant number one position (5.0/13), while also leapfrogging other nets to become the leader in adults 25 to 54 (5.1/12) and teens (3.9/13), according to Nielsen." It was the sort of success that people had said was no longer possible for network television.

As THE TOP twelve contestants took the big stage, yet another round of controversy was unleashed. After the performance of saucy Latina hairstylist Vanessa Olivarez, she took a stool next to Ryan and he asked the singer if she would read his next cue card for him. Olivarez replied, shockingly, "Oh, Ryan . . . I'm an artist, not a performing monkey like you! Read your own script!" Her comment elicited gasps and boos. The following night, she was the first finalist eliminated.

In post-elimination interviews, Olivarez revealed that the questionable comment had actually been scripted by *Idol*'s writers and she had recited it at their behest. This revelation created a wave of conspiracy theories, suggesting that Olivarez had been sabotaged by the "family friendly" network because she had come out as a lesbian. These theories only grew when Olivarez was not allowed to participate in the national tour, despite the opening created when two others dropped out. Nor was she seen in that season's finale.

It seems highly unlikely that the show, which through the years would see more than a few openly gay contestants, had actually tried to sabotage Olivarez with a dumb joke. However, her protests about being forced to read the line after her elimination clearly did not endear her to the production, a warning to contestants to come.

IT WAS RARE that the outside world infringed upon the *Idol* bubble, but in March 2003, it did so in a way that turned out to be a blessing—for the show. As the *Idol* season went into high gear, America went to war in Iraq. Debbie Williams remembers, "We were rehearsing one day onstage. So, we stop rehearsal. The president was speaking. We put it on the big screen and we all sat on the floor and we watched it." The team anticipated that they would be preempted that night, but in the end, even war could not push aside the *Idol* juggernaut. The show aired as scheduled.

Wondering how to respond, someone hit upon having the finalists perform Lee Greenwood's "God Bless the USA." The song was intended to be paired with a more Hollywoodesque message delivered in a rendition of Burt Bacharach's "What the World Needs Now Is Love." However, when the finalists performed "God Bless" at the top of the show, the response from the audience was so overwhelming that Mike Darnell insisted they reprise it again at the end of the night, which they did to great effect, complete with marchlike dance steps and a final salute. The *Idol* contestants ultimately performed the song four times that season. They also released it as a single, with the Bacharach tune on the flip side, which inevitably went to number one on the sales charts. If the notion had been subliminal before this that *American Idol* was the nation's epic voyage, it now became explicit.

As if the gods hadn't smiled upon *Idol* enough, taking the *Idol* stage at this moment was an actual, bona fide, currently serving U.S. Marine, Lance Corporal Joshua Gracin. Having auditioned while stationed at Camp Pendleton, just outside Los Angeles, the crew-cut country singer became an immediate object of interest to the media, with accounts speculating whether he would be recalled to duty in the event of war. As it turned out, the Marines felt that Gracin was doing his patriotic duty representing the corps on *American Idol* far better than he would have been continuing his work as a supply officer on base. The question continued to pester, however, to the point where Cowell felt obliged to bring it up on the air, asking him what he would do if recalled to duty. Gracin responded with a crisp, unwavering, "I'm a Marine," eliciting a round of applause and an approving nod from Cowell.

War, however, granted no holiday from Cowell's barbs. Marine training might have taught Gracin to crawl through the desert under fire, but it did little to prepare him for the verbal body blows he received before an audience of millions. After initially looking favorably on Gracin, Cowell turned on him and turned hard. And Gracin did not like it one bit.

"Josh wanted to punch Simon out several times," recalls one crew member. "I mean, I really thought that that was going to happen. Honest to God. Because he was like a little raging bull."

In the end, Gracin held his fire, but the tension simmered until, driven by patriotic fervor, Lance Corporal Gracin ultimately finished in a very respectable fourth place. Sadly for him, however, once eliminated he was in fact recalled to active duty and sent on a recruiting tour for the Marines, forcing him to miss the big payday of the *Idol* summer tour.

BEFORE THE SEASON could end, however, there was one more unpleasant surprise to come. Corey Clark had been cast as the season's sultry bad boy from the very start. With a long tangle of hair, bedroom eyes, and a beyond laid-back manner, he was the picture of the indolent charmer, turning Paula to butter every time he walked over to the judges' desk and stared deep into her eyes. During Hollywood Week, Corey's decision to blow off rehearsal and go for a night on the town that included a ride on a mechanical bull at a western bar became the episode's recurring joke. Despite or because of the high jinks, he made it through Hollywood Week and was voted into the top twelve. Backstage, others in the cast and crew were less than charmed by the lovable scamp routine.

"What a jerk he was," one crew member recollects of Corey. "I didn't like that kid from the minute he came there. Did not like that kid. He's a punk. When he got ousted we were all like, 'Yes!' because he wasn't really a nice person."

Once again, the Internet intervened and interrupted Corey's journey when The Smoking Gun brought out the information that Corey was due to go on trial for assaulting his teenage sister and a police officer. The matter had escaped the initial background check because the police had misspelled Clark's name on the arrest report. This case required little debate and on the Wednesday night, April 1, results show, it was announced that Corey was being removed from the competition.

Again, however, the way that *Idol* dealt with the disqualification was truly different than anything viewers had ever seen before. Throughout TV history, people had been fired from shows, contestants disqualified, controversies following them. What was new, however, was the way *Idol* dealt with the matter. Rather than sweep it under the rug, *Idol* brought Corey on the air and gave him precious minutes of sponsor time to tell his side. On the controlled, monitored, regulated, corporate product of prime-time network television, this was revolutionary.

When Corey told Lythgoe that the incident did not happen as reported, Lythgoe said, "We had to let him go on. He said, 'This did not happen in the way that it's been reported.' So we felt that it was only fair to let him tell his side of the story to show that on the air. For me it was very important because we are a reality program. We are happening in real time, so deal with it. If we are in real time and if someone makes an allegation, face it and deal with it. That's the joy of being live for me."

While the air might have been cleared for the moment, nobody could have imagined how Corey Clark would come back to haunt *Idol*. His revenge would be served very cold seasons later.

MEANWHILE, THE DREAM of filling that fourth judge's slot just would not die. Before the contestants reached the big stage, another idea was hit upon: celebrity guest judges. Each week in the top twelve rounds, a different star joined the panel. Olivia Newton-John, Barry Gibb, Quentin Tarantino, and Gladys Knight each did single-episode stints at the table. The celebrities were to learn, however, that judging was harder than it looked. Being able to be critical and—occasionally—constructive, takes a bit of spine and creative thinking, while most celebs in our culture have long since been trained to let nothing other than inoffensive blandness emerge from their mouths. Not to mention, if you are going to be at all tough, you have to be willing to look like the bad guy. In their stints at the *Idol* table, the guests mostly contented themselves offering supportive pats on the back to the contestants, their presence adding little and throwing off the chemistry of the original three.

The most productive contribution they made may have been when Gladys Knight gushed that Ruben Studdard reminded her of a velvet teddy bear, giving him the nickname that would stick forever after.

"I personally find it a bit insulting having celebrity judges on the show. To me, it's our role and nobody else's to judge these kids, because we've chosen them from the beginning," Cowell told *USA Today*.

The most important contribution of the guest judges may in fact have been to make clear how unique the chemistry and the contributions of the original three were. While Paula Abdul had been derided for doing nothing but mouthing senseless praise, when seated next to people actually doing nothing but mouthing senseless praise, her value became clear. While always supportive, always finding something nice to say, always putting things delicately, Paula's gentle nudges actually were, on inspection, surprisingly on point. For Cowell, who spent his first season on *Idol* trashing his nemesis in the most personal possible terms, somewhere in season 2, the worm turned. By his own admission, he came to see that there was more there than the ditzy image would suggest, and the relationship changed from contempt to a more complex love/ hate dynamic. With a foundation of actual grudging respect, there would always be a playful, heartwarming quality to their fights to soften the show's hard edges.

WHILE THE JUDGES settled more firmly into their roles, another member of the cast was very clearly growing into his. Freed from having to share the stage, Ryan Seacrest was becoming one of the sharpest hosts on television. At the center stage he grew more confident, ably moving the show forward and keeping the timing on track. Gone now were the surfer dude affects and knee-length T-shirts. Standing at the helm of the biggest show on television, the new Ryan Seacrest wore tailored suits and carefully tended hair.

For a long time, the young DJ from Atlanta had been telling any who would listen about his grandiose visions for himself. Kristin Holt recalls dining with him during the second season's audition tour: "I remember one night at dinner, he told me, 'I want to be the next Dick Clark.'" And now the pieces were falling into place. Before the season started, Fox gave Seacrest his own New Year's Eve special, specifically to rival Clark's.

Seacrest's drive was also fueled by his BFF status with the most ambitious person on the set, perhaps the most ambitious person in Hollywood, Simon Cowell. Since their earliest days in the public eye, both Seacrest and Cowell had been the subject of rumors about their sexuality. Now those rumors spilled over into a ribbing routine between them that was to become a source of discomfort in the years ahead.

Idol's first outbreak of their mock gay banter occurred in the top eight week of season 2. After Kimberley Locke had sung "It's Raining Men," Cowell, who the week before had spent his judging time talking about the flames on the wall behind her, delivered the following ruling this week: "I thought you did one of Ryan Seacrest's favorite songs justice." The remark was met with nervous titters.

The following night, the banter continued. During one segment, Ryan took questions from the audience. When one visitor asked him to respond to the comment of the night before and tell them what Simon's favorite song was, an impish look suddenly spread over Ryan's face and he blurted out, "I don't know what his favorite song is, but his favorite club is called Manhole, where they are listening to 'YMCA.'" The awkwardness in the studio could be served with a spatula. In the wings, Lythgoe remembers looking at the rest of the crew and asking, "What the hell was that?"

As THEY NEARED the final stretch of the season, the stakes were raised considerably by the debut of Kelly Clarkson's album at the number one slot on the *Billboard* charts. While her winner's single had been somewhat predictable schmaltz, "Miss Independent," her first single from the new album, showed off a feisty rocking side that won over the last remaining doubters about the power of Kelly. Whatever the rumors and tabloid reports had been, all was clearly forgotten between Kelly and her fans. Kelly, Justin, and Tamyra all returned to the show to sing their new singles and play up the movie then in post-production. Justin endured one awkward moment; when chatting with Ryan about the movie, the host asked, "What's up with you and Kelly?" The unflappable Guarini could almost be seen blushing. "We're just friends! Nobody wants to believe it!" Indeed, the rumors of romance on the set of *From Justin to Kelly* persisted, fanned no doubt by the unit publicists. Meanwhile, any double meaning in Kelly and Tamrya's duet seemed to float right over everyone's heads.

Entering the top six, the field had at last taken shape, with two unlikely front-runners in the Velvet Teddy Bear and the made-over and spruced-up Clay Aiken. Cowell, however, was beginning to get the hang of this TV thing and started to think in terms of dramatic arc, the need to change the storyline before it gets boring. It was a task that suited his congenital fidgetiness. In season 2, the biggest benefactor of this tendency was Kimberley Locke, who, after being batted around by Cowell for the first half of the year, after suffering criticisms about both her appearance and her personality, was suddenly told that she could win the competition.

Locke recalls how she learned how to stop being scared and angry and figured out how to actually engage Cowell in the competition. "There was so much being thrown at you from hair, makeup, wardrobe, music selection, press, how to work the camera, how to give a sound bite, how to keep it together and be composed and put up with Simon and how to compartmentalize Simon because that's part of it. If you don't learn how to compartmentalize him it will freak you out."

As Locke was transformed from a nerdy law student into a glamorous icon with killer vocals, the audience followed Cowell's lead, and Locke kept dodging the bullet, outlasting even Marine hero Gracin, to make it to the top three. There she found, just as they had prayed to make it happen three months earlier, her friends Ruben and Clay joining her at the very peak of *Idol*. Throughout the entire season, Clay had led in first place in the voting, but Ruben was never far behind.

For the Velvet Teddy Bear, however, the competition was more of a strain than he let on. In years to come, when asked about the *Idol* experience, Studdard would moan in agony about the workload of an *Idol* champion. One crew member remembered: "The whole process was hard for Ruben. I'd let Ruben sit down whenever he could because it was too much work. 'This is too much work,' he'd say. When he came back on season 3 and they asked him a question . . . they asked him like, 'What should we be ready for?' He said, 'It's hard.' I always remember I'd say, 'Rube, come on, Rube, you've got to go. We've got to do this group number.' That's why when he won I thought, *Oh, this is going to be tough on Ruben.*"

PREPPING FOR THE final weeks, Locke remembers one particular ritual that would become an important part of the lives of the contestants: kissing the ring of the man who would take custody of many of their recording careers, music industry legend Clive Davis. "We all went into a little bungalow at the Beverly Hilton Hotel. Sitting in front of Clive Davis I was like, 'Wow.' He talked to all three of us. He said, 'You guys are going to have to learn these songs. I'm going to have all three of you learn the songs because we don't know who's going to win.' We learned the finale songs and recorded them. It's bittersweet."

Season 2 also saw the addition of another ritual, the homecoming. The Idols had returned home in season 1, but those trips had been hurried and impromptu: a stop on a local radio show, a swing by their old high school. Henceforth, the top three Idols would receive welcome homes befitting heroes, complete with parades, concerts, keys to the city, and proclamations from the governor.

The turnout to these events was, and remains, extraordinary. In post-2000 America, nobody gets parades anymore. Astronauts would barely be recognized outside of NASA. Sports stars have become tainted by the money machines of professional athletics. Many people think politicians are beneath contempt, and military heroes are rarely heralded by a wary media.

Only Idols, for that brief moment between their discovery and when they leave the *Idol* bubble, merit the sort of unalloyed affection that gets people to turn out to parades and weep for joy at their joy. Only with Idols does the public feel, "We know these people, we discovered them, we voted them through. They are people like us and their triumph is ours."

. . . .

THE TOP THREE would prove the end of the road for Kimberley, while Ruben and Clay moved on to their showdown. If the previous season's show had been huge, this one was truly on an epic scale. Held at the enormous Universal Amphitheatre (now Gibson Amphitheatre), with Clay's moving rendition of "Bridge Over Troubled Water" and Ruben's gospel choir backing him in "Flying Without Wings," the night had the sense of spectacle on every level, including a return visit from conquering champion Kelly Clarkson to pass on the crown.

In the end, while Clay Aiken had led the voting throughout the final season, on that last week, Kimberley Locke's former voters turned to Ruben and granted him the crown in a nail-biter of a result, only 130,000 votes between them out of 24 million cast. The close result, however, sparked a rare flub on the part of Seacrest, a flub that would fuel conspiracy theories that have not died to this day, driven by what may be the most ardent *Idol* fan group in history, the Claymates.

At the top of the show, when Seacrest first mentioned the margin between the winner and loser—then unnamed—he either misread the number or the number was misprinted on the teleprompter (accounts varied) and he read it as thirteen thousand votes. Later, he tried to correct himself, saying it was by 1.3 percent out of the 24 million cast. Not until the next day did Fox release the correct number, saying 130,000 votes had come between the pair.

On such single-digit gaffes, a thousand conspiracies are born, and eight years later, the Web is still filled with Claymate message boards and sites claiming their champion was robbed of his rightful title.

Worse still, with so many calls, the volume on AT&T was unprecedented, and busy signals abounded, leading partisans on both sides to claim their lines had been jammed. A Fox spokesman testily replied to the postgame avalanche of media queries, "Twenty-four million did get through. The system worked like it was supposed to."

Surpassing the number who watched the Academy Awards, 33.7 million people watched the finale, putting *Idol* second only to the Super Bowl in national viewing. *American Idol* was now officially, unquestionably, without reservation, here to stay.

But its star, Simon Cowell, was already getting antsy.

Chapter 10

DIVAS

The rumblings of discontent were subtle: not quite shots across the bow, more like water balloons dropped off a rooftop.

In the race to get *Idol* on the air that first season, Fox had Cowell sign a one-year contract. In their haste to get the second season of *Idol* on the air, Fox had again extended the contract for just one year. Now it was again up. And in the interim, *Idol* had become not just a phenomenon but an empire.

At the end of the second season, his renewal pending, Cowell had aired a few mixed feelings. Told during a radio interview of a rumor the show was considering Paul McCartney as a fourth judge, Cowell muttered, "Well, good luck to them." Pressed on what he'd meant—wouldn't he be coming back?—he let slip with seeming nonchalance, "No, not really. I may have done enough with the show."

It wasn't the first time he'd used this little tactic—after the end of *Pop Idol*'s first season, he'd made similar noises about moving on—and it wouldn't be the last. Nevertheless, shortly after these comments were made, Cowell's contract was hashed out, and he signed on for three more years at the astronomical sum of six million dollars a season.

Tactic though this might have been, those first vague stirrings of dissatisfaction were unmistakable. While between seasons the *Idol* crew at long last got a break—a full seven months before a new series would go on the air—Cowell returned to England for the second season of *Pop Idol*. The British show held up in the ratings, but something of the magic spark of that first season had faded. The winner, Michelle McManus, attracted more attention for controversies about her plus-size figure and the judges' remarks about it than she had for her singing. The excitement around her victory paled in comparison to the frenzy for Will Young and Gareth Gates. Her subsequent recording career failed to take off, and she was dropped by her label after just one album.

What this meant for Cowell, however, was that by the end of 2003, he had shot four back-to-back seasons on either side of the Atlantic. And he had squeezed in a stint judging the onetime *World Idol* contest. *American Idol* season 3 thus became his sixth *Idol* show in three years. What's more, Cowell, who had created so many stars in his time, was now himself "just talent." He might be celebrated and very well compensated, but a man of Cowell's ambitions wasn't going to be comfortable in that spot for long.

Having dived into the world of television, Cowell was here to stay. And perfect timing too, just as the music business took its first lurch toward the meltdown that would decimate its ranks over the next decade. But just sitting behind the judges' desk wouldn't satisfy his appetite for the new medium. He put his first foot into television mogul shoes producing a show called *Cupid* for CBS, a reality/game/dating show hybrid in which a single woman and her friend toured the country, hunting for the perfect match. Barred by his *Idol* contract from appearing on the air in any other reality show, Cowell served merely as the show's overseer. The complex concept was inventive, perhaps too inventive, and the show failed to find an audience. For Cowell, though, having seen the impact a hit show could have, the TV mogul bug was raging.

Once Cowell's contract was sewn up, however, another judge took her turn at playing hardball with much different results. When Paula, whose salary was still south of one million, attempted to hold out for a major payday herself, sources behind the scenes let it slip to *Variety* that her price tag was out of line with her services. *Variety* wrote, "A sure sign talks aren't going well: Insiders close to the production say execs from the net and production companies FremantleMedia and 19 Entertainment have met with crooner Natalie Cole and Go-Go's front woman Belinda Carlisle in recent days. Singers have been told the network is looking to add a fourth judge—or possibly a replacement judge—to the smash skein when it returns for its third season in January."

Paula quickly came to terms and signed back aboard. After a few seasons of *Idol* and having become the biggest star on television, Simon Cowell's options, were he ever to walk away, were limitless. Paula, on the other hand, while her *Idol* exposure had reopened many, many doors, was still too close to that long dry period in the 1990s to risk going back out there once again. And everyone knew it.

For the producers themselves, the break between seasons was time for another shot at expanding the brand. In the summer months when *Idol* went off the air, its slot was filled by *American Juniors*, an underage version of the show. Starting strong in the ratings, *Juniors* lacked the bite of *Idol*; bringing that Cowell edge of viciousness to bear on ten-year-olds somehow was just one step beyond the pale. It ultimately failed to hold its audience, tumbling 40 percent by the season's close. It would not return.

In December, Kelly Clarkson crossed the Atlantic to compete with ten other *Idol* champions from around the world in *World Idol*. The show was judged by jurists from each of the nations now in the *Idol* orbit, including Simon Cowell for the United States. (Pete Waterman did the honors for the United Kingdom). Wrought by confusion over the language barrier—contestants were required to sing in English but taped with different hosts for different nations—*World Idol* never jelled the way the infamous Eurovision song contest did. Worse still, the one untouchable subject poked its head onto the *Idol* stage. *Idol* could handle strippers, porn stars, and assaults warrants, but when politics appeared, even the most fearless of producers went running. And on *World Idol*, that was exactly what happened.

Although it was widely assumed that Kelly Clarkson would walk away with the title, with the war in Iraq still ranging, Clarkson's down-home Texas girl demeanor didn't ring nearly as charming to the largely European viewers as it did to the folks stateside. As the contest advanced, regional voting blocks formed and Kelly found herself behind the eight ball. Ultimately, a Norwegian country singer named Kurt Nilsen took the prize, singing U2's "Beautiful Day" as his victory song.

Then there was the Christmas show, a reunion featuring stars from seasons 1 and 2. The reach of *Idol* seemed endless.

CONTINUING TO AMAZE, season 3 debuted with an even larger audience than the year before. Twenty-nine million people tuned in to watch the January premiere. The auditions immediately produced one bona fide star, a UC Berkeley civil engineering student named William Hung.

At each audition, as the assembled contestants waited to see the judges, producers would make an announcement reminding them that they were there because "they were really good or really bad." There were always those who didn't quite get what side of that equation they fell on.

Sorting through America's oddest freak show became a pastime in itself, and as the years went on, the audition episodes attracted their own audience—viewers who tuned in for the comedy value even if they had no interest in the competition itself. Every year, the show would soon find, ratings would fall off after the audition episodes, that particular audience moving on.

In season 3, the stand-alone part of the auditions produced its first true star. It remains unclear to this day whether William Hung actually believed his hilariously no-tune version of Ricky Martin's "She Bangs" was a performance that could have taken him to the *Idol* finale. Some seven years later, he expresses little understanding that his music is beloved for any reason other than its high quality. But Hung's case was one true instance in which a singer walked onto that stage a nobody and came back a star. Within a week of his performance, his hastily thrown together Web site had received four million visitors, and he had appeared on every talk show in the universe, from Jay Leno to Howard Stern. He was satirized on *Saturday Night Live* and animated in *Celebrity Deathmatch*. Before the first season was over, his first album was released, and William Hung had stumbled into the sort of career for which more traditionally talented singers would kill. And more important, the path to fame had been opened for a whole new class of performers that, for better or worse, the world had never seen.

While the audition tour was under way, however, Nigel Lythgoe's body would once again revolt. Lythgoe might have outrun the previous year's heart attack, but his body found other ways to fight back.

He had gone straight from *American Juniors* to *Idol* proper, and the schedule was grueling. "In October, I came back from auditioning in Hawaii and had peritonitis. My appendix exploded. . . . They kept taking bits of my intestine. I lost about sixteen feet of my intestine. I missed the

Christmas show. It broke my heart. I said, 'What's happening now, Ken?' 'Don't worry. It's okay.' 'But what songs are they going to be singing?' 'Don't worry,' he told me."

The doctors tried to keep Lythgoe, in his words, "strapped to the bed. " It was so bad that he thought he was going to die. But after six weeks, he was able to rejoin the season and worried *Idol* execs breathed a sigh of relief.

EIGHTY THOUSAND PEOPLE auditioned for that third season of *American Idol.* Yet, somehow, many complained that this army of contestants had failed to produce even a handful with any talent. At least it seemed that way to Cowell, who, as the season began, was notably cranky—even by his standards. "This is the worst day I've ever seen in judging this competition. A disgrace. I didn't want to come in today," he spat during Hollywood Week. In the semifinal rounds, he was so indignant with the whole group that he seemed on the verge of getting up and walking out. "It's good we didn't charge people tonight or they'd be asking for their money back," he told one group.

On his sixth *Idol* stint, Cowell's language of put-downs had grown richer, his metaphors ever more colorful. Joining his traditional "lounge singer" dismissal, he added "cruise ship singer," "wedding singer," and "rodeo singer" to his repertoire. "We were looking for spaghetti Bolognese and that was sweet-and-sour chicken," he told one befuddled contestant.

"In the first season, people said, 'I can't believe he's saying that,' " recalls one crew member. "In the second season they said, 'I can't believe he's saying that, but you know, I kind of agree with him.' By the third season, he was the man who told the truth, and therefore whatever he said, however out there he got, that was what was true."

Cowell's mood had become so petulant that by the end of the semifinals, Seacrest took him on in a less friendly joshing way than usual. After he had told one contestant, "You're a beautiful girl but you're ugly when you perform," Ryan confronted him, pointing out that he and his fellow judges were the ones who had selected this group out of the eighty thousand possible contenders. The implication made Cowell explode with rage:

Cowell: *I'll put it to you since you're the expert: Do you think they all should go through?*
Seacrest: *Yes.*
Cowell: *That's why you are a host and I am a judge.*
Seacrest: *You're the one who put them through.*
Cowell: *Ryan, you find a competition where you can find thirty-two stars and you will be a billionaire rather than a thousandaire.*

One contestant who stood out of the otherwise condemned pack was to become one of *Idol*'s iconic stories. Debbie Williams recalls, "Fantasia is the only *Idol* who, when I saw her in Hollywood Week, when she walked off the stage, I said to her, 'You don't know me. But I'm going to tell you something right now, and I want you to remember it. Top two.'"

All of nineteen years old when she auditioned for *American Idol*, Fantasia Barrino's story already had enough tragedy and heartbreak in it to fill a Lifetime network movie, as it eventually would. Functionally illiterate, Barrino had dropped out of high school, as she would later reveal, after being raped by a classmate. Touring her native North Carolina as part of the Barrino Family gospel group, Fantasia conceived a daughter at age sixteen. By the time she tried out for *Idol* at age nineteen, she had freed herself from a physically abusive relationship with the child's father.

From the start, the highs and lows of Fantasia's journey were right on the surface in her intense vocals and infectious spirit. Almost the only one to receive praise from Cowell in those early weeks, she had been told her after her semifinals performance, "You are destined to be a star."

Fantasia was not to have the spotlight instantly to herself, however, but she instead became cast as one of the "three divas," a trio of sensationally talented African American women who dominated the season. Though grouped together, the three were extremely different outside of their shared demographics. Besides Fantasia, the group also included LaToya London, a cool, understated singer from Oakland whose style was compared with the smooth soulful melodies of Gladys Knight, and Jennifer Hudson, a fiery crooner from Chicago who was cast in the Whitney Houston/Celine Dion mold.

Different as they were, the three did not hit it off. "Those girls fought and fought," remembers one crew member. Most combative of the three was Hudson, who, despite some powerful performances, struggled to win over the audience. She was first eliminated in the semifinals, then resurrected as Randy's choice in the Wild Card round. But week after week, she found herself in the bottom three.

"She was very angry," a crew member recalls. "One day all the girls got out of the car and into the elevator, and they're all screaming at each other and fighting. They go up in the elevator. Jennifer was on the phone in the back of the van saying to her mom or somebody, 'Well, clearly I'm the best. Clearly I'm far better than any of these girls.'"

Hudson's calm was not helped by the wildly shifting verdicts of Cowell, who, whether out of frustration or boredom, seemed to proclaim a new front-runner every week. On the first night of the top twelve, he tagged the pleasantly likable Hawaiian singer Jasmine Trias "the best of the night" and called John Stevens, a shy Conan O'Brien look-alike who specialized in Sinatra-like standards, "the dark horse to win this competition."

The following week, he laid down the glove to Hudson: "Let me sum this up for you. You are out of your depth in this competition." Cowell may have been cranky. Or he may well have been setting Hudson up for a dramatic turn, about to declare she had come back and was now in this competition to win. Whatever the motive, the audience was now following his lead, and that was about to have a dramatic effect.

The top seven results show was to be one of those nights replayed forever in *Idol* lore. When the results were read that night, Seacrest stunned the crowd by announcing that the divas were that night's bottom three while Jasmine Trias, Diana DeGarmo, and John Stevens miraculously were the top vote getters.

Minutes later, when that shock had settled in, he delivered the coup de grâce, announcing that Jennifer Hudson's *American Idol* journey had come to an end.

Randy Jackson was the first to raise an eyebrow at the verdict, suggesting something not wholesome was at work in the fall of the divas. "As a proud American, I hope that America is listening and watching. We want to be proud of whoever wins this. We're proud that Kelly won. We're proud that Clay came in because they were the greatest talent that you could find. That's what this whole thing's about." The outrage was so palpable that even Seacrest felt compelled to lecture the audience, saying, "You have to vote for the talent, you cannot let talent like this slip through the cracks."

While Jackson and Seacrest were ultimately circumspect about the causes behind the vote, the press would grant the *Idol* electorate no such grace.

"Theories flew fast and furious Thursday after the *American Idol* viewer vote went against favorite Jennifer Hudson, ranging from racism to fateful weather to teenage puppy love," wrote the AP. "Questions of racism also came up in the first season, after talented Tamyra Gray was voted off," they reminded readers.

"Another group of people think there's a racist conspiracy to keep *American Idol* from having a black winner two years in a row," the *Boston Globe* quoted an *Idol* viewer.

Watching from the sidelines, Elton John, whose music had been the subject of a theme night two weeks earlier, joined in the outrage. "The three people I was really impressed with, and they just happened to be black, young female singers, and they all seem to be landing in the bottom three. They have great voices. The fact that they're constantly in the bottom three—and I don't want to set myself up here—but I find it incredibly racist."

Whenever a controversial vote occurred, the discussion would be framed in terms of "*American Idol* is getting rid of" or "*American Idol* doesn't want," the conspiratorial mind-set conveniently forgetting that it was the American people, or at least the *Idol* voting segment of the American people, that had made the choice.

But as ever, the controversy did the show no harm. Throughout season 3, ratings continued to soar, continuing to reach unbelievable new highs. The Hudson ouster and the three divas controversy provided a dose of excitement in what had been a fairly uneventful, some said lackluster, season.

THE ANNOUNCEMENTS OF the results were actually one of the earliest tastes of what would become one of *Idol*'s signatures: the delicate ballet staged each week by Nigel Lythgoe to keep the audience on its toes. While in the first season, filling up these half hours had often felt painful, by season 3 the drawing out of the announcement had become one of the show's most delicious elements, the benefit of having a former dancer/choreographer at the helm of the show, with a razor-sharp instinct for what the audience was thinking and a keen visual sense of how to get ahead of and confound those expectations. On the night of the divas' elimination, for example, George Huff was used as a pawn, told to go to join the top three, and then shocked to learn after he'd walked toward the divas, that he had chosen wrong.

In the seasons to come, Lythgoe would create seemingly endless variations of groupings in which to unveil the news. Sometimes he would hit the audience by surprise right out of the gate. Sometimes he would pull last-minute twists that always managed to give the audience a bit of unpredictability no matter how many times they had seen the show.

Lythgoe says of these, "In season 3, that's where the whole thing came together timingwise, lightingwise, and everything else, getting the drama behind it, and that really became the standard. Everybody then copied that, that whole feeling of 'And America said—' and then I could do all the tricks like, 'There are two groups there. One is in. One is out. Go and join the one because you're through this week.' George, with the three divas who were the bottom three, a ridiculous judgment from America. It gave me, though, this wonderful opportunity.

"I'd get the results at something like midnight or one o'clock in the morning. I'd be awake all night choreographing what we were going to do the next day. It was fun. It allowed me to screw around with emotions and manipulate. They say that I'm a master manipulator. I love that. Of course Ryan is so receptive to that. He would love doing it and then when he got blamed, 'You were terribly cruel this week with that.' 'It's not me. It's Nigel.' But it is fun and we screwed around with people, but if you come on the show you know that you're going to get that. Every time someone knew which trick I'd used I'd switch the trick."

BEYOND THE RESULTS night, season 3 was the moment when *Idol* stepped into its own as a production. At last not rushed to air, the look, the feel, the production values of the show finally jelled, and it became something unique on the airwaves, something that took the production of a weekly variety show to a higher standard than had ever been seen.

To that point, variety shows from *Star Search* to the 1970s models such as *The Donny & Marie Show* had been traditional sorts of theatrical stagings. Hosts stood on reflective floors in front of gaudy curtains, overlit, blocked with the finesse and artfulness of a high school production of *Oklahoma!*, complete with cardboard cutout sets.

Because the format had been so long in hibernation in the United States, it forced the crew to reinvent the mold. The awards show veterans who became the *Idol* team were accustomed to working on a massive scale in events like the Oscars or Grammys. They were the ones who conceived and executed *Idol* on a level far above anything ever seen in television variety. The set, tweaked by designer Andy Walmsley (also noted for creating the set of *Who Wants to Be a Millionaire*), became more daring. Its whirling gyroscopes, chrome surfaces, and giant video monitor—video floors, for that matter—were a huge leap from the shiny floor and curtain setup. The direction by Bruce Gowers, a veteran of music videos, kept the show from lagging. Cameras swooped from all angles, searching out the quiet moments of drama in the audience or around the room, to heighten the central tension.

The wardrobe by Miles Siggins and Soyon An, and the makeup team led by Mezghan Hussainy, who would eventually be Simon Cowell's significant other, crafted makeovers of their raw recruits so subtly that the audience was rarely aware they were happening. The lighting team led by Kieran Healy created sharp, distinctive effects, lighting setups more elaborate than anything being done on prime-time television. At the center of every live show, stage manager Debbie Williams operated as the ringmaster, keeping a thousand balls in the air before tens of millions of sets of eyes. Season after season, she'd dodge a million near misses and almost disasters when inevitably one of those balls went flying. The team of vocal coaches—Debra Byrd, Dorian Holley, and Michael Orland—gave a new cast of singers each season sometimes their first introduction to how to expertly use and protect their instrument. Rickey Minor, who would go on to lead *The Tonight Show* band, coordinated a myriad of musical details and led prime-time's finest orchestra. Each week's show would require getting clearance for, arranging, and eventually recording a dozen new songs for iTunes. Come each year at finale time, Minor's studio became the center of a hurricane as he coordinated with musicians, backup singers, guest performers, producers, and the contestants themselves the details of the dozen or so songs that would form the backbone of the season's final two shows.

These are but a few of the people who bring the show together, but to be on the *Idol* set and see the team of professionals guided by Lythgoe and Ken Warwick is to feel you are truly watching people who are the best in the world at what they do. Though the set would be beset by tension, factions, and all the resentments that come with growth and enormous success, the sense on the set of watching a team achieve at the highest level would never change.

O NE BY O NE the divas fell. After Jennifer Hudson, LaToya London went out in fourth place until only Fantasia remained. In the end, it was Fantasia who endured after delivering an intense, out-of-the-park version of "Summertime" that is still referred to as arguably the best performance in the show's history.

She was joined in the finale by Diana DeGarmo, a perpetually smiling sixteen-year-old from Georgia, whose infectious demeanor was paired with a sophisticated cabaret style of singing.

DeGarmo represented a new category of *Idol* performer, the stage child. The show aired images of Diana at five and six years old working the pageant circuit, images Cowell said made her look like "the product of a kept farm." Ultimately, however, he would change his tune, becoming her biggest booster and predicting in the final weeks her ultimate victory.

Along with the new presence of a stage child on the *Idol* stage, Diana brought with her that ubiquitous accessory, the stage mother. Throughout the season, every decision of Diana's would be vetted by her mother, every performance critiqued and picked apart. It made for some very hard days for the sweet-natured young singer.

In the end, there was another epic-scaled finale. Ruben and Kelly joined the two finalists onstage to sing a tear-jerking jumbo-sized version of "The Impossible Dream." After a season of wavering, Cowell gave his vote completely to Fantasia, telling her, "I think you are, without question, the best contestant we've had in any competition," putting her above not only the American contenders but every *Idol* contestant from around the world. The governors of Georgia and North Carolina showed up to lead the get-out-the-vote efforts for their native daughters, Governor Sonny Perdue of Georgia issuing an official proclamation of "Dial for Diana DeGarmo Day."

The audience was down just a tad for the Fantasia/Diana showdown, at 31 million from the previous year's 33 million, indicating at long last, to the competitors' relief, that *Idol*'s rise had to stop somewhere—even if that somewhere was fifty thousand feet above sea level. Sixty-five million votes were cast in the decision to make Fantasia Barrino the third winner of the *Idol* crown and to give the show perhaps the truest incarnation of the *Idol* mythology it had seen yet. And for once, with a healthy margin between them, the finals did not launch an explosion of conspiracy talk and stolen election allegations. There was reason to think that after three years, they had finally gotten it all just right.

Across the Atlantic, however, a decision was made after which the *Idol* world would never be the same. After its just okay second season, ITV announced that *Pop Idol* would be taking a year off. To fill its slot in the interim, they turned to another producer to create a new, rival singing competition. That producer was a man named Simon Cowell.

Chapter 11

SIMON VS. SIMON

This was a big deal. Even by the standards of network television, where stars fought with creators, where writers fought with programmers, and producers fought with everyone, it was a big deal. Simon Fuller was suing Simon Cowell.

To have a lawsuit between star and creator play itself out while *Idol* sat atop the world's entertainment pyramid, a battle with potential to blow apart the biggest thing in show business, well, this was on a magnitude that nobody had ever seen before.

From the start, the two sides made a point of keeping the messy affair "business only" and free from mudslinging. Cowell said that suit or no suit, he would return to work at *American Idol*, where he still had two years left on his contract. Fuller's 19 issued a statement, making clear, "The action is being taken to protect our [*American Idol*] format. It's not personal." Indeed, for the year to come while the legal matters played themselves out, the two sides managed to refrain from name-calling or personal invective, perhaps a reflection of just how much was at stake here and how easily it could poison the well in which the golden goose bathed, to mix a metaphor.

The suit alleged that in creating *X Factor*, Cowell had ripped off *Idol*, the show that had made him a star. "The only thing the two talent shows have in common is Cowell," said Cowell, defending *X Factor* from the copyright infringement charge. Casual observers, however, could be forgiven for noticing a more than passing resemblance between the shows.

Even within the ancient talent competition genre, the similarities between *X Factor* and *Idol* were eye-catching.

The *X Factor* had debuted on British television in October 2004, five months after Fantasia had taken the *American Idol* crown. Like *Idol*, *X Factor* began with regional auditions, building up to a series of live performance episodes where the contestants appeared before three sharp-tongued judges, facing weekly eliminations until the champion was left standing. In look and design, the slick, edgy art direction was very much from the same visual family as *Idol*.

There were some major differences too. *X Factor* was open to groups as well as individuals and to a much wider age range than *Idol*. More important was the role of the *X Factor* judges. In every *Idol* season, Cowell had come under fire for being partisan to certain performers, praising every undulation of his favorites and damning the others no matter how well they did. Whether true or not, Cowell has always chafed at the requirement to be above the fray, to not actively take sides. On *X Factor*, he would need no such restraint. Here, the show's judges were not to serve as neutral overseers but as active mentors to the contestants, to the point of living with their charges during the show. The change had the effect of elevating the judges, who, on *Idol*, have no official role after the semifinalists have been chosen. They sound off with their opinions, of course, but both the contestants and the audience are free to ignore them. Much more than *Idol*, *X Factor* was a show from the reality TV tradition, playing up backstage drama. The contrast showed how much *Idol* was almost stodgily a very pure singing contest.

Today, Cowell recalls the first seeds of *X Factor* to be "rather like the evolution of *Idol* coming from *Pop Stars*. This was nothing more than that. I was on holiday with my girlfriend, Terri, the night it came into my head and I remember asking, 'What do you think about a show whereby young singers could compete with older singers and they could compete with groups and the judges took responsibility for their artists?' And Terri had great instincts, she said, 'I think that's brilliant.' And I said, 'So do I. And I want to make the show.'

"And I called one of my producers in London and said, 'What do you think about this as a format?' and he just screamed down the phone and said, 'Think that's fantastic,' and I said, 'Good, because I want to make it.'

"We had done the second season of *Pop Idol*. I liked it, I didn't love it. I was very, very reluctant to do the second season. This one I really, really had to think it over a lot. I'd say it was because of my relationship with ITV because they'd given us a shot. And that's what they were kind of saying to me, we gave you a shot and we'd really like you to do it. And I reluctantly agreed. I didn't like doing the second show. I didn't have a great time and at the end of it I said to ITV, 'That's it. Don't even think of asking me to do it again, because I don't want to do this anymore. It's too much time.' At that point, America was taking off."

He might have been looking to cut back his judging duties, but that didn't mean that a man like Cowell was just looking for more free time. If he could fill that void left by his withdrawal from *Pop Idol* with a show on which he'd be doing much more, that was another story. "Because I thought it was a good idea, this show. I thought it was a show I'd have more fun on because I had more to do on it than just judge the contestants, so I had more of a role on it. And I thought it would be funny. I thought if I don't make it, there's a chance somebody else would make it.

"It was hard, and that's the point, I think, where you have to say, 'Look. Am I just a judge, or am I going into TV as a serious business?' And I think that's the point where I started to think, 'I'm good at making TV shows. I would like to make more TV shows.' So I made the decision to start producing my own ones. I just didn't want to be a paid judge for the rest of my life."

The first season of the *X Factor* was a solid hit in the United Kingdom. It didn't bring in numbers on the order of *Pop Idol*'s first season, but it was solid nonetheless, with audiences typically in the seven to eight million range.

"There was an awful lot of pressure on me when I launched *X Factor*. I was told this very clearly by a number of people in America: You can't launch a second show in this format. It will fail. It's the show [*Idol*] that is the hit. And if *X Factor* fails, you're not the reason why *Idol* is successful. I hadn't quite thought of it in those terms. All I was thinking was, *I think the show is good. I'm excited to do something different. I'm allowed to do something different, as anyone is allowed to do.* Simon [Fuller] was off making new shows. If I wanted to make new shows I could do what I want. I didn't tell him not to make new shows, I didn't expect to be told I couldn't. So I did it, but I've got to tell you that two-week period when we launched and the ratings weren't great, waiting for the second week to come in, was one of the most stressful times I've ever had in my life."

But *X Factor* became a hit. Almost the moment the show had taken off, Cowell began talking with Fox about bringing it to the United States. Competing with *Idol* on his home island nation would not be enough, it seemed. Having tasted the possibilities of success in America, Cowell was ready to battle the show in which he starred for control of the world's biggest market.

One executive recalls, "Once it became viable in the UK, this was Simon Cowell's obsession and he thought this is something that he didn't share with Fuller."

On *Idol*, he would forever be a performer under the banner created by Simon Fuller, serving under producers and executives who did not report to him. Sony, the record company he worked for (after their acquisition of BMG), owned the winners' albums, but now just being a record executive and doing right by your company were not enough. Understood in the discussions about bringing *X Factor* over was the idea that if and when that happened, Cowell would make the leap away from *Idol* to his own show. He might have had two years left on his contract, but contracts could be altered. If not, two years wasn't forever.

BUT THE TENSION was unbearable. *Idol*'s season 4 debuted just after the first season of *X Factor*. In the year that followed, Cowell and Fuller went about their business, exchanging nary a word. Those caught between the warring creator and star remember it as an excruciating time of go-betweens and messages conveyed back and forth.

"The battle between Fuller and Cowell that played out in the British courts, this was the undercurrent of everything that went on from the beginning of *Idol*," recalls another member of the team. "It was who created this show and who was responsible and which record company was going to have the goods. But it didn't become all-out warfare for a while because no one knew what it was yet. But once *Idol* became a hit, everyone's personal interests needed to be served. That happens with most television shows. So there's nothing particularly unique about it, but the thing that was so unusual was that whatever had gone on in their lives and their professional lives before this, there was blood in the water."

"I just shut it out of my mind," Cowell recalls. "I was more concerned with the ratings of the U.K. show and I thought, *I'll let the lawyers deal with that. I'm still being paid to do* Idol, *I have to.* Our spats have been quite public. When somebody sues you, that's a very public thing to have to deal with. But as I can say today, I didn't steal anything. I just made a new show as he made new shows. But it was a difficult period. I think more than anything I would say this: At the point when *Idol* was launched, we both needed each other. . . . No question about it. I couldn't have done it without him and I don't think he could have done it without me. But we both are people who like running our own businesses, who like owning our own shows, and the inevitable kind of happened, really. Launch something successful together. Simon wants to make new shows, sign new artists, my attitude was, so do I. It's a weird relationship. You've got to have competition, hopefully healthy competition in your life. . . . Enjoy it. But it's been bizarre."

Throughout the first seasons, Cowell had been more than just talent. He had been incredibly passionate about the show, coming in early with the other new members, passionately arguing his side, and sitting through long meetings and days of rehearsal. Now his interest was starting to wane. Outside of tapings, he was showing up less and less. While the others would arrive at 10:00 A.M., he would drift in at three. Visitors to the tapings were struck by how little attention he often paid the performances, watching only the first few seconds before turning to chat with Paula. Cowell says of the time, "You get bored on any show you make. Whether it's *X Factor, Got Talent, Idol,* there's times when it just all becomes quite boring. They're long processes." Clearly, things were not good.

FORTUNATELY, SEASON 4 had something to get everyone's attention. Cowell has described that first appearance of Carrie Underwood in almost mystical terms. "It was almost as though the whole cast were in black and white and she was in color," he would tell Oprah. "That's how clear it was to me. This girl knew what she wanted and luckily we've spotted it."

It was indeed a bold prediction, and to his everlasting glory, Cowell alone made it. Carrie Underwood had been unveiled to *Idol* audiences as the quintessential farm girl; her introductory video featured shots of her feeding the horses, tending to her chores. In fact, as it had been with so many others, Carrie's singing past was a bit more complex. While indeed raised on a farm, young Carrie had been trying to break into the business since before she was a teenager, belting out tunes at pageants and talent shows across the South. While on the circuit, she came to the attention of a manager who secured her a contract with Capitol Records' Nashville division, only to have the deal fall through after a shake-up at the label. After years spent trying to advance herself beyond local contest stages, Carrie finally walked away from the performing dream and enrolled in college at Oklahoma's Northeastern State University. She was four credits shy of a communications degree—magna cum laude no less—when she decided to take a shot at *Idol*.

Simon Cowell may recall seeing her step forward in Technicolor, lights blazing, and indeed on her first appearance he seems for once utterly dumfounded, mouth agape, and at a loss for words. But the impression she made around the set was less glowing. The crew remembers Carrie as a shy, standoffish presence, reluctant to engage with them or her fellow contestants. Says one, "I didn't notice her. I felt she was flat, although when she sang she had a great voice, but I was like, there's nothing else there. She surprised us all, I think. She just kind of snuck in. She kept to herself. She was very quiet. She was one of those people where all of a sudden you go, oh, wow."

"I remember one week," says another, "she did this number where a song was going to change tempo. She wanted to use a mic stand. So we had to figure out a way to get rid of it. Someone suggested, 'Why don't you kick it? Do like a karate kick.' She said, 'Really?' So, she did and everybody commented about it the next day because it was, like, so uncharacteristic that she did something like that."

IN SEASON 3, the show had established the basic formula that would guide it henceforward. But there were still tweaks to be made. The first one was the addition, after Hollywood Week, of the "chair" or green mile episode, so named after the long, hard walk condemned prisoners take on death row. The green mile shows are unique in reality TV: two solid hours of nothing but contestants being told, one by one, whether they will advance to the semifinals. Only a show very confident of its grip on the audience would dare attempt a full episode with no singing, no competition at all, merely contestants learning whether they have made it from one intermediate point in the contest to another.

But the episode works. By season 4 of *Idol*, the stakes had become so high that two hours of seeing people take an intermediate step forward in the competition made for gripping television, especially with each verdict dramatically drawn out through a tearful elevator ride or a long, cold walk to face the judges.

Season 4 also saw a big tweak to the semifinals rounds, changing it from the three heats sudden death plus Wild Card format to what is known as the "boy/girl rounds," wherein each week every contestant, divided by gender, sang, and each week two of them were eliminated. Time has shown each of the two semifinals systems to have their big advantages and drawbacks. With a lot of people to sort through each week, the audience's attention has been found to wane during the boy/girl rounds. However, the three-week period lets the audience meet each contender at least three times before they make it to the big stage, giving them an opportunity to build a personal investment in some early favorites. The sudden death version creates high drama but means that in the top twelve, there will be many the audience has barely seen. Producers have expressed misgivings with each formula, and having now gone back and forth between the two, acknowledge a perfect solution has never quite been found.

The boy/girl rounds were also designed to prevent the marginally talented from slipping through, something that had been an issue in season 3. However, in season 4, one particular contestant managed to create a whole new *Idol* category: the antihero.

In contrast to the glowing presence of Carrie Underwood, Scott "the Body" Savol represented the other end of the spectrum. Pudgy, sullen, and uncommunicative, the R&B singer radiated anticharisma. Yet, as the season progressed, he survived as fan favorites fell. Even after The Smoking Gun revealed Savol had once been arrested for hitting the mother of his child with a telephone, he continued to climb. In the top six week of the competition, Savol finally outlasted one of the season's breakthrough stars, long-haired rocker Constantine Maroulis. The media went ballistic and set off an investigation worthy of the Iran-Contra affair.

"Maybe the conspiracy theorists are on to something. There's little else to explain Scott Savol's baffling longevity on *American Idol*," wrote *USA Today*.

"By 5:00 P.M. yesterday, almost 380,000 people had responded to the show's online poll about Maroulis getting the boot, with 75 percent calling it either 'an injustice' or 'shocking' or claiming 'America let me down,'" the *Boston Herald* reported.

However, in good time the media coalesced around an explanation for the outrage. It was declared that a previously little known Web site called Vote for the Worst had been leading a campaign to undermine the show by encouraging visitors to cast a vote for the least deserving competitor, this season, the press discovered, boosting "Scott the Body." While there was little evidence that this obscure site had reached enough people to affect a contest where tens of millions of votes were cast each week, the story, as they say, deserved to be true. Not only did it explain Savol's popularity, but it captured the influence of this new sector, the blogosphere, upon the contest. Savol's fortunes likely had more to do with his nods to *Idol*'s Christian viewers, but Vote for the Worst was now part of the *Idol* dialogue. The moment foretold a whole new generation of media about to rise from the uncharted depths of the Internet and overrun *Idol* nation in ways as yet undreamed of.

TOWARD THE END of season 4, a bombshell hit the already tense set. *Idol* had weathered scandals aplenty during its short life, but this one was something else, a scandal that threatened *Idol*'s very credibility. The Paula Abdul question had lingered at the back of *Idol* discussions for some time. On-screen, her behavior often went beyond ditsy into the realm of *What is Paula on?*, a question promoted by her often slurred speech—and unpredictable behavior. Offscreen she could be even more erratic. Getting Paula into her chair by showtime was a constant challenge. A no-show often minutes before airtime, her worried producers would send spotters out to Beverly Boulevard to see if she was nearby. On occasion, she would refuse to come out of her dressing room, and a producer would have to coax her to the stage.

Paula was surrounded by the largest coterie of handlers and attendants anyone of this veteran showbiz crew had ever seen: A constantly revolving crew of assistants, publicists, agents, managers, attorneys, stylists, and hand-holders came and went, were fired and rehired. Executives and reporters who wished to get in contact with her often had trouble determining who her current representatives were.

In December 2003, Paula had been arrested for hit-and-run driving after she knocked into another car on the 101 Freeway and fled the scene. She pleaded no contest to a misdemeanor charge and was sentenced to two years' probation.

Then there were the pills. Several witnesses from this period report seeing a veritable cornucopia of little orange canisters in her purse.

In May 2004, as Carrie Underwood neared her coronation, Paula attempted to explain some of the erratic behavior, to make clear that it wasn't about drugs or booze. In an interview with *People*, she said she had been diagnosed with Reflex Sympathetic Dystrophy, a chronic nerve ailment. "If people only knew what I've gone through with pain and pills. I'm dancing for joy at the fact that not even a year ago I was in so much pain I could barely get up." She claimed she had been in pain for over twenty-five years, a battle that began with a teenage cheerleading accident and had been worsened by a pair of car accidents and a near plane crash. To deal with the pain, she had been through everything from bulimia to prescription drug treatments to leechings.

"I love her to death," Lythgoe says. "She is an artist who has been through a lot of pain. I've got one plate in my neck with two fused in my cervical spine. She's got four and I believe that she had a morphine patch for a number of years. You've only got to take a sip of coffee at the wrong time or an aspirin and you're sent. It's not always been the easiest of times for her. I remember carrying her to the studio doors once, running down the corridor literally with her in my arms, dumping her out there and walking her out there. I really love stars. And as far as I'm concerned she's a star and you look after her. That's my job as a producer, to look after her and be protective."

Her explanation of her ordeals with pain, however, could not explain the charges that were about to be unleashed.

It had been two years since *Idol*'s most notorious bad boy, Corey Clark, was eliminated from the show. Now he had a record to sell and a story to tell. On a special edition of ABC's *Primetime Live* entitled "Fallen Idol," Clark laid out a tale of a secret affair with Abdul conducted while he was a contestant on the show. He claimed that a member of Paula's entourage had slipped him the judge's private number, and he had snuck out of the mansion several times to visit her. "When she was dropping me off one night, she leaned over and kissed me in her car," he told. Eventually, as they became fully intimate, he claimed she showered him with gifts and coached him on his performances.

As evidence to back up his claims, he showed phone records purporting to list calls from Abdul, which ABC News claimed to have verified. He played on air a voice mail recording that sounds more or less like Paula's voice, saying, "Listen, if the press is trying to talk to you, you say absolutely nothing. Something's going on. Okay? Call me back."

After the interview, Clark went on a press tour, repeating the charges everywhere from *Good Morning America* to the *Howard Stern Show*.

The reaction from *Idol* was instant and unambiguous, accusing ABC of wanting to destroy a rival network's hit and Clark of fabricating charges to climb back from obscurity and sell an album. Fox said it would investigate the charges and asked Clark for his help in the matter. Clark replied to reporters that he had no intention of helping *Idol*, since they were "no help" to him.

"Regardless," the Fox statement read, "we are absolutely committed to the fairness of this competition. We take any accusation of this nature very seriously no matter their source, and we have already begun looking into this."

On his own, Lythgoe was harsher. Appearing on Ryan Seacrest's radio show, he said of ABC's segment, "The whole show was stretched out worse than one of our elimination shows. It was probably four or five minutes of content. I think it's pretty shoddy journalism, frankly. I think we have to question the motives behind it, both ABC's and Clark's. They would never have done that if we weren't the number one show in America."

On Clark's charges he said, "I know for a fact that a lot of the contestants have got Paula's phone number and contact her and she contacts them. Paula's the den mother. . . . I don't have a problem with that. She's been a star and now she can help them." To Clark's claim that a group number with the refrain "I owe it all to you" had been his attempt to send Abdul a private message, Lythgoe retorted that the serenade had been planned and choreographed by the producers, not Clark.

The response of the media was, of course, outraged and indignant. On *Good Morning America*, a writer for the *Hollywood Reporter* pronounced, "I think it will have very real implications for Paula Abdul. Frankly, I'd be shocked if she was still on the show next season."

And so it might have gone. If *Idol* had flinched or seemed embarrassed about the matter for even a second, the charges might have stuck. Instead, *Idol* did what prime-time network programs never do when they come under fire: They answered the charges immediately and head-on. They went on the offensive, mocking the accusers and giving the impression that they had nothing to be ashamed of whatsoever.

On top of Fox's defense, Abdul pulled the ultimate in bubble-bursting maneuvers. That weekend, she made a cameo appearance on *Saturday Night Live*. Walking in on a sketch about Clark's charge, she interrupted Amy Poehler, who was playing her, and offered critiques of her impersonation. "You need to perfect the clap a little more and be a lot more sexier so contestants will be willing to sleep with you," she said perfectly.

Four days later on the top four performance show, Seacrest opened with a winking reference to the scandal, asking the audience, "How was your week?" continuing with "Lots of shock and outrage surrounding the show. I just want to say, that's what happens when you lose a guy like Scott Savol." When the judges were introduced, at the mention of Paula's name the crowd burst into a frenzy of applause, waving WE LOVE YOU PAULA signs while Randy, in the next seat, blew her kisses.

Three weeks later at the season finale, the show aired their final word on the matter, a satiric video segment titled "Primetime Lies," in which an investigative reporter gets judge Simon Cowell to admit he is having an affair . . . with himself.

By that point, however, the narrative had so clearly changed that that final nail in the coffin was hardly needed. *Idol* audiences had risen up behind Abdul, and journalism monitors wondered aloud to what depths ABC News had sunk airing these tawdry accusations about a singing contest. Howard Kurtz's CNN media watch show *Reliable Sources* devoted an episode to discussing ABC's coverage of the Clark affair, with panelists generally reaching the conclusion that the segment had been a fairly tawdry attempt to lure *Idol* viewers to their show. The panelists, rather than going over the charges and ABC's examination of them, weighed in on the question of whether a distinguished news organization should even be considering such matters. "Everything about it was awful.

But it got the ratings. That's all that matters," opined *Washington Post* doyenne Sally Quinn. The *Philadelphia Inquirer*'s Gail Shister said of the report, "This is not a big news story. The thing that I found interesting, aside from the fact that it was like watching a car wreck, I kept waiting for the big payoff, because they kept hyping and hyping this phone message from Paula Abdul. I thought it was going to be a dirty—talking dirty, you know? I thought it was going to be a sexual message, and they kept hyping it. And then I felt like it was fifty-five minutes of foreplay with no payoff." "This was horrible journalism, but riveting and you had to watch it," was host Kurtz's final say on the matter.

The battle was over and so it was but an afterthought in August when Fox quietly announced its internal investigation had cleared Paula of any wrongdoing and she would be returning to the show.

AFTER THE DRAMA faded in season 4, the impossible happened: The front-runner actually won. After not once sinking into the bottom three, Carrie Underwood cruised to victory.

It had almost seemed like a real race in the final weeks. Almost. After spending the first half of the season in Constantine Maroulis's shadow, Bo Bice, the show's other long-haired rocker, surged in the final month after giving the first real rock performances—albeit a somewhat dated classic rock—the show had seen since the days of Nikki McKibbin. His chances were perhaps exaggerated by producers and judges who, wanting to make it seem like there was a real race on, did everything but sprinkle pixie dust on Bo, praising him and playing up his performances to the hilt. It worked, and going into the finale there actually was a little bit, not a lot, but a little bit of suspense about which way it would go.

But in the end, Bo Bice didn't need Carrie Underwood to defeat him; he was very capable of beating himself. The night before the finale, Debbie Williams recalls, "He went out drinking and got plastered. So, he came in for rehearsal the next day and I said, 'Bo, you look a little sick.' He said, 'I am.' I said, 'You actually look green.' And he did. I didn't know that he had been drinking. I go, 'Honey, you okay? You want to go lay down or something?' He goes, 'I'll be fine.' So, he got up onstage to do something and he had to go offstage and vomit. I mean he was like sick.

"During the rehearsal I said, 'This is not good. Do you need to go home and lay down?' He said, 'Yes.' I told him, 'Do it. Just go. Just go. Get out of here. Go get yourself better.' Then I found out he had been drinking tequila all night long. I joke to him about that now. So, he went and he slept it off that day."

Nearly 30 million people tuned in to see Carrie Underwood sail off to fulfill Simon Cowell's prophecy.

Chapter 12

THE ANTI-CHRIST

I f *American Idol* were America itself, Dave Della Terza would be officially classified as an enemy of the state.

After he finishes his job each day as an IT professional, the twenty-seven-year-old Chicagoan takes to the Internet, where he clocks in as *Idol*'s unappointed heckler-in-chief. The leading antagonist of the country's most beloved pastime, Della Terza searches for the singer who will star in his alternate reality version of *Idol*, the young man or woman whose tortured journey will be chronicled by Dave's Web site, voteforthe worst.com. Della Terza's mission: to undermine *Idol* from within by backing each season's most preposterous contestant.

Since the show's second season, Della Terza has bestowed upon a string of hapless contenders his badge of dishonor, encouraging an army of *Idol* haters to subvert the show from within by propping up the most ill-suited contenders. Della Terza has been denounced by *Idol* champions, waved to by contestants from the *Idol* stage, and reviled by the show's producers. He's been held responsible for some of *Idol*'s most unfortunate soap operas, and has been accused of rewriting the show's history in his own mischievous image.

Messing with a show considered by many to be only slightly removed from mom and apple pie is not for the faint of heart. But for Della Terza, it's all in a night's work. A sampling of e-mails from his in-box:

Mr. Dave Della Terza,

You are such great guy, you work so hard for a living. You are so great . . . not. You are an idiot that does not have a real job. Maybe instead of your stupid Web site, you should be focusing on doing something worthwhile, such as focusing on crime in your shithole suburb of Chicago . . .

Fuck you assholes.

From:
"billy bob"

Dear Funny stone,

You are such a deluesional creep.You need to seek psycohiatric help is your life so empty and worthless that you dedciate it to screwing with a tv show, and destorying people's dreams. You live in a dream world if you think a little bitty group actually fucks with the votes. It doesn't creep you have no control over the votes at all!!!NONE AT ALL!!!!!!!!!!

—Lady Kerns

WHEN *AMERICAN IDOL* was created in the waning days of the last century, the term "blogosphere" had yet to be coined and Vote for the Worst and its chorus of catcalls it summoned could hardly have been imagined. But Della Terza's story is the story of the Internet media in which it grew up, as much as it's the story of *Idol*.

In the early days of the Internet, most of the meteoric ascents to glory, from Facebook to Perez Hilton, seemed parables to the importance of being in the right place at the right time. It was a new kind of democracy and it would call for a new breed of antagonists, more creative, daring, and foul-mouthed than anything that came before. At the dawn of both *American Idol* and the Internet, Vote for the Worst filled that void.

When *Idol* announced its plans to turn the controls over to its viewers, it had fairly straightforward intentions: Let the viewers, rather than cultural arbiters, decide what makes a star. But once invited into the room, armed with the new tools of the Internet, the audience soon claimed the show as its own property. Hence the outrage about "ringers," about accusations of vote tampering, about every tweak and adjustment to the format of what millions in America consider "their show." *Idol*'s viewers would make their feelings about the show known in every possible way.

WHEN *AMERICAN IDOL* premiered, Dave Della Terza was an undergraduate at Northern Illinois University. An early Internet geek, he began his career as a pop culture pundit posting notes on the *Survivor* Sucks message boards that lived on various services circa 2000–2002, dedicated to mocking CBS's island adventure reality show. In the summer of 2002, the board hosted a thread about the new singing competition premiering on Fox.

As he tells it, Della Terza didn't start out to be *Idol*'s public enemy number one. "I said, 'Let me give it a shot and see how bad it is.' I watched the finale of season 1 and I remember saying, 'God, this Justin guy is such shit. If he wins that's going to be terrible. It's going to ruin the entire show.' And then he lost and I thought, *Oh, okay . . .*

"So I watched the next season and I kind of got into it. I didn't really vote, I wasn't that into it, but it was kind of funny to see all these weird characters. I thought the show was interesting. And as the season went on, I thought, *There are so many people on the show who just aren't that good. This isn't really a talent competition.*

"And, funny enough, I was wishing for those semifinal weeks because there are so many bad people. I thought they were so funny. When it got to the finals, I wasn't really enjoying it as much, because I thought, *These people are bad but they're not funny-bad.* I thought it would be funny to keep them around week after week. So I started a thread in *Survivor* Sucks saying, 'Everyone take the Vote for the Worst pledge and let's all vote for the worst next season.' "

Thus are great movements born.

During season 3, the cause lived on as a thread on the *Survivor* Sucks board, urging people to vote for baby-faced singer John Stevens. A friend of Della Terza's moved the thread to its own site, setting up a page on the Geocities service, which was dubbed generically "Vote for the Worst" so the movement could continue with other shows when *American Idol* was canceled. "So we put it up and it was the most ghetto version of a Web site ever. It was like two pages and it just had a giant picture of John Stevens on it, saying vote for him. And then it has 'e-mail us' and it had a tag board on it where you could put comments. And that was the entire Web site."

The site received little attention through season 3. Meanwhile, Della Terza graduated college with a degree in television production and moved to Los Angeles, where he found work in the reality TV industry at Bunim/Murray Productions, makers of *The Real World*.

IF YOU HAD to point to a moment when the Internet took off as a media source unto itself, the day was somewhere in the neighborhood of *Idol*'s fourth season. In 2005, blogging expanded its reach from tech and political topics to make itself felt in pop culture. In 2005, Perez Hilton's Hollywood gossip blog first gained a popular following, TMZ was founded, and Vote for the Worst took off and an entirely different kind of *Idol*-watcher was born.

In season 5, the site endorsed the show's least likely superstar to date, the pudgy, awkward Scott "Scotty the Body" Savol, who, much to the viewership's ongoing shock, survived elimination after elimination, progressing high into the ranks of the top ten. Seeking an explanation, the press dug up the little guerrilla Web site that had been promoting him. "I started having reporters call me and say, 'What's the Web site doing? Why are you voting for Scott Savol?'" It started with a small article in a newspaper in Kentucky and spread. "Why Is Scott Still on *Idol*? Chubby Singer's Online 'Fan Club,'" ran the *New York Post*'s headline. By the end of the season, there were few media outlets not covering the Internet phenomenon that was *perhaps*—without public vote totals, all the media could do was wildly speculate—upsetting the results of the biggest show on television.

So great was the outcry that Fox and FremantleMedia felt compelled to issue a statement dismissing the site's influence: "While it is unfortunate that a small group of people are so caustic that they believe it would be humorous to negatively sway the voting on *American Idol*, the number of purported visits to the Web site would have no impact on voting."

While the furor was breaking out, Della Terza continued to show up at his day job at the bottom rungs of the entertainment industry. "I was like, 'Oh no, I'm ruining a television show on this Web site.' I thought, *Is this going to play out poorly for me?* I didn't want to mention it at work."

The week Constantine Maroulis was eliminated, Della Terza made his first television appearance on *Access Hollywood*. The site, which had moved off Geocities, crashed from the incoming traffic. "So the site was down for five days. Scott Savol got voted off and we thought, *This sucks.* I didn't know how to run a Web site. I didn't know what I was doing. Then I got a letter from FremantleMedia saying cease and desist. We had audio clips of *American Idol* and half the content from the show. And of course that's illegal."

Then the hate mail began, e-mail by the truckload. "These days we have a message board where people can come on and get mad. But back then there was nowhere to really interact. In a normal day, I would get hundreds and hundreds of letters. That kind of freaked me out a little. TMZ—I didn't even know who TMZ was—but they asked to interview me in my apartment. And one of the shots they had was outside of my building. I had people writing to me saying, 'I'm going to find out where you live.' I thought, *Maybe I don't like this.* I'm a very private person. I'm not a very outgoing, crazy, I-want-attention-for-myself person. That's not why I started the Web site. I guess I have to deal with it because I'm the face of the Web site, but it still makes me uncomfortable. I don't like it."

On top of the hate mail, the hassles of dealing with the site made Della Terza wonder, "Is this worth doing?" Then he was approached by an advertising company that offered to manage the site for him in exchange for a cut of the ad revenues. That took just enough off his plate to keep him in the game.

In season 5, the site continued to grow, its selections regularly noted in the press. The site backed Kevin "Chicken Little" Covais before turning to gray-haired soul singer Taylor Hicks. "I didn't think he was going to win. I picked Taylor because I thought Chris Daughtry was going to win. And I wanted Taylor to get second, and I thought that would be really funny."

Season 6, however, was to be the golden age of Vote for the Worst—the year of Sanjaya. Even before the ponyhawked boy entered their ken, the season started off with a bang of publicity. When sultry young singer Antonella Barba first appeared in the top twenty-four, the Internet quickly swirled with rumors that unclothed photos of her or, worse, pictures of her engaged in a sex act, existed somewhere *out there*. This was a potentially explosive issue, as one of the few *Idol* disqualifications to date—that of Frenchie Davis in season 2—had occurred over the issues of racy photos in her closet. Vote for the Worst began to post some of the pictures, sent in by *Idol* gadflies who had unearthed them around the Internet in an early example of crowdsourcing. Suprisingly, the shots ended up helping the soon-to-be-embattled singer by proving she was guilty only of R-rated crimes, not, as had been rumored, of more risqué and potentially disqualifying misdeeds. When the pictures first appeared online, there seemed to be an image not just of a semiclad Barba, but of Barba performing fellatio, an R-rated/X-rated line that in light of the Frenchie Davis precedent could prove critical to whether the show would be able to keep her in the competition. In the end, after examining the evidence, "We were the first site to say those photos weren't real, after which a lot of other sites started saying it too." Barba was allowed to stay in the competiton, ultimately falling to popular vote in the semifinals.

After Antonella and VFTW's next choice, Sundance Head, were eliminated, the site finally focused on the season's emerging plotline involving the emotional, exotically named singer from Seattle. Having initially missed the boat, Della Terza thought, "We'd better vote for Sanjaya because everyone hates him. So we put him up on the site. The first week he came out singing 'Ain't No Mountain High Enough' and then he was in the bottom two and I thought they were going to send him home. Because when a Vote for the Worster is in the bottom two, they always go home. And then Sanjaya stayed, and we were like, wow, that's never happened. And then he came out the next week and did 'You Really Got Me' with the crying girl, and I thought, 'This is awesome.' This is my favorite moment on *American Idol* ever."

After the performance and VFTW's endorsement, the site exploded as never before. "What happened was we were voting for Sanjaya and Howard Stern wanted everyone to vote for Sanjaya too because he thought it was funny. He got everyone to vote for Sanjaya too. And he saw that we were doing it too, so he said, 'Everyone go to Vote for the Worst.' As soon as he said something, our Web site was flooded with Howard Stern fans. Sanjaya would not have lasted as long as he did if Howard Stern hadn't said something."

To the pundits' dismay, Sanjaya continued to survive, his run overshadowing the "serious" contestants as the year's major conversation topic. While other antiheroes had emerged in the past, none so thoroughly overshadowed their seasons as Sanjaya did. Savol, who finished in fourth place, went farther than Sanjaya ultimately, but his impact was minuscule compared to young Malakar's.

"Season 6 got so crazy. I was doing interviews every day, to the point where I was getting sick of *American Idol*. I didn't even want to watch it anymore. These two idiot radio personalities were like, do you want to be on our show? So I was on their show one week, and from then on they would call me like at five in the morning every day and ask 'Hey, do you want to be on our show?' After a while, I just stopped picking up. And I heard, on the show, they were like 'Dave didn't pick up.' It's five in the morning. Go away, I want to fucking sleep.

"It got really obnoxious and I wasn't having fun with it. It was stressing me out. If it wasn't fun, I didn't want to do it. So eventually I decided to cut back some of the stuff I was doing. If I'm not having fun, why the hell am I doing it? I'm not making that much money off it." Della Terza was perhaps the first of the legions to come who would discover that online fame does not instantly translate into offline riches, or even a sustainable career.

By the end of season 5, he had tired of trying to break into the entertainment business and moved back to Chicago, getting part-time work teaching at a local college. Even as its traffic exploded and it became perhaps the most celebrated upstart Web site in America, the site never brought in anything more than pocket change.

"The most money I ever made off the site was the Sanjaya season and it was not even nearly enough to support myself. I made a decent amount of money. I had some health problems a couple years ago and I took care of them with some money I made off the Web site. But it was never a full-time job or anything.

"I took a completely different attitude after season 6, and was just doing it for fun. I thought, *If the news doesn't get up on the site the second it happens, I don't care.* It's just a hobby and I like it that way."

The hobby, however, expanded its scope in the coming seasons, like much of the Web itself, moving beyond mere commentary into citizen journalism, attempting to uncover what it saw as the sins, hypocrisies, and downright lies of *American Idol*. Their greatest mission was uncovering the "plants" on the show, those singers' supposed secret professional pasts.

"Season 7 was funny because we said there are plants on the show who all have previous recording experience. Carly Smithson was the biggest one of all."

Michael Johns and Kristy Lee Cook also, he points out, had made records. "David Archuleta's family knew people on the show. Jason Castro had done stuff in show business before. After Ramiele went home, I think every other contestant had had previous recording experience except David Cook. So when he won, we were like, at least he wasn't one of the plants. In the first two seasons, they said we're trying to find America's biggest undiscovered talent. You notice they've stopped saying 'undiscovered.' Of course, if you're a legitimate singer and you go on *American Idol*, you've probably sang somewhere before or attempted to get a record deal. That's fine. But don't lie about it is what we're saying."

With the tips pouring in, season 7 saw VFTW once again play a critical role in *Idol*'s scandal of the year, the controversy over David Hernandez's past work as an exotic dancer at a Phoenix men's club. "People were coming to our Web site and saying, 'David Hernandez is a stripper.' 'Okay,' we said, 'well, where's the proof?' They said his stripper name was Kayden, so we started looking around trying to find this information. And we found pictures of him at this gay club working. We thought at least we were on the right track, so we found out from one person that he'd stripped at this place called Dick's Cabaret. So I called Dick's Cabaret and I ended up e-mailing with this guy, and I said, 'Did David Hernandez work there?' He said, 'I can't discuss that.' Well, that means yes, then.

"There was a reporter for the Associated Press doing an article at the time about Danny Noriega and if a gay person could ever win *American Idol*. And I told him, 'You need to call Dick's Cabaret' and I gave him the contact information. The next week it was all over that David Hernandez was a stripper. I told him to make sure to quote Vote for the Worst, so we were all over the article. Because clearly I couldn't go to Arizona and try to find out what this Dick's Cabaret thing is about but someone else can."

In the following seasons, the VFTW empire kept growing. Although the official line of *Idol* contestants is always that they never ever look at the Internet, enough have later come clean that it can be safely said that nowhere on Earth are the Vote for the Worst endorsements followed more closely than the backstage at *American Idol*. A subterranean tradition began in season 6 of giving winking-on-air acknowledgments of the site, when Chris Sligh that year called out, "Hi, Dave," during one postperformance moment with Seacrest. The tradition has continued all the way down to season 9, when Crystal Bowersox gave Della Terza an on-air nod.

IDOL'S PRODUCERS HAVE consistently dismissed VFTW's effect on the show, comparing the vast millions who watch *Idol* with the relatively small number who visit Vote for the Worst. Della Terza states that he doesn't monitor the site's traffic numbers. (Sixty thousand monthly visitors during season 9, according to Internet ratings site Quantcast.) But the site has attained notoriety, if not respectability. The announcements of his latest endorsement are heralded in the major news organs of the country, and *Idol* alumni flock to appear on his weekly Web radio show.

As far as the voting goes, *Idol* producers are no doubt right. But as *American Idol* sought to be the first show on network television to put the controls in the hands of its viewers, Dave Della Terza and his merry men have served, in their way, as the authenticators of the democratic process, ensuring through their rowdiness that the larger *Idol* experience never becomes too controlled, too staid, too programmed.

No other TV show has spawned such a camp following of Web sites devoted to it, and in the end, nothing proves how much the show ultimately belongs to the public like the persistence of Vote for the Worst.

"That's the thing," Della Terza reflects, looking back on eight years of mocking *Idol*. "I don't know why they don't embrace Vote for the Worst more. I know we expose their show as being fake, but the thing is, if they would just keep the Vote for the Worst contestant on longer, people will be talking about your show more. They always get so angry and send the Vote for the Worst contestants home so fast that I think, really? Why don't you have a little more fun with it and people will probably get more pissed off and more people will talk about your show. A lot of people think Vote for the Worst is paid for by *American Idol*, but of course we're not.

"I was born two months premature and my mom always said, 'You're going to do big things.' And now she says, 'You were going to do big things, but I didn't know it was going to be an *American Idol* Web site.' We all joke about it. It's so silly. . . . I think it's hysterical that it gets so much attention."

Chapter 13

DÉTENTE

For a little while, there was some doubt as to whether there would be a season 5. With the suit still unsettled and the deal completed after season 2 having lapsed, Fox questioned whether it would be able to even produce the series. Then, as he was wont to do in these negotiations, Cowell put the word out that he was ready to move on.

On November 21, the *New York Times*'s Bill Carter ran the following item:

> Mr. Cowell signed a deal in 2003 that committed him to three more seasons of *American Idol*. But only in the first two of these did he retain the rights to sign the winner and runner-up of each year's competition to his record label, which is under Sony BMG. For the coming edition of *Idol*, Mr. Cowell does not have a deal giving his label such rights. "Simon is not interested in making a star for another label," said one of Mr. Cowell's close associates, who requested that he not be named because the issues are still being debated. Without a deal for music rights, the associate said, Mr. Cowell would have a strong incentive to leave *Idol* and sell *X Factor*—starring him—to one of Fox's competitors in the United States. At least two networks, ABC and NBC, have quietly expressed interest in negotiating to acquire *X Factor*, which this season has been the most popular show on British television.

The "leak" produced the desired effect. Nine days later the parties in the lawsuit reached an agreement. Cowell was given a slightly larger stake in *Idol*; Simon Fuller took some shares of *X Factor*. Sony BMG would continue to own and produce *Idol*'s albums. Fox signed the series for at least four more seasons, with an option on six, and Cowell signed on as judge for five more. His salary? In the neighborhood of thirty million dollars.

What's more, Fuller had given Cowell complete and total victory in the battle of Britain. In exchange for Cowell continuing with *American Idol*, *Pop Idol* would be pulled off the air and the copyright infringement suit withdrawn, conceding the United Kingdom entirely to *X Factor*. For Cowell, it seemed a huge victory, and his people lost no time spinning it that way. The *Independent* quoted one senior music executive as saying, "It has come out 75/25 in favor of Cowell. He is the star. He had all the aces."

But there was a catch, and a very big one indeed. In exchange for getting the airwaves to himself in the United Kingdom, Cowell surrendered America; he agreed to give up his dream of bringing *X Factor* to the United States. In agreeing to serve as judge for another five years on *American Idol*, Cowell would spend the next half decade as "just talent" in America, while racing back and forth across the continents to preside over two empires.

"I am happy that we have been able to sort out our differences and find an amicable solution to our problems . . ." Cowell told the *Independent*. "Simon and I have shown just how well we work together in recent years. We have remained friends throughout this dispute and I think that it was this friendship that allowed us to settle our differences."

In fact, however, as far as the underlying issues went, nothing had been settled. At the core of the dispute had been the fact that locked together under the *Idol* banner were two men each accustomed to unrivaled control of any project they were involved in. In starting *X Factor*, Cowell had attempted to break up this uneasy coexistence. But now they were bound ever more firmly together, the problems merely pushed under the rug, where, in time, they would grow even bigger as the stakes grew ever bigger.

ANOTHER PARTY THAT deserves a great deal of credit for *Idol*'s rise is the other networks. *Idol*'s reign had been aided by the fact that once it had achieved its initial burst of popularity, the other networks didn't dare schedule their heavy-hitter programs against it. Early on, when its highly successful new show *The Apprentice* was surging in popularity, NBC could have used it to take on *Idol* directly. Even if it hadn't beaten *Idol* in the ratings, *The Apprentice* could have taken a big bite out of its ratings, perhaps even prevented it from turning into the monster it became. But NBC got cold feet about risking its hot property and scheduled it on Sunday nights, safely clear of *Idol*'s wake.

Since then, with the exception of *Lost* on ABC, no network dared put its big guns against *Idol*, scheduling only weaker shows against the Goliath and allowing Fox's hold on midweek to go unchallenged. For a while, a rumor had circulated in the trades that Fox was considering moving *Idol* to Thursday nights—that caused a near panic at NBC, where their Thursday comedy lineup remained the last vestige of their once mighty empire—but the rumor proved to be untrue.

By its fourth and fifth seasons, however, Fox's scheduling chief Preston Beckman no longer considered the competition to be just the other networks, but a whole world of entertainment choices available to people at home. By creating a show that became such necessary viewing for so many, such a centerpiece of cultural conversation, he felt you could in fact turn back the clock on declining network shares. "When you look at the collective ratings for networks, the majority of people aren't watching network television. So, our competition is less and less ourselves and the other networks and more and more just going out there and getting the eyeballs. I mean, that's why we put on big sporting events. You don't necessarily see the other networks' shares go down. They get their ratings. In the case with *American Idol*, we're not just cannibalizing the other networks. We've got an audience that doesn't necessarily watch network television but makes it their business to be with *American Idol*." To that end, Fox programmed what they labeled their "shock and awe" lineup: two nights of *Idol* paired with two nights of the hit series *24*. The schedule blew the competition out of the water and established Fox as the absolute dominant force each spring. "It was a psychological thing, to be perfectly honest," recalls scheduler Preston Beckman. "The idea was just to come on and just blow everything away and just get everybody feeling like there's no way to stop us."

It worked. By 2008, CBS's CEO Les Moonves publicly called *Idol* a "monster" and pleaded for somebody to "please kill that show."

. . . .

SEASON 5 IS arguably remembered as the most talented of seasons. Certainly it's the season that produced the greatest number of sustained high-level careers. Chris Daughtry has gone on to huge success, selling millions of albums. Kellie Pickler, the roller-skating waitress, has become a genuine country star, serving as Taylor Swift's opening act during her blockbuster national tour. Bucky Covington has also established himself in the country market. Elliott Yamin advanced from *Idol* without a recording contract, but went out on his own and sold the better part of a million albums. Daughtry won a Grammy for songwriting, as did Ace Young, who also starred in a major Broadway production. Mandisa remains a prominent name in gospel and Christian music. Katharine McPhee has had a consistent acting career as well as recording two albums.

And then there is the champion of season 5, Taylor Hicks.

Idol's oldest winner to date, Hicks was one of its most controversial, too. Perhaps no contestant has ever been as determined to win as Hicks was, and whatever the show might have thought of him, perhaps no contestant was better able to reshape the show to suit his agenda.

When Hicks auditioned for *Idol,* he came to the show with an already viable career. Playing bars and nightclubs across Alabama and the South, his Soul Patrol fan club was already very active. Unique among *Idol* contestants, Hicks came to the competition with this substantial and active backing, which mobilized to support his bid, a boost that certainly did no harm putting him through the early ranks.

Flopping around like a drunk at a wedding, Hicks was the farthest thing from a pop star to hit the *Idol* stage. The judges were perplexed. In fact, midway through the season, Cowell gave up on judging him entirely, declaring Hicks's routine "judgeproof." Still, the good ol' boy who talked about eating ribs for breakfast kept rising as the other talents of the season fell away.

One crew member recalls the crooner, who stood out for his salt-and-pepper hair, his tailored suits, and also for his arrogance. "A lot of people didn't like him. They felt he was rude. What I got was that this is a kid who I don't think was raised with a lot of manners. Sometimes Taylor was in his own little thought world. So, like if somebody did something nice for him and he wouldn't thank them, they'd go like, 'Who is he' kind of thing. But most of the time I felt like he was just in his head."

In his memoir, Taylor gave a good sense of the steely determination that existed beneath his goofy stage persona. In contrast to the typical *Idol* winner who waxes about all the great friends for life they made while on the show, he wrote of the *Idol* dorm, "As you might imagine things could get awkward living with the same people you were competing against. My own way of coping was keeping my eyes on the prize, which meant keeping to myself as much as possible. If you asked my room-mates, they'd tell you there were times when I was fun but other times when I was a monster. And they'd be right. Then again, I was straight up with everybody. I really was there looking for fans. Not friends."

Debbie Williams recalls of Hicks, "He would come to me secretly sometimes and say, 'Okay, I want to do this particular thing. But I don't want to do it in rehearsals. I don't want to give it away.' Okay. The word is, if you're going to do something always tell me. I've got to let the booth know. I won't tell anybody else.

"One night Taylor was going to lay on the floor in his number, but he didn't want anybody to know that. So I told Bruce, 'Okay, at this part of the song he's going to lay on the floor.' . . . So, he had his little secret things all the time that he wanted to pull out of his bag of tricks. I liked that. I liked him. I think he knew he wasn't a great singer. But he had to come up with gimmicks. He had to do that kind of stuff to get himself noticed. And it worked."

BUT IT WAS a long climb up the ladder for Hicks of all people to wind up atop one of *Idol*'s most talented groups.

At the season open, it was the hunky, long-haired Coloradan Ace Young who was quickly marked as the season's front-runner. He recalls hearing that news early on: "I remember telling my brother that first week, 'Well, I'm not gonna win this year.' He says, 'What do you mean?' and I say, 'Dude, it's always an underdog, and I started out on top. I'm screwed.'"

He was right.

Another front-runner from the early days was a lanky but highly likable basketball-playing girl from Boston named Ayla Brown. Other than her clear musical talents, Brown stood out for the presence of her politician father, a member of the Massachusetts State Legislature who sat beaming in the front row during his daughter's performance. Ayla was the victim of one of the season's more shocking eliminations during the semifinals, but she would return to prominence by her father's side when, four years later, Scott Brown would win an upset victory in a special election to the U.S. Senate, replacing Senator Edward Kennedy.

WHEN SIMON FULLER had conceived of *Idol* as the ultimate experiment in entertainment democracy, democracy was still something of an orderly concept. But by season 5, the hounds of the Internet had turned loose and there was no going back. A new generation of blogs and Web sites had descended on *Idol*, making it one of the most searched-for topics on the Internet. Online commentary had lapped up every table scrap from the show.

Sites sprang up devoted to *Idol* fan fiction, imaginary romantic encounters between *Idol* contestants drafted by mostly teenage admirers. One site featured an array of novels devoted to every conceivable pairing of *Idol* contestants, one on one and in ill-fated love triangles, divided up by season and in the forbidden "mixed seasons" category. For instance, *Last Kiss,* a novel of season 5, begins with the following meeting:

> *"You'll wonder late at night, whoever was that girl with those fists of fury?" Her voice was serious, but she couldn't help the smile that escaped past her lips when she said it.*
>
> *"Oh, trust me I'll have my ways of knowing." He gave her a smirk, extending his hand out to her. "Chris Daughtry."*
>
> *"Really now. Guess I'll have to keep my eye out on you." She matched his smirk with her own, and took his hand in hers. "Katharine McPhee."*
>
> *"I'll make sure to give you a little wave every time you're watching, Ms. McPhee," Chris quipped in reply, holding on to her hand for a moment longer before finally letting go.*

On sites devoted to the show, rumors were born and swirled around endlessly on message boards, never to be dispelled. Fan clubs fought vicious pitched battles over whose candidate had been most grievously cheated. Season 7, Archie's Angel duked it out with Carly's Angels over which site had chosen the moniker first. A site calling itself Idoltard sprang up to mock the excesses of the fans and ultimately was shut down after a libel suit from one irate target.

Vote for the Worst continued to issue its anti-endorsements and rile up fan rage. A new site called DialIdol purported to measure the percent of busy signals on each contestant's phone lines and predict who would be going home. These predictions were all over the place: sometimes uncannily accurate, sometimes off by a country mile. Spies outside the studio gates harangued the crowds leaving dress rehearsals and published spoiler lists revealing the song choices hours before the show aired, sending the producers into a frenzy as their element of surprise was spoiled. The Smoking Gun continued to comb their closets for skeletons. TMZ had reporters all over *Idol* land looking for dirt. Among their early season 5 scoops were a report that Taylor Hicks's hair was actually dyed gray and that Kevin "Chicken Little" Covais had dumped his girlfriend to make himself more appealing to female *Idol* voters.

Traveling to Vegas to be mentored by Barry Manilow, Ace Young was to find that what happens in Vegas doesn't stay in Vegas. Not with *Idol*, anyway. He remembers, speaking in veiled terms, of a certain night traveling to Sin City with the others, including his roommate and newly installed BFF Chris Daughtry: "We had an interesting situation everywhere we went, but in Vegas we had a situation that was a dream come true for me, but not for Chris. There was a whole college soccer team that was hanging out . . . I got to have a lot of fun with that whole night, and Chris had to go to bed because he's a married man. It was funny because after that evening, all the girls were putting up stuff that was true about me, but not about Chris."

The reports posted by the women's soccer team began to spread virally. "So we got pulled aside by the producers, who said, 'We need to know what happened . . . Because if anything else happens and it's on our money then we're going to get in trouble.' And I said . . . 'I partied with them and I made Chris go to bed. . . .' Thank God there wasn't Twitter then. MySpace was the biggest thing, and people couldn't access things on their phones like they can now. It was really amazing to go somewhere and have your picture taken, and then get an e-mail from somebody else with that picture in, like, thirty minutes."

IF ONE MAN can truly be said to have single-handedly changed *American Idol*, it is Chris Daughtry. The hard rocker from North Carolina brought to the *Idol* stage an edginess that had never been seen in the pop-dominated show. With other rockers, such as Maroulis, it was like they were playing the rocker character. In fact, Cowell often reminded them that no serious rocker would appear on *American Idol*. But Daughtry disproved that rule. His style arose from a contemporary world of hard rock aimed at a middle-American audience, typified by bands like Fuel and Nickelback. It was the type of music Chris would later label "flyover rock," suggesting rock that was to be enjoyed by average Americans and distinguishing it from the glitzy sounds being produced in New York and Los Angeles.

But more important than the fact that he kicked open the doors to rock music on the *Idol* stage, he showed what could be done with the songs. Since the beginning, contestants had struggled to distinguish themselves with music dictated by the various theme weeks. How do you take songs by Elton John or Billy Joel or Burt Bacharach and make them your own? And how do you do it week after week in front of judges who are pressuring you to show what kind of artist you are? Contestants would play with the keys and the tempo, but few dared to truly mess with the classic songs.

Then came Chris Daughtry.

No matter what the theme, from Queen to Elvis, from love songs to country night, Daughtry made the songs come to him. He'd speed them up, flatten the melodies, and turn them into hard rock numbers, complete with flashing lights, hip wardrobe, and angry strut. No matter what the origins, Daughtry transformed it into a rock spectacle. It was no longer just a question of singing your heart out. It was about performance, energy, and finding a way to take the *Idol* songbook and bend it to your image, make it something contemporary and relevant rather than just an oldies review.

It would be a couple years until a rocker in the Daughtry mold won the competition, but now this element was out of the box. There was no turning back.

. . . .

OFFSCREEN, SEASON 5 was turning out to be another topsy-turvy year for Paula Abdul. In April, she reportedly got in a physical fight at an L.A. nightclub with a former CAA agent. Abdul filed a police report saying the man had grabbed her and thrown her against a wall, resulting in a concussion. The *New York Post* soon reported that the police investigation had been called off, speculating that Abdul had been drunk and "out of it." The paper wrote, "Two witnesses tell Page Six Abdul looked 'drunk' and 'out of it' and was the one kicked out of the party with ex-boyfriend Dante Spencer. Insiders theorize she concocted a story to counter witnesses' claims that she'd been tossed from Xenii for being 'falling-down drunk.' Lefkowitz's lawyer, Michael Nasatir, said yesterday: 'The press accounts of the so-called altercation between Jim Lefkowitz and Paula Abdul at Xenii last Sunday morning are completely outrageous and utterly false. Mr. Lefkowitz did not have an argument with Ms. Abdul nor did he have any physical contact with her whatsoever . . . he was merely an innocent bystander at an unfortunate incident.' A rep said Abdul was unavailable for comment."

AS SEASON 5 wound down, the end of Paula's current contract loomed. Aware that Cowell had wrestled gigantic numbers out of the network, Paula was determined to take a stand. It was not magnificent timing. Given the troubles of the previous season, reports of her car accidents, and off-camera squabbles, this wasn't the moment to play hardball. As in her past negotiating round, sources within the *Idol* camp let slip to certain parties in the media, in this case to *US Weekly*, that talk of some other younger, more current pop starlets was in circulation around the office.

"Paula was being very difficult. [She was] crying all the time and arriving late for meetings," the *US Weekly* story read. The producers, *US Weekly*'s source continued, were actively considering other names. They "liked Jessica [Simpson] a lot. And some were pushing for Britney."

Sure enough, within days of the story, Paula committed to another three years for a mere $1.8 million a year.

It wasn't a payday to sneeze at, especially considering that the *Idol* live season was all of three months long and required two afternoons of work a week, plus six road trips for the auditions. And the *Idol* exposure, as the Fox negotiators pointed out, kept Paula in the public eye, allowing her to launch other ventures like her QVC jewelry line. Also hanging in the air was the fact that Fox had just put itself on the line in a big way to defend her.

On the other hand, a superstar lifestyle doesn't come cheap. After Uncle Sam took his half of the $1.8 million, there was that vast coterie to be paid, not to mention basic living expenses: house, clothes, travel, limos. . . . Her entourage of revolving staff and handlers was the stuff of legend. For one who had seen her opportunities dry up before, living this close to the bone was not a formula to breed security.

And then there was that other matter, respect.

Beneath the ditsy demeanor, Abdul had an incredibly sharp mind and the instinct of a survivor of two decades in show business. After five years of being happy just to be there, she had begun to bristle at what she saw as the lack of respect paid to her by the upper echelons of *Idol*. Never mind how her erratic behavior might have contributed to this problem. After Gail Berman moved on from Fox to become president of Paramount Pictures in 2005, Paula and Cecile Frot-Coutaz stood as the only females in the top ranks of *Idol* among Lythgoe, Warwick, Darnell, Fuller, Cowell, Seacrest, and Jackson. It was a position that Paula often enjoyed—indeed, she would not like it one bit when that changed. But the flipside of being one of the only women in the room was the feeling of being excluded from the boys' club. Now, however, with the wounds of the Corey Clark incident still fresh, was not the time to make waves, but the seeds of discontent were planted.

SEASON 5 ROARED toward another blockbuster conclusion, the year's stand-out personalities having made a major splash in the media. For once it seemed that everything had gone right and everything *Idol* touched turned to gold. The song used for each contestant's farewell montage, "Bad Day," a year-old overlooked novelty ditty by Canadian Daniel Powter, became a *Billboard* number one hit.

Chris Daughtry's shocking ouster in fourth place had been a huge disappointment to the team, but again, the surprise only boosted the interest and drama. Even nerdy Elliott Yamin had found his own in the final weeks, becoming a genuine favorite of many. Typically in the case of a surprise ouster, the other most vulnerable who survive become the targets of fan wrath, as it had been for Nikki McKibbin, but in this case, no one begrudged Yamin his success.

The only asterisk on the season, in fact, was the winner; the fact that as they approached the showdown between Taylor Hicks and Katharine McPhee, it seemed that this unlikeliest of contestants was actually going to win.

In the end however, almost all of the *Idol* winners had been completely unlikely. When *Idol* came to America, the public, and certainly the critics, had uniformly assumed it would be a machine to produce shiny, pretty, disposable, bubblegum stars, inoffensive singers who would be easy on the eyes, unchallenging to the ears, interchangeable, and instantly forgettable. In the first season of *Idol,* the judges' comments focus heavily on appearance, worrying that various contenders didn't "look like a pop star." But cookie-cutter heartthrobs, in the end, were, as it turned out, not at all what the show produced.

Of the *Idol* champions to date, only two, Kelly Clarkson and Jordin Sparks, even fit in the "pop singers" category. Clarkson was a feistier phenomenon, beyond pop pigeonholing, while Sparks, far from being a cookie-cutter type, was an actual plus-size model before coming on the *Idol* stage. Carrie looked the part, but working in country, she had moved *Idol* to an entirely new genre than it had ever planned to be in. Kelly, Ruben, Fantasia, Carrie, Taylor, and Jordin had almost nothing in common. Yet each of them, in their way, convinced America that they were real people with real stories and real talent that had been overlooked by the entertainment machine.

"We'd always said why we thought we were going to be successful both in England and here is the record companies had sort of given up doing their job, which is going around, finding the talent, the A&R, and bringing it back to the record company," Lythgoe reflects. "That wasn't really happening. They sort of sat down like fat cats and had the talent come to them. With *Idol* and *Pop Stars*, we went to the world and brought the talent in."

In his own way, along the path that he very consciously and cleverly carved out, Taylor Hicks was as much a part of that tradition as the rest.

Bringing these talents from all walks of life together and creating that fairy tale made for a great storyline every year, no matter who ended up going home too soon and who ended up winning. Thus the show would find, as the seasons went on, you no longer needed to win to benefit from being on *Idol*. In the early seasons, Seacrest would crack that for those who failed to win, little was waiting but ignominy. "The ones who go home will have a future summed up in three words: paper or plastic," he joked in season 3.

But as runner-up Clay Aiken became a monster album seller far surpassing the sales of Ruben Studdard, the man who beat him, as fourth-placed Chris Daughtry became the biggest rock seller of the year, as eighth-placed Jennifer Hudson went on to win an Academy Award, it became clear that all the contenders who took part in this annual adventure had won a place in the nation's heart. Which is not to say that all of them would become durable stars, but the door was open to many more than just the winner, and even those who did not remain household names would find ways to carve out places on America's broad entertainment canvas.

For those on the inside of that fairy tale, the bond between them often remains very strong. In the early days, the producers scoffed at the idea that the contestants, competing against each other, would become friends and root for each other's success, but year after year, with exceptions and the occasional diva, that is what has happened. They stay in touch, remain friends, and continue to roll down the road of show business together.

Ace Young remembers getting a call a couple years after season 5. "I was on radio tour and I was eight hours away from Birmingham. I found out that Elliott Yamin's mother passed away. I canceled my radio tour. I got in a rental car and I drove for eight hours. And I was there with Elliott and his family and I remember hanging out and being there for the service, and being there for the burial. They actually buried her. I watched them put the dirt on her. It was a beautiful, emotional thing, and I was just sitting there thinking, *If it wasn't for* Idol *I wouldn't have even met this kid*. We're best friends, so much so that we're family. When the real personal shit actually goes down, we have each other's backs. Because we're real friends, not celebrity friends. That's when your publicist sets up a playdate. We're real friends."

Chapter 14

PONYHAWK

W hen it was over, the pundits would not be kind. "There was no disagreement whatsoever on the sixth season: It stunk," wrote the *Biloxi Sun Herald*. "Even staunch fans acknowledge that this season, *Idol* is off," reported the *Washington Post*'s Lisa de Moraes. "They point to the uninspiring crop of jaded Idolettes, whose stated goal in interviews was not to win the competition but to make it to the top ten, securing a place in the summer's *American Idol* tour."

A nation full of bloggers and morning show personalities chimed in with their opinions about what had gone wrong. Too many celebrity mentors. A dull cast. Out-of-date themes. Too much spectacle. As if that weren't enough, Ryan Seacrest pointed a finger at sparring partner Simon Cowell. "Clearly there's been an oversaturation of his character," he said in an interview.

The season began as others had, with a dependable *Idol* subplot: another Paula incident. On January 11, 2007 Paula was interviewed by satellite with Seattle local TV as part of the standard season launch PR run-up.

The public was used to Paula's quirky behavior, her hyperemotional responses, her ability to get tongue-tied over the simplest statements and flummoxed to the point of breakdown by her sparring partner's bon mots. This time, however, she appeared not ditzy but actually intoxicated, majorly trashed. She bobbed and weaved in and out of the frame and her eyes rolled wildly in her head. In response to questions she waved giddily to the camera like she was seeing an old friend across the room. She took long, bizarre pauses before answering. Asked about comments by Cowell that the Seattle auditions had been horrendous, she said uncharacteristically, "You know what . . . I have to agree with Simon," and then immediately contradicted herself, rambling, "You know what, it is what it is. And it was brilliant." The video was a viral sensation, with comments on YouTube kicking off a long and heated debate on the now ubiquitous topic of *What's Paula On?*

The subplot unfolded according to convention. Springing into damage control mode, Paula sat down on the Jay Leno show and offered the explanation that the sound from the satellite feed of two different stations had simultaneously been sent into her earpiece, leaving her struggling to sort out who was asking what. Anyone who has done these satellite tours can attest that such things happen, and there is little more confusing than being in that position. Watching the video, however, her answers and body language seem wacky even when she is responding directly to questions. That YouTube footage was hard to explain away— why would competing satellite feeds cause her to sway, for example—and this one would stay with her for a while. Fox issued its now familiar statement of support. Privately, however, many eyes rolled at Paula's explanation and the always present fears of what else she might do or say in public ratcheted up many notches.

THE AWKWARD INCIDENT would be a fitting opening to a season that flailed and struggled to find its footing. Even to the *Idol* team, it's something of a mystery why the talent resonates in some years and falls flat in others. Funny things often happen on the way to the top twelve. People who seemed promising early on fade under the spotlight. The brightest prospects get eliminated in the semifinals. Some of the most talented fail to make an impression in their ninety seconds before that first reviewing table. Singers who would go on to great careers, including pop star Colbie Caillat and *Glee's* Amber Riley, tell of auditioning for *Idol* and failing to clear the first bar. Others who eventually made it on *Idol*, including season 6 champion Jordin Sparks, had to try their luck in multiple cities before getting a thumbs-up.

Whatever the reason, some years fail to light the public's imagination. Season 6 was one of those years. The sixers as a whole were not without talent. The group initially centered around a trio that was cast as the three divas redux, a cluster of the very able African American female singers Melinda Doolittle, LaKisha Jones, and Jordin Sparks. Beatboxer Blake Lewis still stands out as a truly singular presence on the *Idol* stage, his post-*Idol* albums becoming some of the most critically lauded of any contestant. There were a handful of likable personalities, including wisecracking oversized moptop Chris Sligh and active naval officer Phil Stacey. But after the supercharged personalities of the previous season, it was a lower-key affair.

Except for Sanjaya.

THE SANJAYA PHENOMENON started slowly. When the sixteen-year-old auditioned there was nothing ironic about the judges' praise for him. Sanjaya was first introduced as the quiet sidekick of his vivacious and strong-willed sister Shyamali, both of whom sailed through their auditions. "She has the better stage presence, you have the better voice," Cowell told Sanjaya. His rendition of Stevie Wonder's "Signed, Sealed, Delivered I'm Yours" had, in fact, been well sung and even understated by the good-looking boy with the long flowing hair.

During Hollywood Week, however, Sanjaya was showcased less for his vocal talents than for his emotional roller coaster offstage, breaking into inconsolable tears when Shyamali was eliminated, and he was left to make the journey on his own.

In the semifinals, he gushed, "I guess I've always put my sister on a pedestal. The day my sister got cut I kinda felt like half of me was gone." His singing also came under its first attack from the judges. Randy admonished him for chutzpah in taking on a Stevie Wonder song and Cowell called it, "without question the dreariest performance we've had all night." He might already have climbed above where his abilities could sustain him, but by this time the Sanjaya genie was out of the bottle.

Sanjaya's rise was driven by a remarkable alliance between *Idol*'s tween viewers teamed up with "the haters." To the tweens, Sanjaya's high voice, lithe physique, flowing hair, dark eyes, and laid-back style—not to mention his ability to cry, for his beloved sister no less—made him a viable target for prepubescent crushes. Reminiscent in his manner of a young Michael Jackson, Sanjaya's demeanor was reminiscent of teenage girl's, a quality that called out to the young *Idol* viewers. The

(2009) A pioneer of the reality age, Fox's iconoclastic Mike Darnell pushed for the show to break new boundaries. *(FRANK MICELOTTA)*

(SEASON 8, 2009) *Idol's* greatest fan became one of its unlikeliest stars. Ashley "Crying Girl" Ferl with Allison Iraheta. *(STACY FERL)*

(SEASON 7, 2008)
Teen sensation David Archuleta's rise woke up *Idol*'s sleeping giant—the tween vote.
(FRANK MICELOTTA/ AMERICAN IDOL)

(SEASON 8, 2009) Cast into the middle of the world's most famous buddy act, Kara Dioguardi struggled to find her role amongst the judges. *(KEVIN WINTER/AMERICAN IDOL)*

(SEASON 8, 2009) The founder of American Idol Ministry, Leesa Bellesi with season 8's Danny Gokey and his family, one of the many *Idol* clan that have been part of her subterreanean mission. (*LEESA BELLESI*)

(SEASON 8, 2009) Adam Lambert dominated season 8 as the greatest phenomenon the show had seen in years. Privately, however, the crew was aware there was a ceiling on the controversial singer's support. Ultimately, Kris Allen's victory, while shocking to the audience, wasn't even close. (*KEVIN WINTER/AMERICAN IDOL*)

(SEASON 8, 2009)
Two of the quirky new breed of *Idol* stars, season 8's Nick Mitchell, aka Norman Gentle, and Megan Joy. For Megan, who secretly fought a child custody battle while on the show, *Idol* was the best and worst months of her life. *(RICHARD RUSHFIELD)*

(SEASON 8, 2009)
After leaving the *Idol* bubble, the next stop is the fifty-city concert tour where the Idols for the first time come face to face with their fans. Season 8's Matt Giraud called it his "redemption tour." *(RICHARD RUSHFIELD)*

(SEASON 9, 2010)
It was hoped that *Idol*'s #1 fan Ellen DeGeneres would confer her own star power upon the show. Instead, lacking a musical background, she seemed a fish out of water through the difficult ninth season.
(KEVIN WINTER/ AMERICAN IDOL)

(SEASON 9, 2010)
Crystal Bowersox was the one breakout star of season 9, as well as its major source of backstage drama. *(RICHARD RUSHFIELD)*

ranks of these fans was most notably represented by the appearance of perhaps *Idol*'s most passionate fan, Ashley Ferl, otherwise known as "the crying girl."

It's hard to stand out in an audience of enthusiastic supporters—parents, spouses, friends, and fans who whistle, cheer, clap, and cry for their chosen contestant—but the crying girl did just that. When Sanjaya sang the Kinks' "You Really Got Me," this gawky thirteen-year-old girl was overcome with fits of hysterical sobbing, reminiscent of girls screaming for Elvis and the Beatles in the 1950s and 1960s. For the young fan, it was to be another *Idol* fairy tale come true.

With her emotion beyond the call of duty, young Ashley won herself a permanent place in the *Idol* canon, making her a celebrity in her own right on the *Idol* circuit. A Southern California native from Riverside, about an hour from Hollywood, Ashley had been watching *Idol* since she was in elementary school. Her mother, Stacy Ferl, recalls, "We had to tape every episode, and oh, my gosh, if we weren't home to do something she had a cow about it and called a friend to make sure someone recorded it for her."

"I just think it's a really cool show—giving people chances and stuff," says the now sixteen-year-old Ashley. "Some people, they seem so fake on reality shows. But then *American Idol* is, like, you know they're normal."

Even for an obsessive fan, *Idol* is perhaps the hardest ticket in Hollywood to land, with even people connected to Fox waiting years for a seat in the studio. On the night she stepped into fame, Ashley and her mother had learned that people who attended tapings of *Are You Smarter than a 5th Grader* were offered tickets afterward to the *Idol* dress rehearsal. There, she was spotted by *Idol* producers, who summoned her to return for that night's taping and her moment of fame.

The call to destiny came after Ashley sighted one of her favorites, season 4's Mikalah Gordon, in the crowd. Stacy Ferl recalls, "She just started bawling her head off and the usher comes over and says, 'Is she all right? Is something wrong?' and I told him, 'No, she just really likes Mikalah.'"

Three days after her *Idol* cameo, Ashley found herself flown to New York to appear on the *Today* show. Three years later, she has traveled the country, attending dozens of concerts of *Idol* alumni. Still just as emotional when she sees them, these days, however, she often finds the *Idol* stars recognizing her before she does them. Recently, a high school senior with a driver's license and college plans, she has taken her *Idol* punditry into the media age, beginning a Twitter account largely devoted to *Idol* affairs. Her Twitter bio eloquently harks back to where it all began. It reads, "Ashley Ferl: I cried for Sanjaya."

The haters, on the other hand, were moved by the same things as Sanjaya's young fans—his oddness, his emotionalism, and the growing sense that once this young man got to the big stage, he was in over his head, and in deep.

It remains an open question how much Sanjaya curried his antihero status and how much it was forced upon him. As the season progressed, his songs became louder, screamier. He picked songs like "You Really Got Me" that allowed him to flounce around the stage, screaming his head off. To many he seemed to be just messing around on the hallowed *Idol* stage. Nevertheless, he continued to rise through the ranks. And week after week, the media demanded an explanation. "What Force Is Keeping Sajaya On?" asked the *Florida Today* headline. The Associated Press investigated and reported, "In the Case of *Idol* Star Sanjaya Mala-kar, Clues Add Up to Conspiracy, Kids, and Confusion." His father's native land publicly distanced itself from the young singer. "Sanjaya's Idol Run Not India's Fault" was the AP headline, which quoted several sources who adamantly denied rumors that India's call centers had fueled Sanjaya's rise. "He's an object of ridicule," said one Indian blogger.

Ultimately the finger of blame pointed again at Vote for the Worst, which had endorsed Sanjaya, this time in league with Howard Stern, who rhapsodized about Sanjaya on his radio show, saying he would use him as a weapon to bring *Idol* down. "We're corrupting the entire thing," he told his listeners, taking credit for Sanjaya's rise. "It's the number one show on television and it's getting ruined."

Sanjaya insists he wasn't trying to sing badly or make a mockery of the show. In interviews since and in his memoir, he has said he was just trying to do his best and have fun. That, unfortunately, was not how it appeared to his some of fellow contestants, who grew tired of his antics as they themselves struggled through the difficult season. Blake Lewis later recalled locking Sanjaya out of the rehearsal space during the height of the Sanjaya craze. On particularly tense nights, many of the others were observed keeping him distinctly at arm's length. Blake would later tell in a radio interview, "I was never a fan of Sanjaya. I didn't think he should be on the show at all. It was bad for television. Everyone there was like, why is this little kid who's just annoying in the room? I got pissed every week because my buddies who were super talented were going home and America's ignorant in some things and voted for Sanjaya to stay on *American Idol*."

And then there was that hairstyle.

Debbie Williams remembers the day of Sanjaya's epic hairstyle: "I got off the elevator and here comes Dean (a crew member) and Sanjaya walking down the hall and he's got the seven ponytails. Dean said, 'We've got to take him into Nigel.' Nigel was all for it. I thought, *What a smart kid*. Not the best singer, but he played this other bag of tricks and it just kept him in there. It was fun. It was good entertainment."

Ultimately finishing in seventh place, Sanjaya's final song, a raucous rendition of "Something to Talk About," nicely summed up the Sanjaya meteor storm that had blazed across the *Idol* stage. Indeed, soon after he was eliminated, ratings for the show began to fall off in the biggest slide the show had yet experienced.

For all Sanjaya's goofiness, he kept *Idol* on a very human scale when it was in danger of becoming a slick showbiz machine. What with celebrity mentors such as Gwen Stefani, J Lo, and Diana Ross, guest performers during the results shows, past champions returning as icons, and superstar judges with their superstar issues, the little talent contest was having a problem of size. The production and the brand were becoming so huge they seemed to dwarf the twelve unknowns who stood up on that now historic stage, in the now historic footsteps of Clarkson, Underwood, Aiken, and Daughtry. As the coming seasons would show, some were able to step into that giant spotlight while others, such as the cast of season 6, shrank under its glare.

It was the young man from Seattle, alternately befuddled and rebellious, whose antics deflated a bit of the pomposity that had come with *Idol*'s overwhelming success. It was Sanjaya and his ponyhawk who kept the nation mesmerized. When Lythgoe was asked midway through the year what the season's big story was, he answered, "Sanjaya and three great female singers," the latter referring to season 6's attempt at a three divas redux with Melinda Doolittle, LaKisha Jones, and Jordin Sparks. In retrospect, the memory of those three singers and their place in that season has faded, but the image of Sanjaya Malakar leaping across the stage, his hair in a braided Mohawk, will live forever.

ANOTHER NEW SIGN of *Idol*'s immensity came into play during season 6 and this, too, was unprecedented: the *Idol Gives Back* telethon special. Privately, charity work had always been a part of the life of *Idol*. Simon Cowell had a long-term commitment to a children's hospital back in England. Patients he worked with could often be seen in the audience. On tour and at the show, contestants were frequently visited by guests from the Make-A-Wish Foundation, and former contestants often made visits to children's hospitals on behalf of charities *Idol* was involved with—away from press.

As rewarding as those private involvements were, *Idol*'s ringmasters weren't ones to think small. They wanted to parlay *Idol*'s connections and production talent to produce a spectacle that would benefit children's charities around the globe, and they wanted the spectacle to be even bigger than the *Idol* finale. They came up with an idea that was something entirely new for entertainment programming: Turn a week of episodes into a giant telethon right in the middle of the season.

Once they had had trouble getting anyone even to allow their songs to be performed on *Idol*. But six years later, almost every act in the dying music business would kill for a piece of *Idol* exposure. The plan was to draw the biggest names in entertainment to participate in a super-sized two-night show/pitch for contributions to an array of children's causes. Telethons had traditionally meant nights of humdrum schmaltz, earnest appeals coupled with past-their-prime performers. It was a format that belonged largely to another, lower-pressure age of television. For *Idol Gives Back*, the producers pledged to break the earnestness trap and deliver, first and foremost, a night of great entertainment. The show ultimately drew a litany of stars, including Madonna, Bono, Celine Dion, and Josh Groban, raising over sixty million dollars for the benefiting charities.

Clearly for the crew, the charity became a very personal matter. I witnessed the largest fight I have ever directly encountered in entertainment reporting between a member of the crew and a Fox executive over the subject of how much airtime would be devoted to charitable pitches, with the *f* word liberally employed. To prepare for the show, Cowell and

Seacrest had, in fact, traveled to Africa to see firsthand what the contributions would support. "I've never seen anything like it in my life," Cowell said after the trip, clearly affected. "And I'm glad I saw it because, you know, pictures on a TV screen, they never really show you quite how bad things are."

For the contestants, who performed inspirational songs that week, the show offered them the gift of life in another way as Seacrest announced at its end that there would be no elimination, in keeping with the charitable spirit.

It had been an audacious move. Whatever the criticisms that would be leveled for the inevitable schmaltz and philosophical arguments about celebrity-driven good works, no show before had devoted so much valuable real estate to giving. It made *Idol* about something bigger than just handing out a recording contract.

WITH SANJAYA'S RISE and fall, questions sprang up again about the voting system, whether *Idol* is "fixed" and how much influence haters like Stern have over the show. On the latter question, the answer is clear: very little. Even with the power of Howard Stern behind it, the number of votes the haters can muster are but a drop in the bucket compared to the votes cast each week by *Idol* fans. The number of visitors each day to the VFTW site numbers at most in the tens of thousands compared to the tens of millions who watch *Idol* each week. Even Howard Stern in his satellite era doesn't begin to reach a comparable audience. In the final analysis, Sanjaya's run likely owes far more to the crying girl and her peers than it does to Stern and the Internet.

The question of whether *Idol* is "fixed" remains the subject of perennial rumors and Internet theories; talk of busy signals, crossed numbers, and changed vote totals circulates endlessly. To date, nothing in any of these rumors has produced anything that smacks of actual vote fraud. And surely if the producers could tamper with the votes, the results would have frequently turned out very different than they did. Every year, from the semifinals onward, the show's clear favorites tumble while less marketable personalities blunder on. Further, as the *Idol* team constantly points out, what sense does it make for a show to deliberately thwart the will of its audience? This is not a national health care policy debate where ends might justify means. In entertainment the means—popularity—*are* the ends; winning public support is the entire battle.

Simon Fuller explained that the very purpose of the show was to get around those who would impose their tastes on the public. "You go straight to the public and they tell you, and if they tell you, then, fine. Okay, I'll listen. At the end of the show the winner will be someone that they've all bought into. The power of *Idol* was that connectivity and interactivity of the audience buying into these kids, believing them, voting for them, and it creates a far more meaningful, passionate relationship."

However, to glean the public's will, the votes must be counted, and in the conspiracy universe, *Idol*'s vote-counting has been the subject of endless speculation. As with the Oscars or the major awards shows, *Idol*'s votes are counted by an outside firm, in this case a company called Telescope, which analyzes the data phoned into the AT&T network. Cecile Frot-Coutaz explains the system: "They effectively operate as an intermediate between us and the phone company. The calls are routed from local exchanges to the AT&T network. Then AT&T gives the information to Telescope, who tabulate the votes and give us the results. Over the years it's become more and more sophisticated, so the systems now are better able to cope with the volume than in the initial years. We have now something called the AT&T Labs 39.26, which is a section of AT&T where they analyze the result for us in the event anything looks unusual. They can drill down and look at what's happened per state, what's happened per area code. Anything we may want to look at."

A clause in the *Idol* rules gives the producers the right to invalidate the results of any vote. This clause, Frot-Coutaz explains, is not a device for producers to interfere with the results. It exists in the event fraud is ever discovered, or if major problems occur with contestants' lines. "The good thing is it's never happened that we had a result that was invalid."

Asked what would happen if they ever did discover a problem or fraud, Frot-Coutaz answers without hesitation, "If we had an invalid we would have to say nobody goes away. I think what we do is nobody goes home this week and then two people would have to go home the following week."

There are lots of ways the producers can help move the course of a contest, from the judges' comments to the order in which the contestants perform, but in the end, as far as all available evidence shows, the fate of the competition is turned over each week to the hands of the public and ultimately, the votes are the votes.

WHEN *AMERICAN IDOL* began, it was the center of the lives of all involved in it. For the British expat crew, it was their sole reason for leaving their homeland. Six years later, with the show's monumental success, each of the epically ambitious people involved ruled over far-reaching empires of their own, of which *American Idol* was but one piece. Simon Fuller's 19 productions now employed nearly two hundred people. His interests had moved beyond just music to fashion—he invested in a modeling agency and clothing line—brand management—overseeing the public interests of Muhammad Ali and the Elvis Presley estate, among others—and sports. Most notably, after reconciling with the Spice Girls' queen, Victoria Beckham, he became the manager of both her and her husband, international soccer icon David Beckham, engineering his $250-million-a-year move to Los Angeles.

In 2005, *So You Think You Can Dance*, a show created by Nigel Lythgoe with Simon Fuller, debuted, taking *Idol*'s slot on Fox during the summer months. While Lythgoe had always been passionate about *Idol, So You Think You Can Dance* for him, the dockworker's son who had a yearning to dance, represented not just entertainment but a movement. Talking about *SYTYCD*, his eyes light up as he waxes about how he hoped dance could become a force to improve the lives of all who practice it or view it. *SYTYCD* often seemed to be, in many ways, his antidote to the Goliath *Idol* had become, a competition not about winning a million-dollar contract, but focused purely on the artistry. Indeed, stepping back into the judge's chair for the show, all traces of Nasty Nigel were erased. The *SYTYCD* judging panel was not about delivering zingers, but about giving constructive critiques they could use and grow with, Lythgoe would often emphasize in thinly veiled shots across the bow of another certain judge. "It's not about putting people down or putting them in their place; it's about giving them advice they can use to grow," he said of *SYTYCD*'s judging. After a couple of seasons, in tandem with *Dancing with the Stars*, the show amazingly did spark a dance revival, bringing the form to a more prominent place in national culture than it had been since at least the 1960s.

On top of that, Lythgoe and fellow executive producer Ken Warwick had set up shop as vintners, purchasing a winery in central California. Not ones to let entertainment prospects go to waste, they shot a reality show about their misadventures in agriculture, entitled *Corkscrewed: The Wrath of Grapes.*

Ryan Seacrest had become a virtual hosting machine, helming not just *Idol* but his daily national radio show, which became the go-to confessional spot for young Hollywood and the Paris Hilton set—as well as a news show for the E! network. He was very rapidly filling the shoes he had longed for, those of Dick Clark. Not only did he take over Clark's New Year's Eve duties when the aging star was sidelined after a stroke, but he became America's all-purpose ubiquitous front man, hosting the Emmys and the Super Bowl pregame, for starters. He also set up shop as a TV producer, coming out of the gate with an early unlikely hit, *Keeping Up with the Kardashians.*

Randy Jackson would soon himself become a TV mogul, producing MTV's surprise hit *America's Best Dance Crew,* and Paula produced a pair of cable shows. As for Simon Cowell, besides flying back and forth across the Atlantic to judge *Idol* and preside over *X Factor*, he seemed to roll out a new show every month. *American Inventor* debuted in 2006 on ABC, and in 2007 he launched *America's Got Talent*, another show soon to become an empire unto itself, to be cloned in over thirty countries around the globe. With his judging duties on the British version of *Got Talent*, he was now presiding over three shows each year on either side of the globe. Of those three, the only one where his name was not on the door was *American Idol.*

And it was there that Cowell's restive nature was most evident. On the *Idol* set, there was clearly one man who was king, calling the shots on the floor during each episode, and it was not him. Somewhere around the middle of season 6, the crew began to notice Cowell display a noticable testiness, an itchiness crew members said, about following the orders of Nigel Lythgoe.

Simon says now of their long-running relationship, "We're like Tom and Jerry, him and I. My guess is that there's many times that he was looking at me thinking, *I want to be in that chair.* But then again, I was looking at him thinking, *I want to be in your chair.* So I would have been quite happy to swap places. But I think deep down we had a respect for each other. No question about it, we went through many many times having big bust-ups. But I'm quite comfortable having a bust-up with people to their face, it kind of clears the air. And that happened a lot with me and Nigel."

Chapter 15

THE BUBBLE

I t's an awe-inspiring sight. Hours before dawn, a line of thousands gathers, stretching out into darkness. Some are singing. Some play guitar. The entire mass throbbing with excitement.

On TV, it seems as though the line files straight in to the judges' table. In fact, it's more complicated than that, a multifaceted system taking place over the course of days or months. The legions that line up will be winnowed down to a few hundred in each city who will ultimately be seen by the judges. In the end, six months later, of the thousands who stand shivering in the cold stadium parking lots, no more than two or three will stand on *Idol*'s big stage.

Many contestants spend years preparing for their auditions before making it through. Season 6's Gina Glocksen, season 7's Carly Smithson, and season 9's Lacey Brown, among others, each auditioned in more than one season before reaching the big stage. Others, including season 6 champion Jordin Sparks, have followed the audition tour to multiple cities until they finally got through. Singers are free to audition as many times as they can bear, until they make the semifinals, after which they're not allowed another shot at *Idol* no matter what their fate.

For every one of those hard-striving dreamers, there's the story of one who just stumbled in on a lark or who, like champions Ruben Studdard, David Cook, and Kris Allen, just came to keep their brothers company.

The stadium events, just one part of the audition process, are themselves seven-day affairs. On the first day, contestants must stand in line just to register, fill out paperwork, and get the wristbands that allow them to audition. The following day sees the predawn lineup and the carnival atmosphere of excited dreamers huddling together in the darkness, awaiting their chance at their destiny. There isn't actually any reason for them to line up so early. The numbers on the wristbands determine the order in which they will try out, not the order they get in line. But that doesn't deter the thousands of enthusiastic contestants.

Ace Young remembers getting to Denver's Invesco Field for the season 5 auditions. "It was three in the morning and everybody was singing. Singing their brains out. I was thinking, *Man if you're singing at three in the morning, you're not going to have a voice by the time we get to actually sing.* And a lot of the people actually lost their voice by the time we got in. That first day they cut fourteen thousand people down to four hundred. We sang on a football field, there were about ten tables with a lot of British people sitting behind those tables and we walked up and sang in groups of four, some people got a ticket, most people didn't. When you got a ticket, you just went through and gave them all your information and left.

"Three weeks later and we had to come back to the city that we initially auditioned in. It was hard for a lot of people because they were traveling from all over the place. So it was financially hard for everybody because we hadn't made it at that point. So I came back three weeks later and then again two weeks after that until I got to sing for the actual judges themselves."

Auditioning in a distant city can be an expensive and exhausting proposition, sometimes requiring multiple trips back for follow-up rounds. After having spent years living in Los Angeles and knocking on doors in show business, Brooke White was on the brink of calling it quits between her and music, when her friends and advisors persuaded her to give the dream one last final chance. "I decided to check *Idol* out, and I found out that there was one audition left, in Philadelphia. I spoke to my husband and my manager and we all decided it was worth a shot. We scraped money together and I got a plane ticket, and I waited twenty-one hours for my first audition, and I made it.

"I was in a turnaround city [the rare stop on the tour where all the rounds from stadium to judges are packed into consecutive days], so everything happened the same week. I didn't have callbacks. I was there five days in a row. The waiting was insane. There were so many people there, and you're hearing people sing, people who are amazing, and they're leaving. Fifteen hours go by. People start leaving because of the wait, and I got up there and said to myself, 'I don't even care if I make it. I'm so tired, and I just want to go home.'"

After the day at the stadiums, the remaining contestants return to sing for the producers. If they make it past that round, they sing once more for the judges. These rounds can be months apart or, as in some cases, occur on consecutive days. It's at this point when the stark divide between the talented and "alternately talented" is most acute. Matt Giraud remembers sitting with one of these hopefuls. "I can't remember the guy's name, but he was an astrophysicist. He wore a suit and was singing really low. The thing is, all the crazy ones think they're going way further than we do. I didn't know how far I was going but he sure as hell was going all the way."

Of finally stepping before the judges, he remembers, "Singing for the judges was weird. It was like stepping into the TV. You can hear their voices, you can hear Simon and Randy, and it just kind of felt like the TV was on in the background. It was just really weird knowing you were going up for your epic, big audition. It could be nothing, it could never be shown, or it could be everything."

ONCE CONTESTANTS ARE given their golden ticket, the veil of secrecy descends, beginning with their first stern lecture from the *Idol* staff. Season 8's Jackie Tohn recalls, "After you get through the judges, they [the production staff] sit you down and say, 'This is the deal, Hollywood Week is coming. You can't tell anybody where you're going. You can't tell anybody where you're staying. You can't tell anybody when it is. No information except to a very close loved one and you have to make sure they don't say anything.'

"And then they tell you these horror stories. 'Three years ago we had to change hotels when someone revealed where we were. And the person whose fault it was got cut. We're not saying it's why they got cut, we're not saying it's not why.' They pretty much put the fear of God into you from the word *go*."

This need for secrecy creates no shortage of complications for the young contestants. As Ace Young recalls, "By November I knew I was in the show. I had a job selling copiers but I didn't know how to tell them that I needed the time off because I couldn't publicize that I was on the show. So it was a very interesting time, because you have this life-changing opportunity that's coming your way but you can't even tell your parents you've made it because if it makes it to press then they kick you off."

Then there are the awkward situations of other sorts, such as the incident that happened to Carly Smithson en route to season 7's Hollywood Week. "Because there was a shot of me in the ads for the new season, I'd been warned to come in disguise, to put on a baseball hat and cardigan. Well, my flight stopped in Vegas, where I became very hot, so without thinking I took the cap and sweater off but tried to keep my head down because I was terrified someone would recognize me. When I got on the plane, I was walking through first class, looked down at a man, and saw John Mayer. At that moment, he looked at me and his eyes lit up, and he yelled out to the whole plane, 'Hey, that's the girl who's going to be on—' when I shushed him, cut him off, and raced back to my seat. I was petrified that I was going to be disqualified. At the baggage claim, he sent his people over to ask if it was really me. When I got to the theater, though, and confessed it all to the producers, they laughed and said it was the funniest thing they'd ever heard."

"EVEN IN THE early days they called it the *week of hell*," recalls RJ Helton of Hollywood Week. To the two hundred or so people who emerge with a ticket to Hollywood, it can seem as though they have won the lottery. The iconic *Idol* image will always remain that of the hopefuls racing out of the audition room, golden ticket in hand, leaping into the arms of a cheering family. The euphoria is so overwhelming they can be forgiven for believing that they are but a mere technicality away from their dream.

But in fact, having beaten such odds, they face an equally stiff challenge in the days ahead. Each year, somewhere in the neighborhood of two hundred singers enter Hollywood Week. Before it's over, that number is shaved down somewhere between thirty and fifty. (It varies season to season.) At this point, contestants are not competing with the deluded masses, but with the best of the best—mostly.

Hollywood Week is also the part of *Idol* that most resembles a reality show like *Survivor* or *Road Rules*. There's a very specific set of challenges to overcome in a very specific order. Ace Young tells of his week, "I remember sitting down, and the very first song we started singing, the judges started cutting people. Literally, they just got there, and people are getting up on stage and saying, 'Hi, my name is so and so.' 'Sing. All right, you can go home.' It was almost like we were just the cattle and we had no control over anything. So much so, that when you missed something they'd send you home right there, on the spot, on the stage. I saw a lot of talented people get up and not do very well. And I saw the opposite. I saw people who didn't have as much talent get up onstage and do amazing, because this was everything to them and they couldn't let anything get in the way. It was a really interesting time. And I remember, nobody wanted to talk to anybody because we didn't know if we were going to be there, you had no idea who was still going to be there. Nobody wanted to befriend anybody."

"When you're cut, it's like, gimme your papers and your number," recalls season 8's Alexis Grace. "Go up to your room. Pack your bags, and then they slip your itinerary under your door for your flight the next day."

Pleasing the judges often feels like luck of the draw. Season 8's Jackie Tohn recalls how another member of her group persuaded her to sing "Mercy" by Duffy. "I said, 'I know eight of these songs out of ten choices we were given. We're not doing "Mercy," which I don't know.' He said, 'We have to, it's a sick arrangement.' In the end, everybody in the group gets cut but me. Simon goes, 'So, Jackie, I guess you used your feminine charms to convince these boys to sing a song that's perfect for you.'"

Perhaps the most intense moments come during the group numbers when the singers are thrust together to plan those quickie song and dance routines. Megan Joy recalls the tension that can take over the groups: "Everybody picks groups immediately. I'm the last one sitting there without a partner. They're, like, okay, we're going to need to put you up here with some people. So they put me in a group. So it was really embarrassing. Then you have to rehearse it until, like, five in the morning. So you don't sleep that night. You get, like, three hours of sleep if that. That's why people fight. There were a couple of, like, testy moments where someone would say something bratty. . . . That day I remember right before we sang, I was done. I was exhausted. We couldn't get along. No one was getting along. There was nowhere to practice so your groups are taking turns in the bathrooms or corners. It's just really crazy by that point. I was just, like, this is not worth it. I'm not going to make it anyway. I'm going through misery to get rejected, so I need to go home. I remember in the bathroom I started to cry and I turned around and my mom was there. I really started to cry. I was, like, I'm done and I want to quit. She said, 'No you're not quitting, you're here and you're doing it. You're going to be great no matter what happens.'"

The ultimate torment of Hollywood Week takes place when the judges deliver the fate of the young performers. Season 8's Alexis Grace recalls, "At the end, they put people in three rooms. So all seventy people were in this one room. You had to be silent for three hours. If you whisper they said, no no. And you want to talk some *Temptation Island* stuff! They keep switching the room that Tatiana [season 8's outright drama queen, Tatiana Del Toro] is in. So the room that she's in knows they're going home, or maybe she's so crazy, they're going through. Either way, whichever room she's in is scared. Every single one of us became mathematicians, trying to figure out what our chances were."

"They said you can't go to the bathroom. It was hours," remembers Jackie Tohn. "And I had to pee, and when we're at the point when they came in, Paula, Kara [DioGuardi], and Randy, our room was last, and we hear another room screaming with joy. And we're like, oh, my God. And Randy looks right at me and says, 'For some of you it's your last opportunity, it's your last year and we're really sorry to say . . . that you made it through.' And everybody's crying and screaming. People were, like, punching each other, not in a bad way, but they're saying, 'Oh, my God!' People just go crazy. Adam [Lambert] and I were crying. Adam was holding me like a baby and we're sobbing. And Paula's hugging us saying, 'I'm so excited to see how this unfolds for you.'"

AFTER SURVIVING HOLLYWOOD Week, the contestants return home for a few weeks or months, depending on the season. The schedule varies from year to year. The field has been shaved down to a manageable size by this time, so the show can conduct the background checks on each of the surviving contestants. In most seasons, Hollywood Week is shot in December and the green mile episode in February, just before the semifinals live shows begin. The green mile is the most exquisite piece of torture on the *Idol* calendar.

Alexis Grace remembers returning to Los Angeles for the episode. "The green mile was the longest day I've ever experienced. We got up at 5:00 A.M., and went until 10:00 P.M. It was just sitting, doing interviews, and it was emotional because I did about four interviews, and they all emphasized how make-or-break the day was, asking questions about my daughter—stuff to really make you emotional."

Brooke White remembers the tension. "Knowing this was going to change my life completely either way was really intense. If I didn't make it, I didn't know that there was much more for me in music after that. I broke down, and totally started bawling. Michael Johns turned around and hugged me and they made me get in the elevator, and I thought, *I want this more than I thought I did.* When you sit down in front of the judges, there's cameras around and people are everywhere and the camera guy gives a thumbs-up and you don't realize that your life is changing so fast."

Megan Joy, alone in Los Angeles from her Utah home, recalls her day after learning she was going to be a semifinalist on *American Idol.* "I hugged everybody, hugged the judges, and then at that point I still didn't have any friends. So we were all done and so everyone went off in their groups to celebrate. So I went by myself and I went to a pizza place on Hollywood Boulevard to get spaghetti. I got a pitcher of beer to celebrate and I made a friend with the guy who was there. He was really funny and really interesting and we just talked. I couldn't tell him what I just did but I was, like, 'I'm celebrating I just progressed on a TV show' and he's, like, *awesome.*"

HAVING MADE IT out alive at Hollywood Week, the singers step onto *Idol*'s little semifinals stage. Finally, each has their chance to perform live before *Idol*'s millions of viewers, but close as they are to the dream, half will fall before making the big stage. (In some years, the number is more like two-thirds, as the format switches back and forth between boy/girl rounds and the three-heat sudden death version.) While most who make it to the big stage manage to make careers in the music industry, history has not been kind to those who fall during *Idol*'s semifinals.

Whatever the stakes, the remaining contestants are at last singing live underneath the *Idol* logo for tens of millions of people. Ace Young recalls of the experience, "Doing the actual show live was ridiculous. Just doing a show that was live for the whole world was more nerve-wracking than the judges. I was sitting there thinking, *My grandparents are watching this, my family is watching this in Colorado, all my friends are watching it.* I remember that first week after we all performed, we walked out to the car and went back to where they were putting us up and we had two hours to wait before we got to see what we just did on television. We're all sitting there going, 'Are you going to watch?' 'I don't know. Are you going to watch?' Everybody was sitting there talking about the fact that they didn't know if they wanted to see it or not because it would get in your head. And everybody ended up watching it."

On the final night of the semifinals, after the top twelve are announced, a coronation party complete with red carpet is held for the anointed, and the newly minted Idols get their very first taste of the limelight. "You walk down a red carpet and people are screaming," remembers Brooke White, "which was weird for all of us. You're trying to look at every person. You're shocked. It's such a new situation. We did a press junket the first few weeks on the show. The first ten interviews were torture for me. I would go home and lie in my bed and analyze everything I'd said."

"You can't even comprehend how intense it all is once it gets to that point, and it's crazy before then, but it continues to get crazier and crazier," says Megan Joy. "I remember my face hurting from smiling so much. I remember I loved it."

Alexis Grace tells, "I'd never experienced this before. Pictures, interviews, people calling out our names—one thing after the other. It was super long, and I was still in shock that it was really happening. That's when we all realized what a big deal it was."

Each year, the producers encourage—beg, even—the contestants not to look at the Internet, warning them it doesn't help to have all the trash that's spewed out there in your head. Each year, few listen. Almost all read the reviews, the message boards, the hater sites. Having struggled so hard for this moment in the limelight, it's a lot to ask these young people not to look once their moment has arrived. Some of the more methodical, like season 9's Adam Lambert, say they study the Internet to see if what they are attempting to communicate is coming across. Others just can't resist taking a peek. Brooke White recalls glancing in the Web's closet of horrors. "The one time I caught a small glimpse of something and it was mean, I realized that I wasn't capable of dealing with it. There were other contestants who said it didn't bother them, and I don't believe that."

"By the time we got to top twelve," Ace Young recalls, "there was already scandal press, like 'Is Ace sleeping with Paula?' or there was a three-page spread in *Star* magazine that says, 'My son's not gay,' and it's all about me. My dad literally answered the phone and said to the reporter, 'Sorry, my son's not gay.' Click. They made it, like, this epic thing like he yelled it on the phone. We were the *Twilight* of the time."

A BIG ISSUE for those locked inside the bubble is how to manage contact with the people on the other side. Naturally, when your friend or family member is on the biggest show in the world, you want to share that moment with them, be a part of the excitement, support them, encourage them, and most of all, offer advice—lots and lots and lots of advice, from suggestions about song arrangements to comebacks to use against Simon.

"Dealing with family and friends on the outside is a massive stress on everyone on the show, and it's something I struggled with," says Brooke White. "People start acting really weird when you're on the show. You're very busy, and you get maybe five minutes a day to talk to anyone. That's hard for a lot of people in your life. You talk about a song and people question it when I'd feel excited, and it deflates you. I got to a point where I was very careful about who I would talk to about what. Nobody understands what you're going through, and it's not their fault. They have the best intentions, and they think that they're helping. They can't fathom what it feels like to be in this situation, which, you know, is life."

Idol accommodations have varied from season to season. During years when their home is used in on-screen segments, they have been put up in lavish mansions in the L.A. hills. Other years, the contestants have lived in a nondescript apartment building in Hollywood. Non–cast members are strictly prohibited from visiting the accommodations, a rule that has been more rigorously enforced in some seasons than others.

Ace Young tells of life in the dorms during season 5: "You're not allowed to hang with your family. You have a curfew. Chris and I were grown-ass men and we had an eleven o'clock curfew, and we couldn't have family in the room with us. It was weird. And it made sense from their standpoint that nobody gets hurt in their facility but it didn't make sense in the family side of *American Idol*, so that made it hard. But it made all of us come together even closer because if I'm having an argument with my girlfriend, or Chris is in an argument with his wife, or Elliott's having something going on with his family or his girlfriend, we only have each other to talk to about it. We're on the phone with that person but we can't really resolve it."

NOTHING ULTIMATELY AFFECTS a contestant's progress more than the dreaded song choice question. Each week, with only days or hours to do it, the contestants must choose a song from within a week's theme that is beloved by both the audience and the judges—God help you in the eyes of Mr. Cowell if you pick an unfamiliar ditty—and that you can make your own. Contestants are expected to define themselves as artists without being "self-indulgent." It is a dilemma that could drive an Idol to madness.

Although ultimately the choice of what an Idol sings and how he sings it is made by the contestant, there's an array of hoops to jump through before that choice is made. First of all is the question of song clearance. Each week the contestants are given a list, sometimes a very short list, of songs that *Idol* has acquired the rights to perform. If the contestants want a song that's not on the list, the show will often try to acquire the rights, but there's no guarantee. Some artists will refuse to license their songs to *Idol*, not wanting to see them turned into fodder for a "game show," although this happens far less than it did in the early years. Other times, the price will simply be too high. Often with the clock ticking toward showtime, this decision can come down to the wire.

Ideally, after each Wednesday's elimination, the contestants will choose a song the next day. They'll spend Friday working with the vocal coach and music director, coming up with an arrangement. Over the weekend, they rehearse with the band while the producers review their work. Monday, they hit the studio to record the versions for iTunes release. That's when they also work out the blocking and choreography onstage. Tuesday it's showtime.

Ace Young recalls of the process, "The producers have to okay the song, so they'll come into the room when you're working with the vocal coach and they listen to it. But I remember when I sang 'Butterflies,' they asked me not to. Everything was leaning rock, I was getting ready to sing 'Butterflies,' and they literally came in and said, 'I don't think it's a good song, I don't know this song, I don't think it's a good song.' And I said, 'Listen, I've sung this when I'm the only white dude in the room for two and a half years and I promise, this is a good song. It works very well for me.' So I actually had to tell them I'm not going to sing another song. And they said, 'That's your decision, so if you're sitting out there and you've got nobody supporting you on it, then that's your decision.' And I said, 'That's fine.' Turned out that it was my second-best song performed on the show. I knew it—I didn't have to think about the words. When I was done with that Randy jumped on and went, 'Dude, you could sing songs in your falsetto all day long.' "

Negotiating with the band over the arrangements was also often a delicate dance. Brooke White recalls, "It was 1970s week, and I knew my stuff. I'd even practiced 'You're So Vain' before the show, hoping I might get to sing it, and initially I wanted to play the guitar. [Music director] Rickey Minor said, 'You're lovely, but you're not quite a good enough guitar player to play on the show.' He was very kind about it, but I was devastated. I felt like this was an important element for me. I went home, and I told my husband, and he told me to practice and see how I felt tomorrow.

"I was seriously doubting myself, and I prayed, looking for an answer. And I decided to play it. I adjusted some things, and I felt like I could play it pretty well. I told Rickey that I appreciated his feedback, but that I wanted to play, and he was very cool about it. We compromised—I told him I'd play during the chorus and the first verse, and it worked out beautifully. That was the first night the judges really got it. Simon insisted I was singing it about him, and I knew he was going to say that. But it was a moment where I was, like, 'You need to trust yourself.' You learn that there are so many voices, and you can't hear your own, and you have to learn to get into a place where you can hear it."

The schedule runs the Idols ragged, so sickness is a constant threat that most succumb to at some point. Flu, bronchitis, mono? The show must go on. Megan Joy remembers when her turn came to fall ill, "I got really sick. For dress rehearsal, an hour before the show I couldn't sing a single note. I started sobbing and they pretty much carried me off-stage. That's how weak I was. In that hour, I didn't practice. I didn't do what everyone else did. I sat in a dark room with IVs in me and tried not to cry. I was lying down as the makeup people were putting on my makeup, like passing out while they were doing it all. It was really intense. I was so sick. I was trying to find the humor in it. I was, like, I'm going to be the first person to pass out on the *Idol* stage. That's going to be hilarious. That's just what I kept thinking. I'm, like, I'm probably just going to drop on the stage. So I walked out there and once again, magic. I guess the adrenaline just canceled everything out and pushed me through it, because it was my best night."

STANDING ALONE ONSTAGE before an audience of tens of millions with your entire future hanging in the balance is the world's most terrifying experience. As is being ripped to shreds by *Idol*'s expert panel. "I think it's everyone's worst nightmare, that you look like a fool in front of thirty million people," said season 8's Anoop Desai. "That's a nightmare for everyone. It's a combination of pressure, criticism, how we felt about our own performance, whether we're happy or disappointed in ourselves. It all comes down to that one moment."

Ace Young fell under the lash. "I sang Daniel Bedingfield's song 'If You're Not the One' and I remember the judges just ripped me. They just cut me up. And I remember I sat there and I just didn't care. Before it even happened, before the song started. And also, I didn't pick the song. I had to sing it because it was on a list of six songs that were cleared. And I was just going, 'Well, all right, this is interesting.' And it was a weird time for me, because it was the first time they were all mean and I was so out of it that day because my mind was elsewhere. It was like kicking a dog when it's down. Simon was mean to me and it didn't affect me because I didn't even care. My brain wasn't about that. I wanted to get off the stage and deal with my stuff. The problem with a show like that is you have too much time to think about everything so you overprocess everything instead of just remembering to go out, have fun, sing the damn song, and have fun with it."

After each performance, an odd dynamic reigns in the holding room backstage, as some want to celebrate their triumphs and others struggle not to fall apart. "People come backstage after getting abused by the judges and it's scary, and then some people are on a high," said Brooke White. "You want to be very careful when you're back there. I would try to be calm and not say much, even if I was feeling amazing. Some people would get chewed up—they were just awful to Kristy [Lee Cook] all the time, and she took it like a champ. We'd all hug and give reassurance. You always knew you weren't alone. Most people got picked on."

FOR EVERY *IDOL* contestant there comes that moment when they realize their lives have changed forever. And it usually comes once they step out of the *Idol* bubble. The contestants know they're at the center of something big, but it's hard to truly grasp the phenomenon.

Idol contestants are different from actors or other musicians. The audience has met them in their homes, seen them progress, watched them celebrate and mourn. Joining them from the first steps of their journey, the public feels that they know the *real* them, and that they are responsible for having made them. Unlike with movie stars, the public feels that they *own* them, and that sense of ownership has led to some scary moments.

RJ Helton recalls the experience of leaving the show and going home, where he first got a glimpse of what he was a part of. "I was at the Mall of Georgia by myself shopping. I walked into a clothing store and this huge trail of people were behind me and I had to have mall security called and escort me back to my car. It was pretty weird. That type of stuff was strange to me, surreal actually. I didn't understand the big deal. I was just a very normal, regular person from a very small town. It was kind of scary at times."

Nikki McKibbin remembers a similar moment, also at a mall. "It's scary to some degree. It's awesome, but I remember coming back home and since Kelly and I lived so close to each other, I was in a mall here when Kelly was. I remember getting mobbed when I walked in. I didn't go with Kelly but there were people running up to me asking if we were all there and I was, like, 'What are you talking about?' 'At the mall, are you guys all here?' 'No, it's just me.' Then they'd get mad. 'Why are you lying? Kelly's just right over there.' I walk over and poor Kelly is face to the counter, hat on her head. I walk up, and you get to know the sound of someone else's voice even when they're messing with you, and so I walked up to her and screamed, 'Oh, my gosh! Kelly Clarkson!' She knew immediately. She turned around and she looked at me like, 'Help.' We were both standing there, like, 'Holy shit, what's going on?'"

On the tour, if anything, the fans become more voracious. Ace Young tells, "We had people literally try to run up onstage and try to give us their address, or try to get into our dressing rooms and get into our stuff. On numerous occasions we would walk inside the tour bus and there'd be fans on our bus. They snuck in, and they're going through our stuff. And we can't go and tell them they have to leave. We'd walk off and tell security, because if you physically grab their hand and pull them off the bus they could sue you, so on numerous occasions we had people sneak in and go through our stuff. I remember Chris and I went shopping. We had to go to the mall to grab outfits for the next week. We were in a store looking at jeans and we had two to three thousand teenagers outside. We said our hellos, and walked through it."

LIVING INSIDE THE bubble is a lot to contend with, but it eventually comes to an end with elimination. Early in the season, the eliminations are celebrated with a good-bye dinner, where all the contestants' families are invited to say farewell to the departing singer. The tradition holds that they go around the table and each contestant tells the eliminee how much they mean to them.

But first, they have to face that moment onstage, in front of the cameras—alone.

Melinda Doolittle remembered, "I hated Wednesday nights so much. They were hard either way. If you stayed you were crying so hard for the people who left and then if they said your time was up you were, like, 'Okay, here we go. What do I do now?' You can't really celebrate because you're next to someone who's headed home."

"You feel like you're being pushed off the edge of a cliff," said Brooke White. "You just do the best you can and it's very solemn. It becomes very solemn toward that stage of the competition. When it was my day, I just had a gut feeling. I called Kristy Lee and told her I thought I was going to go home, and she said, 'No, you're crazy.' That whole day, though, I started packing. I knew it was getting close. You have to be ready to go. I was packed, and I just remember standing there and emotionally preparing to sing. When it was time to go, I felt a deep, deep sadness hit me. Just devastated. It's not good enough anymore. You want to go farther. Top five was my ultimate goal. Five out of 107,000 people. I looked at everybody onstage, though, and I was sad to leave. I was sad that I would not see the *American Idol* family anymore. I loved those people, and that was a part of me I knew was gone. I told them I couldn't sing, and finally I took the microphone and I remember being just so, so sad. Saying thank you. As soon as I was done, I turned around and walked away and sobbed. Cameras were in my face, and I didn't think I was going to be able to stop crying."

Alexis Grace recalls, "Getting eliminated was one of the top ten worst feelings of all time. I might be alone in feeling that horrible, but it was so awful. I think that I should've still been there. Not in a cocky way, but that's how I felt. I felt like I needed more time there—it was cut so short. I got through it, though. I was fine once I got home, but it was really hard to keep watching the show. I'd wish I was there performing. It was, again, like a breakup! You're so in love, and you get dumped, and then plastered everywhere is them, out with someone else. That's what it feels like. It's horrible. As much as I wanted to support the other contestants, it was so hard. Eventually it's fine, and luckily I got a radio show to distract me."

As tough as it is to leave, by the time the end comes, many are ready for it. After the long journey, so many contestants are exhausted, drained of the will to fight on, and just wanting to go home, to see their families and sleep in their own beds. Matt Giraud remembers his number finally coming up in much rosier terms: "It was actually really exciting to go out after and meet everyone. See the people who supported you and meet the fans and do press. It was all fun. It was a little bit lonely because you're separated from your people who you've been with for so long. And you're sitting in your New York hotel room by yourself just thinking about what just happened to your life. But I liked it. I was ready to go home. I couldn't wait to get home, I really couldn't. I'm best friends with the mayor, so they had a big welcoming party for me. I told them I didn't really want all that. I was kind of nervous about it. There were news cameras and kids waiting for pictures. It was insane, it was an emotional moment. It was almost like you get a hero's welcome. They make it seem like you saved a hundred people from dying or something. I kind of take it a little more lightly. I was on a reality show. But they love you for that. They love you for putting Kalamazoo on the map. They took me home in a limo, and my room was decorated all crazy. It said, 'Welcome home, Matt,' and there were balloons. It was really cool. And your friends were so proud to have you home. It's just a cool moment. Everyone just looks at you differently. They look at you like a star now."

Chapter 16

TWILIGHT OF THE VALKYRIES

When twenty-one-year-old Kyle Ensley, a junior at Oklahoma State University, auditioned in white oxford, red tie, and thick glasses—presenting himself as the image of a hard-working computer nerd running for student council—few could have imagined that his candidacy for *American Idol* would tear the show apart. Yet it's on such stones that empires stumble.

It was the year after Sanjaya, and the ponyhawk's shadow loomed over *Idol*'s annual postmortems. The team agreed that the year before had become cluttered with sideshows and distractions. So, as each season reacts to the excesses of the previous, *Idol* execs agreed to retrench. Lythgoe recalls, "I said, 'Let's not do any gimmicks this year. Let's just go for talent. We can bring gimmicks back later on. This year, just talent.' So we all agreed to *not* have a Sanjaya again."

Then in walked Kyle. He didn't have a terrible voice. He had just enough of one to make it through the auditions, through Hollywood Week, and to the green mile, where, at last, a decision had to be made. Lythgoe recalls that he was "one of those where you could see people voting for him and other people going, 'How can this person be on *American Idol?*' I said, 'Look, please, don't take this guy.' Randy and Paula didn't want him. Nor did Cecile or Ken. But when it came to Cowell, he wanted him. I said, 'You're outvoted.' He said, 'I don't care. I want a character on the show. I want someone I can pick on.'"

Lythgoe remembers the encounter as extremely unpleasant. "'I can't let you have him,' I said to Cowell. 'Everyone has voted against it.' He said, 'I want him.' This must've gone on for three hours, and they're all waiting there, and he's just dug his heels in. I said, 'Well, sort yourself out. I'm saying no.'"

Lythgoe's voice grows softer, becomes uncharacteristically wistful as he continues. "This was the final year that I did it. We had really good talent and he wanted the geeky guy. I said, 'No geeks this year.' If the other two had said yes then I'd have been outvoted. I stood my ground, though, and it was just like that was the straw between us. I respect him tremendously and as a producer I respect him. I dug my heels in there, and if you like, I won, but it was a hollow victory. You're not winning anything. You're just standing your ground and if anything, you're losing because everyone hangs their heads, like, 'Oh, he's not happy.' So that was frustrating."

The anger over this particular issue did not die down easily. When Kyle took his seat on the green mile, he was paired with another contestant. The duo was told that only one of them would make it through. In announcing the decision, Cowell issued a rare public protest, fuming with rage out of all proportion on whether or not the bespectacled nerd, clearly not destined to be the next American Idol, was allowed to go forward. He said, "Kyle, I want you to know, from me, wholeheartedly I disagree with this decision. I think you had done enough because you were different and unique to have made it through to the next round, and I completely and utterly disagree with this decision. I think you should have been given a chance based on the impact you made in Hollywood to be competing further in this competition. I don't think you're the best singer, but I think you have something that people will enjoy. And I'm really disappointed. Really disappointed."

Looking back on the dispute, Cowell has a dramatically different re-collection of the argument. He agrees that it was one of the major fights, perhaps *the* major fight between him and Nigel. "That was probably the most serious one. . . . You can see it on camera. I was furious. I was abso-lutely furious. The argument went on for a long, long time before. And I couldn't shake it off when we were filming."

However, he strongly disputes the notion that he backed Kyle just to have a whipping boy. "I felt really passionate about this boy, because he was so popular with the fellow contestants. I'd seen that in the Holly-wood round, and I felt that . . . he'd be a popular contestant on the show. He'd be controversial. He was feisty himself. And it was like casting a show. I felt it was a different type of contestant and therefore interesting. And all of the people being offered in his place, therefore, to me were boring."

That he wanted to keep Kyle just to beat up on him, he says, "is absolutely not true. And I resent that. I'd given him a hard time, but if I don't think they can take it, we don't put them in. He was more than capable of looking after himself. And that was a very weak argument to say that I wanted to beat up on a kid. The irony was, I was the only one standing up for him. There are definitions of beating up on a kid. My definition was by not giving him a chance, he was beating up on a kid."

As for whether the fight was the last straw between them, Cowell recalls, "It left a sour taste, to be honest. I guess it was principle more than anything else. I felt we as judges had a right to put who we wanted in. Nigel obviously felt differently. And at that point you kind of think, this is going to happen again and again and again. They don't need the aggravation. I don't need the aggravation. And yeah . . . that was a turning point."

The crack was, in retrospect, inevitable. A split had almost come during the lawsuit, but the settlement had allowed them all to take a step back from the brink. But the personalities had grown along with the show, and the underlying issue—one kingdom and too many kings—had not been resolved.

SEASON 7 MARKED another turning point in *Idol* history: the end of domination by female pop singers. There had been male winners, of course—Studdard and Hicks, to be precise—but with the possible exception of season 2, the show had been ruled by its female stars. It wasn't just that the women's ranks had supplied the show's two supernova-sized breakouts of Kelly Clarkson and Carrie Underwood, it was that even when the women didn't win, they were always in the upper ranks.

That all changed in season 7, which ushered in the gritty new era of the boys. For the next three years, a bare handful of female performers would struggle to compete at the highest ranks. The women, who in previous years had benefited from the music choices—heavy on the oldies, the Bacharach, the R&B numbers, the big-note pop songs—now tumbled like cannon fodder before the boys. And not just any boys. It appeared this new era would become a time for "cute" boys. The men of the first epoch who triumphed were markedly not the stuff of teen idols; Ruben Studdard and Taylor Hicks appealed to many, but no one could call them tween bait. That was about to change.

While the singers of the first years were, in essence, inventing *Idol* around them, those who tried out now knew exactly what they were getting into. In fact, many of them were reared on *Idol* from their earliest days. They prepared for it and, in some cases, spent years auditioning for it.

The first sign of a new era came in with a roar. In the bowels of You-Tube there exists a video of a young David Archuleta, aged about nine, meeting the cast of *Idol*'s first season in an airport. To their amazement, the youngster broke out in a powerful voice to sing for them. The moment of Kelly Clarkson hugging young David prefigures a torch of destiny being passed to the young boy who would someday rule the *Idol* stage.

Archuleta's pre-interview reveals an almost unbelievably sweet, pathologically shy personality punctuated with nervous giggles that stand in contrast to a flawlessly strong singing voice capable of enormous runs and heartbreaking high notes. He was the perfect *Idol* candidate, and almost instantly the season was dominated by the legions of tween fans whose screeches punctured the air whenever he stepped onstage.

In private, his sweetness and shyness never ceased; the world has yet to produce a single story of diva behavior on the part of David Archuleta. However, that shyness also revealed the hothouse flower nature of his youth. Raised singing since he could walk, David was like an Olympic athlete whose entire development had been funneled into his performance. Talking with him offstage, you rarely found him totally relaxed or unguarded. But when a strand of music would float through the air from a neighboring room or down a hallway, he would latch on to it like a lifeline, reciting the lyrics quietly to himself, moving his head with the rhythm.

In an interview at the end of the season, when asked for the millionth time when he might get a girlfriend, and when he explained for the millionth time that he was focusing on his singing, I pressed him, saying, "You know, this is not how teenagers typically think about life." He became quiet and thoughtful before whispering, "I've just always loved to do this." When I pressed him further about what music had meant to him, he explained that growing up, like so many awkward young people, he had never felt comfortable expressing himself in words, had never felt he could say what he meant, but in music he could let people know what he was feeling, what was going on inside him. "And you don't even have to get the words right. If you sing, they can connect with you," he said.

The girls had had their mini-heartthrobs before: Anthony Fedarov, Kevin "Chicken Little" Covais, and of course, Sanjaya. But none had matched that call with such powerful vocal skills. That visceral connection to the girls of America would awaken a sleeping giant.

And standing in its way were the women of season 7.

IDOL HAD BEEN hit with cries of "ringer" before, but those revelations usually came after the season ended, when, inevitably, word of an earlier recording career and stint in Hollywood tumbled out. It was a tradition that dated back to Kelly Clarkson, but despite its recurrence throughout the years, the mythology of *Idol* was so strong that anything that threatened to shake it, as one singer was to find, would be met with fury.

At age fifteen, young Carly Hennessy had moved with her father from her native Ireland to pursue a singing career in Los Angeles. The angelic-voiced, raven-haired teen had been singing onstage since she was all of four, and had toured as a youth with a production of *Les Miserables*. Before she could even get her driver's license, Carly hit the jackpot, getting signed to MCA records. She was prepped for stardom by legendary music mogul Miles Copeland III, founder of the iconic I.R.S. Records. However, in between the recording of her album and its release, disaster struck and the label went belly-up. It was the beginning of the decade-long implosion that would sweep the music industry, and the album was dumped on the market with no promotion and no support, all but unloaded for scrap. Worse was still to come, however. A *Wall Street Journal* article on MCA's meltdown would credit practically the entire overhead of the company in those final months, two million dollars, to promoting Carly's album—even though no promotion outside of the offices had occurred. Not yet eighteen, Carly had become the poster girl for the reckless ways of the recording industry.

She spent her early twenties carving out a living on the margins of entertainment. Her early jobs included recording a demo of a Diane Warren song for presentation to Carrie Underwood. In 2005, running out of options and open doors, she traveled to Las Vegas to audition for *Idol*'s season 5 and won a ticket to Hollywood Week. At the close of that year's auditions, Simon Cowell had told the *New York Post* about a season that included Chris Daughtry and Katharine McPhee: "The only person I can genuinely remember from the auditions that I've done for this season is an Irish girl that we saw in Las Vegas who now lives in America. I think she sang a Chaka Khan song and afterward I said, 'I think we may have found someone as good as [*Idol* winner] Kelly Clarkson.'"

Unfortunately, the winds of fortune were still not blowing for Carly, and she learned before Hollywood Week that her visa status would not allow her to appear on the show. Forced to withdraw, she left Hollywood and moved with her recently wedded husband, a tattoo artist named Todd Smithson, first to Atlanta and then to San Diego, where she kept the barest embers of her dream alive by singing in a pub where she waited tables.

Until season 7. That year, *Idol* auditions came to San Diego and Carly stood in the same line with David Archuleta to give her dream one more try. Yet again, *Idol* was stepping into the gap that the imploding music industry was leaving behind. That, however, was not the fairy tale held dear by *Idol* viewers, and, more to the point, not the story that legions of *Idol* haters and amateur sleuths felt *Idol* was obliged to live up to. Whereas at *Idol*'s dawn, it had taken traditional muckrakers months to dig up the dirt, now whatever people had buried in their past—naked pictures, an arrest, or a recording contract— was up on the Internet within hours of a singer's first appearance. "Smithson's Secret Past," touted Yahoo!'s music blog. "Pick the Plant," Vote for the Worst challenged readers. Everywhere, the old *Wall Street Journal* misinterpretation was dredged up as fact.

Lythgoe leaped to Carly's defense, pointing out that David Archuleta had appeared on the *Star Search* revival—and won—when he was eleven. "Nobody said this is an amateur competition. This is something that people are making up for themselves. It doesn't matter if you've had a professional contract. Kelly Clarkson had a professional contract. Bo Bice had a deal. Taylor Hicks has got records that are out there. This is nothing new."

Once again, *Idol* was faced with viewers who were more Catholic than the pope, wanting the show to enforce rules that didn't actually exist. The immediate furor blew over, but it would remain in the background for Carly during her entire *Idol* run.

THERE WAS ANOTHER change introduced to the rules in season 7 that, of all the tweaks, would perhaps turn out to be the most important. In season 7, the show first allowed singers to use instruments. It was an example of the fellowship between the different *Idol* incarnations around the world, each of which had grown along their own lines. Instruments had first been introduced on *Australian Idol* and had been adopted on *Norwegian Idol* and *Canadian Idol*, the latter of which was much more strongly rock oriented than its American counterpart.

The change had an immediate effect, opening the door to a more diverse pool of musicians than had previously been seen. Bar rockers, jazz pianists, and contemporary singer/songwriters would all be represented in the coming years. Perhaps the greatest beneficiary of the inclusion of instruments was the man who would become *Idol*'s first rocker champion, David Cook. A bar rocker from St. Louis by way of Tulsa, Cook finished the revolution started by Chris Daughtry, each week brazenly reframing his song choices, whatever the genre, in a gritty rock key that ground down the melodies and slowed the tempo to an angry crawl. Little did it matter that some of his reinventions were borrowed from other bands, such as Chris Cornell's version of Michael Jackson's "Billie Jean." Cook's sultry renditions so electrified the set that each week the thrill of wondering what trick Cook would pull off became the season's growing storyline, even competing with Archuleta's.

Chris Daughtry, of course, managed to dominate the stage without the benefit of instruments, as would Adam Lambert in season 8. But it would be no coincidence that the next three champions of *American Idol* would all be guitar players, cute white male guitar players, to be specific. The edge that playing an instrument gave in performance would prove unbeatable in the years ahead.

In season 7, four of the top five were musicians who leaned heavily on their instruments. They would include, in addition to bar rocker Cook, pianist prodigy David Archuleta in the Josh Groban vein, Jason

Mraz–inspired, guitar-and-ukelele-playing hippie crooner Jason Castro, and Brooke White, a Carole King–inspired singer-songwriter. It was a range of styles entirely new to the *Idol* stage, but these more esoteric traditions would come to dominate the show in the years ahead.

There was another singer-songwriter who made a splash with his story in the early days of the season. Nineteen-year-old Josiah Leming's story was heavily featured in the auditions and during Hollywood Week. A native of a severely impoverished family in East Tennessee, Josiah told of coming to Nashville and living in his car while he tried to make a singing career. The tears flowed in rivers down the intense young singer's face as he told his story. Offscreen, however, the other contestants who dealt with him remember a highly erratic mischief-maker who could turn the waterworks on at will and who, after his on-camera interview, bragged to his fellow contestants that he had "told them I live in my car," leaving the others to wonder, "Well, how are we supposed to top that?"

The end of auditions also brought the annual parade of skeletons tumbling out of the closet. This time it was Arizonan David Hernandez who was revealed, thanks to a research assist by Vote for the Worst, to have worked as a stripper in a gay nightclub. The previous year had seen the revelation of nude or scantily clad photos of semifinalist Antonella Barba. When *Idol* had ruled the photos were not disqualifying, that ruling had sparked a mini-flood of outrage as some commentators, including Rosie O'Donnell, wondered why Frenchie Davis had been ousted four years earlier but Barba was allowed to stay, speculating that Barba was the beneficiary of a racist double standard. The Hernandez accusations, however, barely even prompted a debate, the show declaring almost immediately that they would leave the judgment to the voters. As it turned out, the voters were, in the short term, okay with it, voting Hernandez through from the semifinals to the top twelve. He was, however, the first to be eliminated on the big stage.

ONCE THE CONTESTANTS arrived on the big stage, the Archuleta frenzy put the female contestants behind the eight ball. Their awkwardness was increased by the addition to the set of twin mosh pits in front of the stage, which, filled with gushing recruits from local high school water polo teams and the like, became hives of gale-force shrieking for Archuleta and the contingent of his sultry young companions, David

Cook, Jason Castro, and Michael Johns. Syesha Mercado remembers trying to perform before the eyes of the mosh pit. "I tried to be as comfortable as possible with the audience, because it's those people who I'm really performing for, and sometimes it was a little hard because those little girls would be staring at me like, 'Where's David Archuleta at!'"

There was also, they would soon find, the letter gap. "My fan mail was, like, three letters," recalled Ramiele Malubay. "At the most I got, like, six letters. That's at the most, six letters a week," says Mercado, who climbed to the pinnacle of third place. The boys would get hundreds.

Their struggle against the prevailing tween winds was made no easier by the judges, who seemed poisoned against the women from the start. Ramiele Malubay and Kristy Lee Cook never received a second glance from the panel after their initial dismissals. Brooke White found herself ricocheting back and forth between being the judges' darling and their target, and fought to control herself from talking back. After embracing Carly, Cowell turned against her with a particular venom. Some speculated that after marking her as a favorite early on, Cowell was knocking her down in order to dramatically bring her back up later on. Others thought he was incensed that she had failed to live up to his early hopes for her. Whatever the case, it was not pretty. On the second of the two Beatles weeks, he trashed her choice of "Blackbird," saying she had squandered her opportunity by singing a song "about a bird," a choice he called "self-indulgent." Two weeks later, when David Cook sang "Little Sparrow" on Dolly Parton week, he said to Carly as he went onstage, "Here I go, about to sing a song about a bird." In this case, Cowell loved it.

Cowell himself denies ever self-consciously tilting the contest for dramatic effect. He says, "Let me tell you, this audience in America, they're not mugs. They make their own decisions. Everyone says that I can influence the audience at home. I genuinely don't believe that. As was proved with Taylor Hicks. I couldn't have been more negative and he won the show. That wasn't planned so he could win the show. I just called it like I called it. If someone's got it, the audience is going to back you. They might listen a little bit, but I can't change their minds."

The audience will support his narrative, he says, "only if I'm right. I like the times when Vote for the Worst suddenly became popular, and it shows the audience that they're in control. The idea that I can manipulate them is crazy. But you have to have a strong opinion one way or another. I've never been just ambivalent about anybody. If I like them I like them. If I hate them I hate them. But it's all done with a sense of humor as well."

That same night, after struggling to overcome the judges' mixed feelings, Carly finally turned in a performance that seemed to set her back in the upper echelon of the race. Simon responded with a curt, "It was good but not great. And I think you've got to have a word with whoever's dressing you." A gasp went out in the room.

Three long weeks later, Cowell finally seemed ready to make the dramatic turn. On the top six week devoted to the music of Andrew Lloyd Webber, he finally conceded a measure of praise, ready to declare her back in the race. But it was too late: In the shadow of the screaming girls, the time for a breakthrough had passed for Carly, and she found herself the victim of another shocking *Idol* elimination the following night.

THE ARCHULETA FRENZY continued as he turned in flawless performances and won over ever more fans with his sweet and humble demeanor. But he was falling victim to the old *Idol* front-runner disease: too much praise too soon. Flawless began to be taken for granted. Meanwhile, the low-key Cook, who had been no one's prediction to win, kept surging.

On Mariah Carey week, David Cook broke through completely. Lurking in the background of the private young man's story was the fact that, all the while he had been on the show, his brother in Missouri had been extremely ill with cancer that ultimately would prove terminal. That night, his brother visited the set and watched from the audience, his condition grave. Cook's heartfelt, melancholy take on "Always Be My Baby" became one of the great star-making moments of *Idol* history, and as he waded into the crowd after to embrace his brother, the crowd went wild with enthusiasm.

For the women, however, Mariah Carey night was an ordeal of another sort. As they had on Dolly Parton night, the women confronted the question of how to perform a song by one of America's greatest female singers and not just have your version compared to hers. "It was not like we could just slow it down," Smithson said. "Then they would just say you sounded like Mariah Carey but slow and not as good." In the end, the judges gave them few points for effort. "I don't think you had much choice other than to do what you did," Cowell said to Brooke White of her stripped-down version of "Hero" sung at the piano. "Having said that, it was a bit like ordering a hamburger and only getting the bun. The vital ingredient, the bit in the middle, was missing because I don't think your voice was strong enough to carry that song." Later in the evening he referred to the renditions as "karaoke hell."

AND OF COURSE, season 7 saw the inevitable Paula moments. Before the season began, Paula had made herself the centerpiece of her own reality show, *Hey Paula*. The VH1 production had been intended to dispel the rumors about her wacky personal life and depict her as a hardworking, serious businesswoman. But the series, rife with meltdowns and near hysteria, only fanned the flames. The *What's Up with Paula* question was not to be vanquished.

Still, season 7 was refreshingly free of Paula mishaps. Until, that is, the top five week, mentored by Neil Diamond. The episode caused a particular production challenge, with each of the five contestants performing two songs squeezed into a mere hour of airtime. The crew struggled to make everything fit, but the night's format ended in a confused jumble. To keep the show on schedule, the initial plan had been for the judges to wait until after each singer had performed their second song, and then to review both numbers. However, in the seconds before airtime, Mike Darnell had the notion that after the first round of performances ended, the judges should review all the contestants at once, in one massed group. As the studio lights darkened and Ryan Seacrest began his introduction, Executive Producer Lythgoe raced to the judges' table to explain the new plan.

Abdul, never one to roll with the punches, was flustered by this arrangement. When the time came for her comments, she confused the notes she had taken from the dress rehearsal with her live show notes and offered dreadlocked crooner Jason Castro a critique of a song he had not yet performed. As Castro smiled uncomfortably, Randy Jackson jumped in and ever so gently cut Abdul off, causing another historically awkward moment to go down in TV history with Tom Brokaw and Tim Russert's half minute of confused silence on election night 2000.

The next day, the press and the Internet were on fire, mocking the greatest example to date of Abdul's loopiness, some wondering if she had hallucinated. For others, it was proof of *Idol*'s persistent conspiracy bugaboo—that the competition was "fixed." Had Abdul nakedly revealed herself to be reading notes given her by the producers, ordering her to trash Castro? To this day, legions of Castro partisans believe the incident was the smoking gun that the fix was in to knock Jason off the show.

For once, *Idol* didn't try to make a joke out of the incident. Sensing no doubt their judge was near her limit, Seacrest opened the following night's show with a heartfelt statement of support, denying Internet rumors that she would be replaced, saying, "She is part of our family and we love her."

THE SEASON 7 finale delivered the first surprise verdict in *Idol* history. While David Cook's popularity had surged, the country remained convinced that David Archuleta was the season's unstoppable phenomenon. Impressive though it had been that a low-key, scruffy rocker like Cook could make it all the way to the finale, in the end, this was a show about pop stars. The crown would not be wrested from the head of the chosen one, David Archuleta. On this the pundits were nearly unanimous.

Cook's surge, visitors in the *Idol* dome noticed, seemed to be taking a bite out of Archuleta's core demographic. In the final weeks of the season, the shrieks for Cook grew almost as loud as the mosh pit screams for Archuleta, with a segment of the junior high set looking for something a bit scruffier in their icons. And there was another new demographic unit that was about to enter the *Idol* fray: cougars. For whatever reason, Cook's appeal to women in the 35- to 55-year-old demographic was unmistakable. When that summer's Idols Live tour came to Cook's former home of Tulsa, I decided to visit the bar where he once played. I found the small honky-tonk room packed beyond capacity with women in their forties and fifties, camera phones extended, recording for the historical record every cranny of the room where Cook once sang.

In the finale show, the night seemed to belong entirely to Archuleta. His voice effortlessly filling the vast six thousand-seat Nike theater, he seemed to dominate every round. "What we have witnessed is a knockout," Cowell declared.

The next day, however, Cowell sheepishly retracted his ruling, saying that watching it back on TV, the effect of Cook's performances had been completely different from what he had seen in person. "I was almost horrified when I went back home and watched. It was literally like watching and listening to a whole new show. What you thought was good wasn't very good and what you thought was bad actually was a lot better." The admission was part of Cowell's enduring appeal, his ability not to take his opinions too seriously, to admit mistakes, which projected the unfailing sense that this is one man who tells the truth, no matter what.

He was right about being wrong. David Cook, to the screams of horror from a million little girls across the nation, became the seventh American Idol, beginning a new dynasty of rocker guy champions that would stretch on for years.

BUT ANOTHER THING would have to change. With the break on the set now between Lythgoe and Cowell, the tension was again becoming difficult. And what was worse, for two seasons in a row, the ratings had sagged. Not horrifically—they were still the sorts of numbers any show would kill for—but in a world where every ratings point meant tens of millions of dollars, any bump in the road was like a bomb blast. It seemed that after seven years, *Idol* was showing the first signs of age. In the postmortems that began before the season even ended, there was a sense that things needed to be shaken up, the format tinkered with, and big attention-getting changes needed to happen to keep the audience interested. And the man who stood in the way of big changes was one Nigel Lythgoe.

Since the dawn of *Idol,* one item had dominated Lythgoe's agenda, that at all costs it must always be about the talent. He had fought many a battle, sometimes winning, sometimes losing, against any element that would take attention away from the central narrative of watching, considering, judging, and ultimately rewarding the talent. From the early *Real World* elements to funny twists in the rules, holding at bay nonessential funny business had been the battle.

But with the ratings beginning to sag and with discontent on the set, that fight was becoming harder. With the thought of tweaks and changes it was clear the one thing everyone was feeling must not change, could not change, was the man who after seven years remained the subject of endless fascination, the still unshakable center of *Idol*, Simon Cowell.

After season 7, two years remained on Cowell's contract. But with the star looking increasingly bored and restless on the set, at odds with Lythgoe and once again making noises about "everything comes to an end" and "time to move on," two years felt dangerously close. It was time to start thinking about making Cowell happy, really happy.

A month after David Cook won the *Idol* crown, the announcement was made that Nigel Lythgoe, the man who had guided the production since its birth in the United Kingdom, who had invented the mean judge character, and who had served as its flamboyant ringmaster, would be moving on.

The changes were just beginning.

Chapter 17

THE PASTOR

We're all just going where the Lord sends us. Some are sent on missions around the world. Somehow I was sent to *American Idol.*" Leesa Bellesi, an engaging blonde in her early fifties who resembles a young Florence Henderson, sits back at her kitchen table and begins her story. Her home, located in a hilly, semirural section of south Orange County, seems another world from the *American Idol* bubble. But at this table, a long line of mothers and fathers of *Idol* contestants have prayed for their children, watched them perform, and mourned when their *Idol* journeys ended.

The unofficial host to dozens of *Idol* families, Leesa Bellesi has in her time penetrated the protected space of the most high-profile show in the world. She has roamed backstage, attended *Idol* dinners, and sat in the audience beside *Idol* families.

And it all began "the day a clown fell on my head," Leesa told me with a laugh.

Actually, just before the clown, there had been a warning.

"It just goes back to the book of Job being put inside *our* book," Leesa said. Several years before the *Idol* ministry, before she had even watched the show, Leesa was sent a cryptic warning that her path was about to take a dramatic turn. At the time, her husband, Denny, was serving as a pastor at one of the congregations in Orange County, California, a church that was in the orbit of Rick Warren's famed Saddleback, nexus of the sunny, upbeat, and outgoing brand of Fundamentalist Christianity that has reshaped evangelical America in recent years.

As a side project, Leesa and Denny founded the Kingdom Assignment ministry, a traveling event wherein they would appear before a church, pass out one-hundred-dollar bills with the challenge to the recipients to *pay it forward*—that is, take the money and see how much good they could do with it, how many ripples they could start across the pond. In the years they had been doing it, the program had spawned scores of miracle-working stories and a pair of Kingdom Assignment books put out by a leading Christian publisher, and eventually the holy of holies, an appearance on *Oprah* to talk about the mission.

So it came, or it should have come, as a warning when in the midst of Kingdom Assignment's success, they were approached by a woman bearing a copy of their latest publication asking why her Kingdom Assignment book had the book of Job in it. Looking inside, they found that the biblical book detailing the suffering and trial of the Lord's most ardent servant had indeed been misprinted inside the woman's book.

If you were still looking for harbingers after that, a few weeks later, the clown dropped.

Leesa and Denny were sitting at a local performance by Cirque du Soleil. Denny had given Leesa the tickets for her birthday and had upgraded to front row seats. Just before intermission, the couple noticed "this 250-pound Darth Vader–ish guy with propane tanks on his back, fire was shooting out of his arms. And he started stumbling around the stage. I lost track of him, and all of a sudden his back was to me and I thought he was going to fly or something and he just fell right on top of me. And immediately I had pain at the top of my head and it was from my neck snapping and getting a bulging disc in my neck."

Leesa was in constant pain for three years; only after extensive physical therapy could she begin to get out of bed and move around. To make matters worse, the injury led to an acrimonious lawsuit against Cirque du Soleil, in which the troupe had photographers trail Leesa, snapping photos to try and prove she was not, in fact, disabled.

In her forties, largely bedridden, in pain, often delirious from medication and financially near ruin thanks to the medical costs, Leesa found herself for the first time in her life questioning her faith, wondering where all this lay in God's plan for her.

It was at this moment, lying in bed, that Leesa happened upon the audition episodes for a little show called *American Idol*, which was just starting its fifth season. Somewhere deep inside, something told her that she was supposed to be watching this. She recalls having no idea what this notion was about or why, wracked in pain, God was steering her toward a TV talent competition, but she prayed: "Here I am, Lord. Send me where you need me." The words *backstage at American Idol* popped into her head.

Having been handed that instruction, Leesa had no clue what she was supposed to do with it. Certainly it was one of the odder pieces of direction she had received. But as the new season unfolded, she kept watch, trusting that somehow the path to *backstage at American Idol* would be made clear. Soon she stumbled upon the audition of a then twenty-one-year-old singer named Katharine McPhee singing "God Bless the Child." "I started praying for her in my living room in Orange County. And I Googled her. What's going on with this girl? I just had a real propensity toward her. I just felt like she was an amazing singer but I loved her. I thought she was just a precious girl."

The messages she received—backstage at *American Idol*, Katharine, "God Bless the Child"—hung in the air as Leesa continued her physical therapy. But within weeks, the path would become material in the first of a series of coincidences that would take Leesa not just backstage, but deeper inside the *Idol* beast than any viewer, any reporter, could ever dream of.

Two weeks after watching McPhee's audition, Leesa accompanied Denny for his Sunday services to the church in Pasadena where he was doing a stint as guest pastor. As the services ended, a couple approached the pastor and his wife. The worshipers explained that they were looking for a church to join and had been touched by Denny's sermon. The young woman told them that she was about to start on a TV show, that she'd be living with the show in a bubble cut off from the world, and as she was newly discovering the spiritual path, would Leesa and Denny pray for her during her trials to come?

Standing before her was Katharine McPhee.

Leesa recited to Katharine her favorite biblical passage, the one she had turned to to sustain herself through the past years of physical pain. From the book of Jeremiah (29:11) it went: " 'For I know the plans I have for you,' declares the Lord, 'plans to prosper you and not to harm you, plans to give you hope and a future.' " They exchanged numbers and as

Katharine entered the *Idol* bubble, Leesa frequently texted her the citation, reminding her that she was on God's path.

A couple of weeks later, Katharine still in her mind, Leesa received a gift from a friend—a white rubber bracelet, similar to the once-ubiquitous Lance Armstrong bracelets, bearing the Jeremiah citation.

"I woke up one morning," she recalls of the bracelet, "and I just really heard the Lord say, 'That's not yours. It's Katharine's.' I was like, I have no idea how I'm going to get it to her. Maybe I was going to see Nick [Katharine's boyfriend] at church, maybe I could give it to him. But He said, 'No, you need to give it to her today.'"

It was a Wednesday, the day of the results show on the first week of the season 5 finals. The night before, Stevie Wonder had served as the guest mentor and he was scheduled to perform that night.

Visitors in the *Idol* audience often wait years to get tickets to the show. With Wonder scheduled to perform, you'd have an easier time getting a private meeting with the pope. Even Nick couldn't get an extra ticket, Leesa, heeding her marching orders and working the phone, soon learned. "My niece works for Fox, I called her. No. I have a producer friend. No. Nobody can get tickets, Leesa. Nobody can get tickets for *American Idol*. And I'm, like, 'Right, right, nobody can get tickets.'

"I went home and I remember I was lying on the floor exercising and all of a sudden I flipped back over to Fox and it said, 'Okay, the eleventh caller will be receiving two tickets for *American Idol* tonight.' . . . And so I grab the phone. I'm writing down the number. I'm dialing the number. All I know is I never heard it ring and all of a sudden I heard, 'Hi, you're the eleventh caller.'"

Hours later, Leesa and Denny were backstage passing along a bracelet to Katharine and to Katharine's roommate Kellie Pickler, who it turned out, had her Bible bookmarked to her favorite passage, Jeremiah 29:11. Throughout the rest of the season, Leesa continued to visit the set and check in with Katharine. The message got through and out to the world. On an elimination night toward the end of the season, Ryan asked Katharine if she was nervous, and she replied with a cryptic, "Oh, I know God has a plan for me."

The season ended with Taylor Hicks's narrow victory over Katharine and the bracelet-adorned Idols dispersed. The following year, Denny presided over Katharine's wedding ceremony, but it seemed to Leesa that her *Idol* journey had come to an end. She had, as requested, found her way backstage, she had delivered the message, and the message and the bracelet had made it through Katharine on the air to tens of millions of people. Was that, she wondered, mission accomplished?

Until one day at an Emmys' gifting suite . . .

A nephew of Leesa's was in the event business in Hollywood, and each year put together a space at the Beverly Hilton Hotel, where stars would come to collect jewelry, handbags, and lotions that designers hoped they would wear or mention on the red carpet. Leesa had helped him staff the suite with young people involved with her various ministries. As Leesa supervised her charges, into the suite walked none other than Paula Abdul herself.

"She was going through the gifting lounge," Leesa recalls, "and I told her my story really quick. And she said, 'Will you pray for me?' And we did." Leesa and some of her wards formed an impromptu little prayer circle in the hallway, asking succor for Paula.

"And then she said, 'I want you at every show praying for me in the audience.'" And so, of course, she would be.

THUS THE MINISTRY returned to the *Idol* tent. On hand to visit with Paula, Leesa ended up as ordered, backstage. There she met that year's contestants, a flock that included a strong active Christian contingent, including Virginia church administrator Chris Sligh, naval officer Phil Stacey, and eventual champion Jordin Sparks, with whom Leesa talked of Katharine McPhee. "She said, 'Oh, I'm using Katharine's extensions' for her hair. And so we were talking about her a little bit. Later I wrote a letter connecting the dots of Jeremiah 29:11 and telling her that story and I put [one of the white Jeremiah bracelets] in a box. I gave it to a stagehand and they delivered it to her before the show. I'm sitting out in the audience wondering if she got it and she walks out onto the stage and she's got it on. We just connected."

Sparks would wear the bracelet right through to the season's finale.

Leesa also introduced herself to Sligh, who, with his mop top, roly-poly physique, and sardonic wit, had been a singular presence on the *Idol* stage that year. She chatted with him about a mutual acquaintance they shared, a youth pastor from Orange County. "And I said, 'You know what? How can I help you? What can I do for you?' And he said—and it was kind of one of those Prayer of Jabez moments of just asking somebody what can I do to help you—and he said just right away, 'I need a place for my wife to stay.' We had a house in Sherman Oaks that we were selling and we had two empty rooms and I said, 'You got it. What can I do?' Then a week later I picked her up at the airport with his cousin and brought her to the house and she stayed."

While the *Idol* production is generally an impregnable fortress, built to withstand season after season of ravenous fans, stalkers, paparazzi, and tabloid reporters who besiege the set, Leesa had stumbled upon the one chink in the security fence: the families.

Each year, when a dozen young singers enter into *Idol*'s protective custody, their loved ones find themselves left outside the fortress walls; not brought into the bubble, but they're not quite at liberty on the outside either.

In general, *Idol*'s guidance to the families is more or less: If you find your way to Los Angeles, we can give you four tickets. The families are left to contend with neighbors, hometown papers, TMZ reporters, and passersby who recognize them from a glimpse on the show. To make matters more confusing, while their son/daughter/husband/wife/boyfriend is going through all this, they are more or less incommunicado. With the punishing *Idol* schedules, free moments to phone home are rare, let alone Sunday brunches. Even worse for many families, dying to be a part of the excitement, to stand by their loved ones during these days of trial, the show provides no financial help to families to get to Hollywood. For many from *Idol*'s celebrated humble beginnings, the cost of a flight and hotel in Los Angeles is beyond their reach.

The intent is not as heartless as it seems. The kids have a show to put on and that requires a brutal schedule and every ounce of their concentration. Having dozens of relations hanging around the set, distracting them, tiring them out, causing them stress, putting ideas in their heads about whether they should sing more country or more R&B, doesn't do anyone any good.

But it leaves a lot of very confused people, looking for guidance. Into that void, for the families of the Christian faith, stepped Leesa.

FOR THE NEXT three years, Leesa and Denny's two homes (they also owned a beach house in nearby Huntington Beach) became way stations for *Idol* families. In season 6, the houses bustled with tension as the families of Jason Castro, Syesha Mercado, and Kristy Lee Cook all passed through. The house saw nights of tension as both Castro and Mercado competed for a diminishing number of slots at *Idol*'s highest ranks, their families huddled in opposite corners of the living room awaiting the news. (Syesha ultimately finished third, Castro fourth.)

The Bellesis' spiritual counseling skills were put to use, however, with the Mercado family. On air that season, Wanda and Oscar Mercado had referred to Oscar's struggle with drugs, but had not gone into the depths of their difficulties. Oscar had, in fact, spent the past years at the lowest rungs of the addicted, living on the streets, estranged from his family. Their reconciliation and its accompanying sobriety came just as Syseha entered the *Idol* competition. Under the Bellesi roof, the reunited couple fought demons harsher than Simon Cowell as they struggled to rebuild their marriage and Oscar wrestled with sobriety, while the eyes of the world were fixed on their daughter.

The Bellesis provided not only shelter, but plane tickets and general aid for *Idol* families at loose ends. Asking each as she met them simply, "What can I do for you?" she learned that many were unable to afford the flight to Los Angeles. For these, she turned to her Orange County community and was able to raise the money to fly more than a few families to be with their children during their *Idol* run.

Throughout these years, Leesa saw more of Idol's backstage life than any noncrew member ever has, certainly more than any reporter ever has. During this time, *Idol* producers quietly acknowledged *yes*, when asked if they were aware of her presence, but otherwise seemed not to want to touch her or the question with a five-thousand-foot pole. Some members of the production would acknowledge they were aware of her work, roll their eyes, and change the subject. While the show did nothing to actively encourage her, on some level there was knowledge of the hornet's nest she represented: *Idol*'s most loyal audience long kept at arm's length. If they were to give her any trouble, the show might well be looking at the nightmare of this woman, connected with some of the largest congregations in the nation, going public to say *American Idol* wants to ban Jesus Christ Himself from its set.

The crew's relations with Leesa in many ways paralleled the show's with its Christian viewership. While the Fundamentalist audience may well be *Idol*'s largest demographic—drawn by its family friendly appeal and the frequent prominence of singers who learned their craft on the stages of America's megachurches—the show goes to great pains to wink to this following without explicitly acknowledging it. Singers will vaguely reference their ecclesiastical backgrounds, but they won't elaborate at any length. Despite the fact that so many contestants hail from deeply religious backgrounds, explicitly Christian music is practically never heard on the show, the exceptions being the group performance of "Shout to the Lord" performed during season 7's inspirational week, and sporadic covers of the Carrie Underwood hit "Jesus, Take the Wheel." Whatever their audience may be, however, *American Idol* plays by the rules of Hollywood, wherein explicitly acknowledging religion, particularly of the Fundamentalist Christian variety, is the industry's greatest taboo.

Over the years, one can find more positive portrayals of Communist dictators, drug dealers, serial rapists, and child abusers than conservative Christians (the sleeper hit film *The Blind Side* was such a rare exception that it actually startled many audiences and critics). The overseers of *American Idol* are not immune to these prejudices and thus, throughout most of its history, Christianity has remained the crazy aunt in the attic on the *Idol* set: tended to, cared for, but rarely allowed to show her face at the dinner party, even if she's the one holding the title on the family estate.

LEESA CONTINUED TO find her way to the innermost sanctums of the world's biggest television show year after year as the producers turned a blind eye.

It was only in season 8, however, that the ministry reached its apex, as for the first time, Christianity edged out onto the stage in a very public way. That year's group saw no less than five Fundamentalist worship leaders make it to the top twelve, as well as the rise of a contestant whose story was interwoven with his religious background and became central to his appeal.

Many *Idol* contestants had hailed from church-singing backgrounds before, but none embodied that world as did season 8's smiling, barrel-chested, famously bespectacled Danny Gokey, for whom the religious message was at the core of not just his identity, but his rationale for appearing on the show.

Four weeks before season 8's auditions, when he was twenty-eight years old, Gokey's wife, Sophia, died during surgery for congenital heart disease. Gokey himself had not been raised in a particularly religious household but had become deeply committed to Christianity through the influence of Sophia, who brought Danny into Faith Builders, the Beloit, Wisconsin, megachurch to which she and her family belonged. Danny's involvement with the church grew as he became more active both as a worship leader and a participant in the church's musical program. The Faith Builders' musical style—upbeat rock with a country edge described by the church as "Contemporary Christian"—became Gokey's style, matching easily with his perennially cheery, ebullient nature.

It was to Faith Builders that Gokey turned after Sophia's passing, where in prayers and grief he decided that the greatest way to honor her life would be to go through with his plans to audition for Sophia's favorite show, to use his time on the show to carry a message that sadness and pain can be overcome with the help of faith.

Gokey lined up with the thousands in Kansas City, Missouri, and in short order, the grieving spouse found himself whisked away from the cocoon of church and family into the center of the *Idol* whirlwind, which was where Leesa found him. Shortly after watching Gokey's story in the audition episodes, Leesa reached out through the Christian network and got in touch with his pastor and then his family. She spoke on the phone to his mother, who asked for help getting Danny's friend and co-auditionee Jamar Rogers back home to Milwaukee after his *Idol* stint ended. Soon after, Leesa received a call from Gokey's sister-in-law, Demati, checking in. "We had a great time, a fellowship on the phone."

Before long, the extended Gokey family—brothers, sisters, in-laws, cousins—were trooping through the Bellesis' homestead. Feeling that there was something important going on in Danny's journey, the Bellesis donated some of the Kingdom Assignment ministry's money to flying out the many family members—"the season nearly bankrupted us"— while also acting as a conduit between the Gokeys and friends in the Christian community who wanted to support their cause. "A lot of people were very interested in their family and helping Danny. We got some donations and stuff. It was a woman who had lost her daughter. Friend of ours. And she donated for the family's flights."

Of Danny's struggle during this time, she says, "He really was going through a lot. It hadn't been that long since Sophia's death. None of them had a whole lot of time to grieve. So that was really hard."

The Christian themes continued to play a huge role in Gokey's on-screen journey, as he overtly framed his *Idol* stint in religious terms, making reference to his struggles and the ability to overcome, choosing songs heavy on the uplift. Offscreen, in the rare free time afforded *Idol* contestants, Gokey immersed himself further in spiritual work, sneaking away with his fellow top twelve worship leader Michael Sarver to visit and volunteer at L.A.'s Dream Center, a massive homeless shelter outside of downtown Los Angeles.

While Gokey's journey was perhaps the most public outing for Fundamentalist Christianity the show had seen, it was also the most public appearance of Leesa Bellesi and the *American Idol* ministry. On a trip to a taping with the Gokey family, Leesa found herself interviewed on the *Idol* spin-off show *American Idol Extra* and seated in the front row with his brother-in-law the night Danny was eliminated in third place. Audience shots labeled "Danny's Family" focused on Leesa in the foreground, and many assumed her to be his mother or close relative.

"I felt like it was the truest form of the ministry that year. Because there was such a huge need. Financially it was just breaking everybody's backs to be able to get out here. And it was such a big family. And Sophia was just a big part of this. And then you had Sophia's Heart foundation starting up. I just think it was kind of in its truest form, and in his heart for the Lord. Totally," Leesa says, referring to the music education charity Gokey started in his wife's memory immediately after leaving *Idol*.

In the aftermath of that year, the Bellesis, reeling from the experience and its costs, are scaling back, spending time with their newly born granddaughter. Pending God's call, Leesa mostly sat out season 9, and was planning to downsize the annual show put on by her Kingdom Assignment ministry, the Well Done Awards, which in the past had featured many from her *Idol* flock as guest performers.

"I think the ministry's needed," she says. "I really do. Something that's called *American Idol*. I mean, it's so interesting because Denny just did a message on the second commandment, 'There will be no other gods, no other idols before you.' The word *idol*—it's a word that displeases God. So it's very interesting that it's something like this—that God is using. And God's using it because it's giving a lot of these

Christian kids a platform to really tell their story and to live out their purpose. Their God-given purpose. It's been an idea that the Lord's allowed me to be a part of but I can't—I'd love to see it go on with other people. It will be interesting to see what happens this year and I don't know. And that's okay."

Chapter 18

TWEAK HOUSE

If Paula Abdul were listening for signs from the gods, the message sent at the opening of *American Idol*'s eighth season could not have been more ominous. It came in the form of a corpse. Of a former *Idol* hopeful. In Paula's driveway.

A woman who had stalked Abdul for years, and whose obsession had been depicted, even mocked, on the show, had made her final statement on the subject, taking her own life in her car directly in front of Abdul's home.

The fact that this happened just as Abdul was actively looking for signs about her *Idol* future would be enough to unhinge the steeliest of nerves. Paula did not have the steeliest of nerves.

As she showed up for the first days of shooting on season 8, Paula looked ahead to the crucial turning point of her career: the season when she would stand up for herself and demand decent treatment (and payment) from the show that had resuscitated her moribund pop career and put her back on the cultural map. So serious was she about demanding the respect she felt was her due that she told all around her she was prepared to do the unthinkable and walk away from *American Idol*.

And now this.

It was November 12, and as the *Idol* crew was filming Hollywood Week at the Kodak Theatre, word trickled in that something terrible had just happened at Paula's house. When the woman's identity became known, for Abdul, it was as though the sum of all her fears was playing out before her eyes.

For a few seasons now, many commentators had rebelled against the audition episodes. As high as their ratings were, the crew often acknowledged that this segment of the show represented *Idol*'s not-so-pleasant side—the open mocking, not just of the untalented, but of many who seem at least borderline emotionally disabled. In season 6, the outcry had grown a bit too loud, especially after it was revealed that one young man who had been a victim of Cowell's mockery was actually a former Special Olympics competitor. For their part, the Special Olympics said they were all for Cowell's assault, that it proved their ranks were capable of being treated like anyone else. Nonetheless, in season 7, the show had dialed back the meanness factor, the judges even seeming to soften their barbs.

Considering that *Idol* takes some of America's most unstable people, raises them up to believe that their deluded dreams are about to come true, and then smashes those dreams in the most brutal possible way before an audience of tens of millions, it was incredible that no explosion had ever occurred.

But even among this cast of the marginally stable, the woman who lay dead in front of Paula Abdul's house represented a whole other category.

Two years earlier, Paula Goodspeed had appeared in the Austin, Texas, audition episode. Her "quirk," as portrayed in her intro video package, was that she was obsessed with Paula Abdul—*extremely* obsessed. She had spent her childhood drawing pictures of the singer-turned-judge. She dressed like her, even changed her name to Paula. According to Abdul, she had been aware of Goodspeed before the auditions, aware enough to be alarmed by her fanatical devotion, and when she learned she was slated to appear before the judges, she claims, she begged the producers not to let her. (The producers would later dispute this account.)

In the aired segment, Goodspeed is shown displaying her gallery of Paula Abdul drawings, her obsession portrayed as a charming idiocy. In her audition, Goodspeed sang a predictably horrible version of "Proud Mary" before being shown the door, her dreams dismantled, following three "no" votes, including one from an uncharacteristically subdued Abdul.

And now, two years later, Paula Goodspeed lay dead at the foot of Paula's driveway.

The news disrupted the filming of Hollywood Week. As friends rushed to comfort a very freaked-out Abdul, the production went into its all-too-familiar crisis control posture. Statements of sympathy were issued to the press as well as blanket denials that the show could have in any way anticipated such tragic behavior on the part of an auditionee. All knew, however, that this was not some singer's bikini pics showing up on the Web; the media firestorm over this one was going to take more than a news cycle or two to blow itself out.

"Paula Abdul Fan Who Was Mocked in *American Idol* Audition Commits Suicide" ran the headline in the *Times* of London. "Did *American Idol* Play a Part in Former Contestant's Death?" was how it was played on no less than Fox News.

Executive Producer Ken Warwick, now solo at the show's helm, appeared before the press to assure the world that the show would never put a "dangerous person" in front of the judges, and that psychological examinations were conducted on all potentially problematic contestants.

After absorbing a few strong cycles of nightmarish publicity, the media storm was on the brink of blowing itself out when Paula Abdul herself finally spoke up.

After initially hunkering down and avoiding the press, Abdul emerged and made a lunge straight off the reservation. In an interview on *The View* she told her unedited side of the story—how she begged producers not to let Goodspeed on the show, how fearful she was and astounded that they would do that to her.

This was a PR disaster of the highest magnitude, eclipsing the Corey Clark flame-up and the Jason Castro mistake.

Within days, Abdul was reminded of how the show had stood by her through her many scandals, of how the show had supported her. She pulled herself together and fell into line. Appearing on the David Letterman show a few weeks later, when Letterman prodded Abdul to "sue these baboons"—that is, the producers who had exposed her to that threat of a stalker—a contrite Abdul became notably uncomfortable, stammering and refusing to take the bait, before finally saying only "You're going to get me in trouble" and "I'm lucky we were filming Hollywood Week when it happened."

Abdul's contract was up at the end of this season, and after stewing about it all summer long, she had decided, insane as the idea sounded, that unless things changed, she would walk away from *American Idol*.

FOR TOO LONG, Abdul had felt like *American Idol*'s poor step-cousin. Now, she determined, that had to change. When explaining her resolve to at last stand up for herself, Abdul would tell a hard-to-believe story of flying with the rest of the crew to an audition city. At the airport, when the group learned that there weren't enough first-class seats for the entire A-list, Simon, Randy, Ryan, and Nigel and Ken, the executive producers, were naturally placed up front, while Abdul was sent to the back of the plane, directly, as she told it, next to the bathrooms. With a mind given to obsessing over the little things and a mountainous insecurity complex that had remained intact all through a music career during which she had sold 54 million albums, Abdul clung to the memories of these petty insults, reliving them over and over in her mind until they became the meaning of her *Idol* existence.

Then there was the money, which in its way was really about respect. But the money questions are also very much about money. Eight seasons in on the entertainment Goliath, the paycheck of one of its *stars* remained a paltry $1.9 million a year. Not bad by any real-world standards, but by network TV scale, a pittance. It had been a hard enough figure to swallow, but when, the previous year, Nigel Lythgoe had let it slip that Simon Cowell earned $39 million, Paula reached her breaking point.

As if all this were not enough, she had an even bigger concern than whether she wanted to come back to *Idol*—did *Idol* want her to come back?

After the Castro incident, the producers were asking if Paula was more trouble than she was worth. And there was another element that shaded that question in a different light: Suddenly there were new faces at the table asking the question. In addition to Lythgoe's departure, there had been a change of the guard at Fox, with Peter Rice, the suave British head of the corporation's indie film arm, stepping in as head of the network. When these discussions had come up in the past, there was always a sense that whatever massive amounts of hand-holding were required in the Paula sphere, what she brought to the show was irreplaceable. The Paula/Simon/Randy buddy act was one of the historic relationships in television, and it was to be preserved at all costs. The phrase "lightning in a bottle" is commonly used by television professionals to describe on-screen chemistry, something that can't be manufactured, is very hard to capture, and something that once you've got it, you never ever let it go.

But with a new guard on board and the thought that *Idol* was due for a shake-up, that iron law was being questioned. Maybe it was time to revisit this whole judges thing.

As much as Paula was on the producers' minds, they were more concerned with the five-hundred-pound gorilla in the room—the looming specter of losing Simon Cowell. In their minds, they had gamed out different scenarios for a Cowell succession—various replacements or reconfigurations of the panel—and they all came down to one thing: Tens if not hundreds of millions of dollars each season rode on keeping Cowell with the show.

In the summer of 2008, as preparations were being made for season 8, a new contract was placed at Cowell's feet. It was the mother of all contracts, enough money to make Oprah look like a pauper. The executives took into account every possible cent Cowell could make if he left *Idol*—from bringing *X Factor* to America to appearing on other shows—added them all together, and came up with a number far, far bigger than that sum. They wanted to make sure there was no possible way Cowell could feel that leaving *Idol* made any financial sense for him. The amount, at that time, was said to be in the range of $100 million a year or $2.5 million an episode. Not bad for three hours of work a week.

His reaction: We'll see.

So the tinkering began. Iconic though it was, by season 8, the three-judge combination, with its familiar nice-to-mean spectrum, was so widely imitated that it was hard to remember that *Idol* had, in fact, been the show to popularize it, if not create it. Eight years later, the three-judge spectrum seemed integral to the fabric of the *Idol* universe. But now the show that had invented the panel was about to take it apart.

KARA DIOGUARDI HAD always wanted to be a star. Growing up in New Rochelle, the daughter of a U.S. congressman, young Kara, like so many *Idol* contestants, sang around the house and at local stages as soon as she could speak. In videos of Kara as early as her tweens, her father can be seen egging on his gawky reluctant daughter, who magically comes to life once she begins belting out "Hello, Dolly!" for a family dinner. Coming to Los Angeles after college, she attempted to break into the industry as a performer herself, but instead became fabulously successful as a writer of other people's songs, churning out a string of hits for Christina Aguilera, Britney Spears, Ricky Martin, Natasha Bedingfield, and Kelly Clarkson herself.

Working with the latter and with other *Idol* alums, Kara came to the attention of the show, and when the time came to return once again to the dream of a fourth judge, her name was quickly mentioned. She was younger than the rest of the panel, attractive and opinionated, and she also had a track record of producing hit records. And with a hint of feistiness, she seemed the woman who could stand up to Simon Cowell. On many levels, Kara seemed the perfect mix of ingredients to spice up the series. For her part, when approached about joining the biggest show on the planet, it was as though the dream of stardom, long since shelved, had suddenly been brought back to life. It didn't take her long to think the offer over.

If the addition of Kara DioGuardi wasn't actually calculated to make Paula's stomach lurch, it certainly didn't help. With her contract renewal looming, she could not help but notice the fact the producers had added not just another judge, but another *female* judge. And if she didn't get the message on her own, the media was there to point it out for her. "*Idol* Judges Abdul Unreliable, Takes Out 'Insurance'" was the *Arizona Republic*'s headline on Kara's hiring.

When the decision to add DioGuardi was abruptly announced, a stunned Abdul didn't wait long to make her feelings known. She mentioned during a radio interview that she was "concerned about the audience and acceptance," noting that previous attempts at having a fourth guest judge had not been successful.

Watching now from the sidelines, Lythgoe made his feelings about the changes clear. "I don't like fourth judges. I think once you've been told 'You suck,' you don't need to be told another three times," he said to the *New York Post*.

For DioGuardi, these statements were just the beginning of the season-long hazing coming her way. As preseason shooting began, Kara was thrust into the middle of the most famous panel in entertainment with little more than a pat on the back to guide her. In the audition episodes, Kara seemed not to know whether she was to be another mean judge or a nice judge. Sometimes she took Paula's side, as if attempting to bond against the boys; at other times she came off as brutally shrill. Her most memorable moment of the audition tour was in her harsh dismissal of Katrina "Bikini Girl" Darrell, which degenerated into an out-and-out catfight. Particularly noted by critics was her sarcastic employment of the term "sweetie," which gave many the chills.

But the new panel was just the beginning of the season's problems. The audition weeks were largely seen to have been a wash—delivering few "star is born" moments, or any of the particularly memorable "freak" contestants to achieve breakout anti-stardom. Following the Goodspeed suicide, *Idol* showcased their deluded contestants with a far gentler hand than in years past.

The show then devoted two weeks of airtime to the drama-rich Hollywood Week segment of the competition. But after the bland auditions, this seemed to swing too far to the other extreme: turning every last snit into an epic drama, and giving the lion's share of airtime to contestants such as the aforementioned "Bikini Girl," chosen for her shameless antics and ability to stir up anger among her fellow contestants rather than any particular performing skills. Even at two weeks, the season's best singers hardly made it onto the screen during the Hollywood episodes. And thus, five weeks in, viewers were left feeling the competition still had not begun and that—the most unpardonable of sins—the show had given them no one to root for.

But whatever demon possessed season 8 was just getting warmed up. The green mile episode became the stage for yet another semipublic debacle. Since the show had first introduced a perky, raven-haired singer named Joanna Pacitti, the cries of "Ringer!" had once again sounded across the Internet. During her audition, the show had taken a "cards on the table" approach to revealing her recording past, remembering how it had been accused of covering up Carly Smithson's. Telling of the album she had recorded at age twenty-one and the heartbreak she had felt when it had failed to take off, the show tried to paint hers as a redemption story. This tactic, however, only seemed to bait the Internet catcalls, spurring on the amateur detective corps. It was soon revealed online that not only was Pacitti a former recording artist, but one with deep ties to *Idol* itself. Internet reports also claimed, and were rapidly repeated in the mainstream media, that Pacitti was housemates with 19 executives Roger Widynowski and Michelle Young, a fact that, if true, would be in clear violation of *Idol* rules stating that all relationships with the show's staff be disclosed.

The truth, however, was far less nefarious and it would be the first of many stories the press would get very wrong that season. Pacitti had not been housemates with Widynowski, but merely lived in the same gigantic West Hollywood apartment complex as he. She later described Widynowski as a friendly face she knew only as "Roger" who worked somewhere in the music industry. "We'd see each other in the elevator. 'Hey, how are you doing?' He's a really, really funny guy. I adore him. He's unbelievable. He makes you smile and makes you laugh and he would sing my songs and make up really funny lyrics. So that was our *relationship*."

Michelle Young had briefly been Pacitti's manager years before, but they had not spoken in over a year. Pacitti knew that, long before, Young had once been an intern at 19, but says she had no clue that that was still active or what she might be doing there.

Pacitti would not get to tell her side of the story, however. On the night the green mile episode aired, Joanna and her two new BFFs, Alexis Grace and Adam Lambert (they called themselves "The Smoky Eye Club"), were celebrating their admission to the hallowed ranks of *Idol* semifinalists when Pacitti was summoned to Warwick's office. Briefly and with little explanation, he told her that "for the good of the show" they had decided she was being removed from the competition. She was asked if she wanted a ride home, shook her head no, and stunned, drove herself back to her boyfriend's house.

"I had just finished my interview packages for my performance, for my solo performance. They reassured me that, like, 'Your piece tonight was great. It's going to be good for you. You can really take advantage of the press that you're going to get from this.'"

For viewers who had seen Pacitti celebrating on Thursday night's pre-taped episode, it was a shock to wake up and read she had been eliminated via an official statement that offered no explanation other than stating the rumor. In the past, *Idol* had always addressed its issues publicly, with humor and sympathy. But this time, there was nothing. It felt to some as though the show was somehow losing its rudder.

And then came the semifinal rounds.

AFTER A NEARLY two-month preseason, fans were ready for the singing competition to get down to the business. However, thanks to yet another format change, that was exactly what they were denied.

In a preseason interview, Mike Darnell said that the biggest challenge for *Idol* was keeping it fresh, keeping people interested in a show that was at an age when most pulled up the stakes and called it a day. To that end, *Idol* dramatically shuffled the deck on the format, throwing in a host of rules and tweaks. Some of these changes—such as the Save Rule borrowed from *French Idol*—were to prove brilliantly successful, increasing the dramatic tension, highlighting, not undermining the basic narrative thread.

In the semifinals, however, the changes, the tweaks, and the attempts to spice things up only underscored the alienation viewers felt from the contestants. The show reverted back to the original semifinals format, the three heats plus Wild Card version. The semifinals formula of recent years had its problems, not least of which was that the stately progress of calling the field often put the audiences to sleep. But with this change months in, the audience still hadn't spent enough time with any one singer to develop a connection. Worse still, slow though the original format had been, the sudden wiping out of all but three of the contenders each night felt brutal and uncaring in what ultimately was considered a nurturing family show. Original format though it had been, years later, it felt gimmicky.

If the previous seasons had reacted against the Sanjayas, this season had a surplus of them in the early weeks, including the borderline-unhinged pageant queen Tatiana Del Toro and the first contestant to openly, flagrantly satirize *Idol* in all its years, the brilliantly funny Nick Mitchell (aka Norman Gentle), who got on his knees during his semifinals performance to sing a song of worship to *Idol* itself.

However, the changes showed one thing, the boldness of the *Idol* team. With most long-running TV success stories, from *Law & Order* to *The Tonight Show*, the edict is once you've got a hit, you don't move a single hair on the star's head. The show's bible remains sacrosanct until well after the novelty has worn off and the audience slide is unstoppable, by which point the changes made are transparently desperate and ill-considered.

As a result of the changes and chaos swirling around the show, by the time *Idol* at last lurched onto its big stage, the press smelled blood and with the ratings for the first time significantly off year after year, a new genre of stories appeared in the media as reporters fell over themselves to proclaim every problem, every off night, the beginning of the end for the Goliath. "*American Idol's* Ratings Slide: Speed Bump or Bad Road Ahead?" asked the *Los Angeles Times*. "Idol Juggernaut Shows Signs of Slowing" was UPI's headline. Throughout all its trials, *Idol's* absolute dominance over the airwaves had never in eight years once been questioned.

However, despite the issues, a funny thing happened on the way to the apocalypse. From the crazy process emerged perhaps the most talented group ever to step on the *Idol* stage—a group to rival the fabled fifth season cast. In the long run up, they had struggled to bond with the audience, but season 8's group was filled with such a high level of accomplishment that the entire season hardly saw a single belly-flop performance, something that was generally an *Idol* guarantee on any given night. To a singer, it was a truly capable, deeply likable group, and for the next months, whatever wackiness *Idol* went through production-wise, on pure talent alone this group would hold up the *Idol* season, led ultimately by perhaps the greatest phenomenon of a performer ever to step on the *Idol* stage, and ultimately won by a young man who in his quiet way captured the very best of the *Idol* spirit.

Little known to himself, Adam Lambert had been preparing for *Idol* for years. A theater nerd from San Diego, he had graduated to a career on the stage, winning a high-profile role in the cast of *Wicked*. Lambert was the first major *Idol* contender to bring professional theater experience to the show. He was also one of the most flamboyant singers to make it to the *Idol* dome, most comfortable dressed in black alligator-skin bat suits accessorized with rhinestone-studded handcuffs.

A veteran of the Southern California rave scene who had experimented heavily in it in every possible way, Lambert was a world away from the cluster of prayer leaders who filled that season. However, with his theatrical background and alternative culture fearlessness, he was able to build on the changes Chris Daughtry had brought to *Idol* and push them to another level entirely. While Daughtry and then David Cook had reinvented the arrangement of songs, bending them to create an artistic persona, Lambert created something else out of them entirely. Working with the *Idol* crew on the arrangements, costume, makeup, and lighting, he turned every performance into a fully realized theatrical spectacle every week.

His reinventions were audacious but also polarizing. On country night, when he took one of the most beloved songs of all time, Johnny Cash's "Ring of Fire," and turned into into a psychedelic dirge complete with Indian sitar, half the audience leapt to their feet elated while the other half sat on their hands outraged. *Idol* had never seen anything like Lambert, and the question reigned throughout the season: How far would *Idol* audiences be willing to go along for this ride?

Another element put a question mark on the Lambert trajectory, the matter of sexuality. *Idol* had had a few openly gay contestants before, but they had not gotten far. David Hernandez, the season before, had finished in twelfth place. Vanessa Olivarez, in season 2, had likewise finished at the bottom of her season. Clay Aiken had asserted he was straight while on the show, coming out only years later. Adam Lambert entered the show refusing to speak about his sexuality, but once photos were released on the Internet showing him in heavy glitter makeup making out with another man at the Burning Man festival, his active participation in the story became a moot point. The question was whether *Idol* nation was ready to make this leap forward.

MEANWHILE, *IDOL'S* RECORDING fortunes were not what they had once been. There had been enormous success, of course: Clarkson, Underwood, Aiken, and Daughtry. Each year the winner's album, even that of the star-crossed Taylor Hicks, had gone platinum—nothing to sneeze at in a time of implosion for the industry. But it had been a few years since one had broken out on the level of that big four, selling records by the many millions and filling stadiums with their fans. The past two winners, Jordin Sparks and David Cook, had each had hit singles and achieved a certain recognition, but neither had rocketed to the absolute A-list, and each continued to perform in clubs and smaller venues rather than moving up to arenas. Short of that there were dozens of others, for whatever reason, whose records had fizzled in the market-place, a line stretching back to Justin Guarini and the huge disappointment of Tamyra Gray's album, onward to Katharine McPhee and Blake Lewis. There were plenty of acts on the *Idol* register making plenty of money. But the *Idol* dream was based on the promise that it created not just moderately successful singers, but megastars; that was what only *Idol* could offer, what set the stakes of this competition apart by an order of magnitude from *Survivor* or *The Bachelor*. The stakes of *Idol* had to remain huge, life-altering, for the myth to function. And that proposition was looking more like a hit-or-miss thing.

As the show on the big stage got rolling, however, the problems only seemed to deepen. The bickering act between the judges, always a popular runner, got so out of control that it swallowed the show whole. Just as the finalists were desperately needing oxygen to introduce themselves to the audiences, the high jinks between Paula, Simon, Ryan, Randy, and the new girl often made the contestants seem like interlopers at someone else's dinner party. With the whole group bristling against the arrival of an awkward newcomer in their ranks, without Lythgoe on the floor to step in (Warwick guided the show, as he always had, from the control booth), the panel became uncontrollable, using their time to make inside jokes, ignoring the contestants' performances.

Worse still, the show ran overtime week after week, cutting off the final minutes for those who watched on TiVo or DVRs. The low moment came when Adam Lambert closed the show with what was probably his or anyone's finest moment of the season—a haunting rendition of Tears for Fears' "Mad World." It was one of those quintessential moments when a singer leaps beyond the ranks of contestants, forges a bond with the audience, and is transformed into a star.

But thanks to the overrun, a good share of the viewers never saw it. The number didn't begin until after the hour had ended, causing it to be cut out on many stations and all DVR recordings. The omission was so egregious that the following night Seacrest commented on it on the air, advising viewers to look it up on YouTube. Two months later, when Lambert lost the *Idol* crown, some grumbled that the fact that audiences had missed his greatest performance couldn't have helped anything.

Backstage, the frustrated contestants strained to establish themselves on a show where it seemed they were becoming but a footnote. Despite being widely praised by critics, the group struggled to deal with the wildly conflicting advice they were receiving from the distracted judges, keeping them at a constant level of frustration about where they were supposed to go. It got so bad for singer Anoop Desai, a Indian American nerd from North Carolina reborn as an R&B star, that one night after having followed the judges' previous weeks' orders to a T but receiving a bawling out nonetheless, he went backstage and punched the wall so hard he was forced to hide his bleeding hand when he returned before the camera.

From the sidelines, Lythgoe took another jab, saying, "There's been so much talk on *Idol* about the judges, the judges; it's not about the judges. It's about the talent."

THE TALENT ALSO had another matter to deal with, a little issue of the supernatural. In another tweak to the season, the show had put the contestants back in a mansion together after years of housing them off camera in a nondescript apartment building. The hope once again was to capture some *Real World*–like footage to use on the show, perhaps a fight or two, but the result was disappointing: The little time the contestants spent at the house, they were too exhausted to stir up much drama.

Off camera, however, a certain unexpected visitor came into their lives in the mansion. Alexis Grace had decided to name the presence Phyllis after her first couple sightings. Megan Joy said, "I remember the day I saw her. We were all pretty scared of certain rooms. Well, the electricity was all crazy, so lights would turn off by themselves. Things would make the electricity change. That was scary. One day I was in the bathroom brushing my teeth. I turned around and I was facing the mirror and I saw something go past the window, and it felt. . . . It was like somebody went past it but it wasn't really clear and it was more of just like a light. I can't really even describe it. Like maybe someone was wearing a light color or white, just real fast. I was, like, that really scared me. No one was in there."

"She lives in my room," Allison Iraheta said during the season. "If you spent one night in my room, you'd see. . . . I've heard growls. I'm not lying."

Megan Joy, however, had matters of the all too earthly variety to deal with during the season. The quirky tattooed blonde from Utah noted for her refreshingly uncoordinated dance style, and her propensity for breaking into birdcalls while onstage, had a story perhaps as close to the *Idol* myth as any contestant ever had. Before *Idol*, Megan truly had not sung for any audience larger than her immediate family, having failed to even win a part in the school play. Recently divorced, with a still young child, Megan worked at home as a graphic designer when she decided to audition for *Idol*, and to her shock, she made it through the auditions to Hollywood Week, past the green mile, and then after getting eliminated in the semifinals was called back and put through by the judges on the Wild Card night. It had been a wild ride, but behind it, unseen by the public, a horrible drama was playing itself out.

In the middle of her divorce and custody negotiation before auditioning, Megan's ex had decided to use her decision to go on *Idol* as evidence that she was abandoning her child and was an unfit mother. She traveled back to Utah secretly to testify in the custody hearing, spending her time on the show locked in battle with her ex, talking daily with her lawyers. She lived in terror that *Idol*, which she hoped would earn her enough money so she could buy a house for her and her son, might in fact cost her the child himself.

She recalls of her child at the time, "It was pretty crazy. He felt like I didn't care about him and I was chasing a dream. It wasn't that, I was trying to better our lives. I'm always going to be his mom raising him every day no matter what. I don't care, that's number one always. So, he was hurting. He was going through a lot and confused at how I could be away from him so much. Trust me, being away from him was the hardest thing I've ever done. I was a stay-at-home mom every single day. It tore me apart. It was really, really hard.

"People were always confused when I say that the *Idol* experience was the best and worst time of my life and it truly, truly was."

As the season drew toward its close, Paula Abdul still wondered about her contract, still strived for respect from the production team, still fought to be taken seriously by the audience. Ironically, it was the arrival of Kara DioGuardi that provided her the only bit of reassurance she had, giving her the chance to bond with her fellow judges to all but freeze out the new girl. During the season to come, visitors to the live show were shocked when during breaks the original three judges would step outside for a cigarette (or more precisely, to watch Simon have a cigarette) and leave Kara sitting alone by herself at the judges' table, her humiliation in full view for the audience, which she anxiously scanned for a friendly face.

Younger and more energetic than Paula, Kara made her play to draw Simon's attention away from his longtime sidekick, but he was having none of it. On the set, she would laugh uproariously at his asides and lean over him to muss his crew cut, to his visible annoyance. On one occasion, to the gasps of many in the room, Kara climbed into Cowell's lap, wrapped her arms around his neck, and whispered in his ear. The normally flirtatious Cowell drew back harshly.

Cowell says now that Kara "drove me crazy. It's no secret, year one, we did not get on well for whatever reason. But then year two, it suddenly clicked on the live shows. She and I genuinely got on with each other and genuinely ended the season on a good friendship."

Looking back after they have both left the show, he says, "She did something recently where we were both chasing an artist, and she said to the artist, 'No, if Simon's in, then I have to wait to see what he does. I'm not going to outbid him or compete with him.' And she didn't know that I knew, and I said, 'You're a very honorable person.' I called her on that and said, 'Thank you.' I liked her. I'm not saying we didn't have our moments, but you know what? You've got to have those moments."

But before they would find that happy balance, for Kara it would get much worse.

Part of the hazing ritual included a Hang Kara Out to Dry routine the other judges practiced on her. With the panel enlarged to four, the producers decided to mix things up by rotating the order in which they spoke, a move that inadvertently gave the original three the perfect opening to stick a knife between Kara's ribs.

One night, halfway through into the season, singer Lil Rounds took the stage and gave one of her more creditable performances. Up first, Kara gushed that Lil had given the performance of the night. She was followed by Paula, who, strangely for her, chimed in, "You know, I just didn't feel it from you tonight." Up next, Cowell played up the disagreement, saying, "I'm going to agree with . . . Paula." Then even kindly Randy Jackson joined with his old comrade, saying, "It wasn't good for me." As the season wore on, Kara's reviews were devastating. *Entertainment Weekly*'s *Idol* watcher Michael Slezak virtually declared war, calling her Kara the Terrible and demanding her removal from the show. His popular *Idolatry* video series regularly mocked her grating overuse of "sweetie."

In an interview with the *Los Angeles Times*, Kara openly wondered about her future with the show, saying, "I could be fired at any time. Done. Axed. Probably even during this process."

The tension finally boiled over halfway through the season after Paula gave yet another interview saying she thought bringing Kara aboard had been a mistake. Before that night's show, Kara confronted Paula outside her dressing room. Paula attempted to explain, "I wasn't talking about you, just the format." But months of residual tension came seething out, and soon, with minutes to spare before showtime, the crews' walkie-talkies buzzed with the exclamation "Catfight!" as the two judges tore into each other in an open corridor. When they were finally wrangled into their seats, they sat side by side without exchanging a look or a word throughout the show.

Despite the small comfort afforded by bonding with her fellow judges in hazing Kara, Paula Abdul felt only more insecure about her place on the show as the end of her contract loomed. With hints small and large, she had sent out the signal that unless she was afforded more respect under the *Idol* tent, she could not allow herself to return to a place that in her mind, especially in light of the world falling all over themselves to appease Cowell, treated her as a third-class citizen.

She had begun the season by attempting to up her game. Abdul had begun privately rehearsing her critiques and had secretly hired a writer to draft some more orderly rejoinders. Slowly, as the season progressed, some of the more observant *Idol* watchers took notice that the panel's resident scatterbrain was actually making sense, often sounding like the most informed, insightful person on the panel.

However, the train wreck narrative on Paula had been too long established for it to be turned around overnight.

With an episode in late April, Abdul planned to take her pre-negotiation campaign into high gear. Her latest album of pop songs was due out and for the first time since joining the show, she planned to step to the *Idol* stage and perform a live dance number to showcase the first single, "(I'm Just) Here for the Music." To accompany the reminders that she remained a vigorous force of music and dance, Abdul's people planned a little bombshell certain to get the attention of the *Idol* powers that be.

Days before Abdul's performance, I received a call at the *Los Angeles Times*. Members of Abdul's camp suggested that it would be interesting for me to do a story on Paula's return to the stage, offering to bring me out to the rehearsal space where she was preparing the elaborate number. They filled me in that with her contract coming up, this performance would certainly showcase the fact that she was a woman with a lot of options. And, they told me, they were willing to share one little fact that they thought would underscore why she was so serious in her demands for respect: They were willing to publicly reveal Paula's salary.

While it was assumed that Abdul's salary was less, significantly less than the thirty million Cowell was known to make, no number had ever come out. A newspaper report when she had signed her last contract had put the amount, according to "sources," in the eight million range.

Not even close, was the word from Abdul's camp, revealing the disparity between their takes from thirty million for Cowell to the paltry 1.8 million for which Abdul served.

In the dressing room of the Burbank rehearsal space where Abdul ran through her number with a dozen backup dancers, complete with a plunge off a staircase fifteen feet high into their arms, she sat in her makeup chair and talked about the pending contract and her place in the *Idol* firmament. Paula became visibly shaken, refusing to say that she was returning to the show, only saying she was leaving everything to the "negotiation people" and trusted that it would work itself out as it was meant to.

On the Tuesday morning, my story was released and picked up around the world with headlines aghast at the disparity between the judges' take-homes. The revelation certainly delivered as intended, getting the attention of *Idol*'s producers, but behind the scenes, her plea for sympathy and demand to be taken seriously was greeted by an eye-rolling sense that this was just the latest Paula antic.

Her week from hell was just getting started.

On Wednesday morning, the day of her planned dance number, *Ladies' Home Journal* hit the stands with an interview conducted a month earlier in which Abdul admitted that she had fought drug addiction and gone to rehab to deal with it. This was in direct contradiction to what she had told ABC in an interview at the season's open and what she had been saying for years.

Actually, on closer inspection, the story told less than met the eye. The revelation of addiction might have been the story's author reading too much into Abdul's garbled syntax as she never, it seemed, said exactly that. As for her supposed confession that she had attended rehab . . . the story cites her saying she had gone to the La Costa center for drug rehabilitation. In fact, La Costa is a resort and spa that offers no addiction treatments, a mistake that lent credence to Abdul's frantic response that the piece misunderstood and misquoted her.

But in the white-hot vortex of *Idol* news cycles, there is rarely room for explanations and reconsiderations. As Abdul took the *Idol* stage Wednesday night, the performance was cast in the light of her supposed drug confession. And then even the performance was torn apart as reviews the next day criticized Abdul for lip-synching her song as she leaped through the vigorous dance steps.

The year that had begun with a death in her driveway seemed to be fulfilling all its ominous potential. As the clock ticked toward her contract's end, the producers wondered if this person had really incontrovertibly become more trouble than she was worth.

IRONICALLY, FOR ALL its problems, it would be season 8 that would break *Idol*'s long exclusion from the Emmy race. Since the reality categories had been conceived at the beginning of the decade, they had been the sole property of CBS's *Amazing Race*, which year after year took home the trophy while the far more popular *Idol* seethed on the sidelines. At last, however, for season 8, the technical expertise of the *Idol* crew having been honed to a fine point, the Television Academy acknowledged their work with awards for Bruce Gowers for Best Direction, Andy Walmsley and James Yarnell for Art Direction, and Kieran Healy, Joshua Hutchings, and George Harvey for Lighting Direction.

WHILE LAMBERT CONTINUED to dominate the coverage, as the contest came down to the wire, the final weeks were ruled by the Arkansan prayer leader, Kris Allen, a highly likable and endearing soft rocker whose John Mayer–inspired performance demonstrated the diversity of musical styles emerging from America's megachurches. In eight years of *Idol*, never had there been a darker horse than Allen, who even three weeks before the season's end seemed unlikely to make the finals, let alone take the crown.

Adam Lambert remained the season's huge phenomenon in terms of the enthusiasm of his fans. Much noted around *Idol* events, the Glamberts were becoming the most devoted and voracious fan collective since the Claymates, surpassing even the commitment of the previous season's Archies. But with his polarizing performances, there was a cap on his fan base, and in the final weeks, Adam was no longer generally the top vote-getter. When Danny Gokey was eliminated and Kris went on to face Lambert in the finale, it was widely assumed that Kris would take all the votes from his fellow prayer leader and win.

At the final, as it turned out, it was Kara who stole the show. When her old nemesis Katrina "Bikini Girl" Darrell took the stage to sing before the vast Nokia crowd, Kara snuck up behind her and joined in, then opened her dress to reveal her own bikini. It was the show's unforgettable moment and the bravery it required of Kara won her a grudging admiration she had been denied all season.

The moment actually provoked a fairly major incident of backstage drama. Not having been filled in beforehand that she was to be sharing the spotlight with Kara, Katrina had looked ahead to her performance as a veritable coronation. Her hopes had been raised even further when, during the rehearsal, guest performer Cyndi Lauper, who had not watched the show, heard Katrina practicing and became alarmed that no one was helping her sing properly. "She's not hittin' her notes!" Lauper exclaimed. Working these days as a vocal coach, Lauper took it upon herself to sit up with Katrina and get her in shape for the big day. Thus, when Kara intruded, it produced a highly incensed reaction. Katrina raced backstage and locked herself in the women's dressing room. She had to be pried out by security and was taken away, cursing her fellow contestants of the season to the sky.

Ultimately, the crown went to Allen, continuing the cute rocker boys' dynasty. Once again, however, there was an incident that would launch an armada of conspiracy theories. Days after the finale, no less than the *New York Times*—there were by now no holdouts in the media to blanket *Idol* coverage—ran a story about some parties thrown in Allen's home state of Arkansas by *Idol* sponsor AT&T where special phones were passed out to allow the users to text votes in far faster than on normal phones. The world immediately cried foul, but *Idol* asserted that in a hundred-million-vote universe, the votes cast at a few parties could hardly swing the results. It had not been, they hinted, a close election. Privately, *Idol* sources were even more determined on the subject. Several have revealed that even if every vote from the state of Arkansas was disqualified, Kris Allen still would have won easily.

No information would likely satisfy the Glamberts, who remain the most ardent of *Idol* fan clubs, and to this day continue to post evidence on message boards, e-mail reporters, and even write books attempting to prove that the eighth *Idol* crown was stolen from its rightful owner.

The voraciousness of his fans would seem to get to even Adam himself. On the tour, he was forced to tweet warnings to the Glamberts that he could only give so much of himself to sign autographs and greet after the show. So dedicated did they stay that Matt Giraud remembers one night on the tour standing backstage with Kris and looking out over a sea of Lambert signs. "Who voted for me?" Kris half jokingly wondered aloud.

For his part, Lambert immediately became one of the most watched people ever to leave *Idol*. When he finally chose to discuss his sexuality during the interview for a *Rolling Stone* cover story, the issue became the magazine's best seller of the year.

AT THE SEASON'S end, Abdul had brought on a high-octane new management team led by David Sonenberg, who also managed the Black Eyed Peas. Sonenberg duly informed the powers at Fox that he was standing by and ready to begin negotiations. He heard nothing. He placed more calls and was assured that they would be in touch soon; still he heard nothing. He sat still until days before it was announced that host Ryan Seacrest had signed a new contract with the show, increasing to the neighborhood of twenty million his annual take from *Idol* and related Fox activities. Somehow, *Idol* had found time to hammer that out with Seacrest, while they still hadn't gotten in touch about Paula's contract.

Finally, determined to make clear that he wasn't messing around, Sonenberg called me to let me know, for the public record, of his frustration with the process. He told how in previous years, when it came contract renewal time, the producers had called Abdul up days before the new season started and said, "If you can be in Boston for auditions Monday, we'll take you back"—a process that led to her still receiving a relatively minuscule sum for her services.

With weeks left in Abdul's contract, Sonenberg told me, "Very sadly, it does not appear that she's going to be back on *Idol*." He went on, further venting his frustration with the production, saying, "I find it under these circumstances particularly unusual, I think unnecessarily hurtful. I find it kind of unconscionable and certainly rude and disrespectful that they haven't stepped up and said what they want to do."

In eight years, no member of the show's cast or crew had ever publicly spoken out against the show in this way. Abdul had shattered the illusion of a happy family that had been so carefully tended to. She might not have fully realized it at the time, but she had crossed a brink from which there was no going back.

But even as they shook their heads at this ongoing debacle, the producers' minds remained intensely preoccupied with the Cowell question. During the summer, there had been a showdown meeting with all the parties involved, a summit akin to the meeting of the Five Families in *The Godfather*. Gathering in Hollywood were representatives of 19 Productions, FremantleMedia, and Sony (which owned not only the music contracts for *Idol* but most of the *X Factor*). Fox was represented by Rupert Murdoch himself, and Cowell was accompanied by Bryan Lourd of CAA.

Put on the table was a staggering deal: To continue his services on *Idol* as well as to bring *X Factor* to America, Simon Cowell would be paid in the neighborhood of $130 million a year. Even in this elevated company, the number took people's breath away.

Cowell's response: I don't think that's good enough.

Cowell had been taking steps toward this crossroads for a long time; nevertheless, making his decision was much harder than he ever anticipated. Asked why it was so difficult, he says, "It was my relationship with Fox. These were the guys who had given us the chance of a lifetime when nobody else would—and were incredibly loyal to me, decent to me, kind to me, supportive. You've got to turn around to those people and say, 'I'm going to leave when you want me to stay.' It was a personal issue. It wasn't a financial issue. The money was never a problem.

"And at the same time I was also looking at a competitor who also offered me the most crazy deal I've ever seen in my life. . . . And I looked at it and I said, 'We can't even look at this deal. . . . We said we'd love to talk to you but we absolutely can't. It's just too tempting.' So I had to stay on track about my relationship with Fox and it was really difficult because it was like saying to a friend, I'm not going to be your friend anymore but at the same time I want to do another show with you. And that's eventually what was agreed upon, but it was very, very difficult."

While the issues and the feelings were sorted out, the talks dragged on.

Into this breach stepped Paula Abdul and her demands.

To renew her contract, Abdul demanded she be paid ten million dollars a season. Fox countered with three. At first it seemed they were bluffing; after all they'd been through, they couldn't possibly expect her to accept that. But the number did not budge. While they claimed they wanted her back, Abdul and her people could not help but note that if *American Idol* really wanted something, they certainly wouldn't let a little matter of a few million dollars stand in the way of them getting it.

On August 5, 2009, Paula Abdul made history by breaking the biggest story yet broken on Twitter. She tweeted, "With sadness in my heart I've decided not to return to *Idol*. I'll miss nurturing all the new talent, but most of all being a part of a show that I helped from day 1 become an international phenomenon."

After eight seasons of making entertainment history, the iconic panel that had guided *American Idol* was breaking up.

Chapter 19

LEAVING *IDOL*

hat's on the other side of the rainbow? When the season ends, the exiting Idols face their greatest challenge of all: how to convert their *American Idol* experience into a real-world career. How do they make it in an increasingly difficult marketplace, entering not just a music industry that has all but imploded, but a world where, after nine seasons, more than a hundred *Idol* finalists roam the landscape?

After leaving the show, the top ten finalists of each season have one last *Idol* duty, the national "Idols Live" fifty-plus-city tour, a stage spectacle directed by noted spectacular specialist Raj Kapoor. For most of the finalists, the tour represents their big payday, paying them over $100,000 for four months on the road. An audacious gambit when it was first rolled out in the United Kingdom, the *Idol* tour had stayed relatively secure against the downturn in the music industry, holding its audience through season after season. However, in 2010, the summer of doom hit America's touring industry and acts from the Eagles to Christina Aguilera to Lilith Fair were forced to cancel shows. For once, *Idol* was not immune and was forced to call off seven shows.

Despite the recent troubles, for *Idol* the tour gives alums a chance to live out their pop star fantasies, singing to arenas night after night. That first year's tour marked the first time in recent music history that the stars of a television show managed to transform their fame into success on the concert circuit, where they were competing directly with the biggest acts in the music business. RJ Helton recalls of that first year's tour, "It was insane. We had people following our tour buses. We were selling out arenas across the country and that's obviously something none of us had ever done before or were ever even prepared for. It was just crazy, the fans that we had and the money that we were making. All of those things none of us had ever dreamed about or even thought about or thought was even possible."

Life on the buses would be another test of endurance for the *Idol* contestants. Season 2's Kimberley Locke remembers, "Tour was very tough. A lot of homesick people. A lot of people missing family. Getting up in the middle of the night and getting off the bus and into a hotel, the constant nonstop, only having a day off here and there. If you don't have the work ethic, then you can't do life on the road. It's very hard."

Megan Joy recalls of the schedule, "On tour you work twelve to twelve. Twelve o'clock it's the meet and greet with fans. Press. All this other stuff. Then you get ready. Then it's the show. Afterward, you do another meet and greet. Then you go outside to the fans and sign. That's a long day."

During the season, the singers exist in the unnatural situation of living with people who are actually their competitors. Once the season ends, however, when the contest is over and the rivalries are dismantled, many *Idol* contestants look back on the tour as a time when they can at last let their guard down, when they can just hang out with the only people who know what they've gone through.

Ace Young recalls, "On the tour we're all on the same level. It was a crazy tour because we had forty-four dates initially and they sold out in, like, ten minutes. So they added sixteen more dates. So we did sixty arenas in two and a half months and we were 93 percent sold out on the whole tour. It was the biggest tour of the summer. We beat out Madonna."

Season 5's buses, however, bore some rather distinct gender differences. "The female bus was pretty chill," Ace remembers. "The one thing that caught me off guard the most was our bus was cleaner. The female bus . . . was the nastiest thing I'd seen in my life . . . the nastiest thing ever."

One part of the tour that divides rather than unites is the question of what to do next. After the season ends, the winner and the runner-up are generally picked up for management and record contracts and are whisked off to put together their albums. Those on this track spend the off days of the tour flying back to Hollywood to work on their album, their free moments on the phone working on the songs, the album cover, and the myriad details of their careers to come. For the rest, the tour is something of a limbo period while they ponder the next step.

Carly Smithson remembers, "Everyone was thinking about what they were going to do next, but you didn't really talk about it. Late at night, I'd be the only one up on the girls' bus writing. We'd pull into a little truck stop at four in the morning, I'd get out, and hang out with the boys."

With the end of the season, the tour gives the singers at last a chance to perform without the worries of competition. Free of the judges' glares, with weeks to choose their songs and work on the sets, the Idols perform much better than they ever had on the show. And the critics notice. For many who struggled during the season, the tour is a chance to let America see them at their best. Matt Giraud recalls, "My favorite part of the tour was really redeeming myself. I felt like I really changed the minds of a lot of critics who were tough on me. Jim Cantiello from MTV and Michael Slezak from *Entertainment Weekly*. They weren't fans of mine at all. They advocated against me a lot. I took it light-heartedly, but when I got the judges' save, MTV was saying 'Why did you save him?' It hurt me. And they all came out, and when they saw me live they all changed their minds. They all wrote these amazing reviews. That's a good feeling. I called it my redemption tour because I had some haters out there and when they came out for the live show they really came around."

ALAS, EVERYTHING COMES to an end. The last day of the tour is the deadline for Fuller's 19 Entertainment to inform each contestant whether the option to manage them will be picked up. (This is stipulated in the contract that each signs at the beginning of the process.) Each season, 19 selects the singers they feel have the most viable commercial prospects, typically taking two to four Idols under their wing. For those picked up by 19, life becomes a whirlwind, as managers race to hook them up with a record label and get an album to market before a new *Idol* season begins.

For those not picked up by 19, it can be a rude awakening. A year after they first auditioned, the former Idols are now cast back upon the world. Stepping out of the *Idol* bubble, where their every need was taken care of, every moment scheduled, the young performers often find themselves on their own, with little experience to guide them and few advisors to turn to.

RJ Helton recalled of the experience, "They prepare you to be a huge success, but when you have to go back to reality and all of a sudden you're going back home and there isn't any security around you, there isn't any manager or producer or agent, there aren't those people who have protected you throughout this whole process, and all of a sudden you're now a normal person going back to the public eye—it was probably the scariest time of my life.

"There was no private life. I couldn't go out to dinner. I stayed at home for the most part. I mean, we did the tour after the show but in between that time and then after the show or after the tour you're on your own. They don't prepare you for the aftermath. They prepare you to be a star and then once your star is gone they don't know who you are."

Carly Smithson remembers stepping out of the bubble: "I was standing on the curb at Burbank airport and the city felt so huge and overwhelming, like it was going to swallow me up. But I said to myself, 'I'm not going to let it destroy me. I need to make a plan to move forward. I need to map out week by week what I have to accomplish.'"

Ace Young recalls facing his future. "After the *Idol* tour it's complicated, because you were just on the biggest show in the world and anything you do has to be big. So most people try to put stuff together and they fall on their face because they don't know how to compete with the people who are doing it for a living. All those people whose songs we sang are making a living right now. And they're performing, and now we're competition to them in the marketplace. But we don't have their support because we haven't had their success as an artist. So it's very confusing at that moment because you need the support of a major label, but no major label will pull you on because you're directly linked to *American Idol*, 19 Entertainment, and Sony, and they really don't know what to do with you."

Season 3's Jon Peter Lewis recalled, "I figured that since I'd been on this TV show that if I released any kind of record, it would sell pretty well. I went right away into the studio. I was off the tour beginning of October, and by the end of October I'd recorded three songs. I didn't really know what to do with them. I didn't have great business sense, so I sat on them for a year before anything was released. I think that's the case for a lot of people—they have big ideas but there's no infrastructure to support them. It's all people at the top—you don't know any producers, label people. You also feel a little like there's no one you can trust—you have a short amount of time to produce something, and you don't know or feel like you're really ready for it. You don't want to make the wrong decision. There's a lot of figuring out."

Natural-born businesswoman and almost-law-student Kimberley Locke remembers her sense of the ticking clock while she was on that year's tour and her race to get ahead of it. "My goal was to have a record deal by the time the tour ended in September. I was hounding 19 management. I called them every day. 'Are you going to sign me?' because time was wasting. I knew that I didn't want to come off the tour and not have something lined up. Between my lawyer and a few other people who were making phone calls on my behalf, Curb Records was interested. Mike Curb met me in Memphis and signed me in Memphis at the concert.

"My thing was that I realized that the window of opportunity was closing because *American Idol* was at the height of its run, and I knew that as soon as they started picking the next season of contestants, people were going to get ADD and they were going to forget because they wanted to see who the next crew was coming in. As soon as I came off the tour I went right into the studio. If they weren't going to sign me, I needed to be on top of my game, because what people don't understand is if they don't sign you, they're done with you. They don't hold your hand. They don't help you. You're no longer their client, which is fair. That's how it is. That's business."

For many former Idols, however, the expectations would prove debilitating. Their enormous year of *Idol* is followed for many by a difficult process of figuring out where they fit in the challenging landscape of the music business and trying to put together a team to get them there. It can take years. Season 6 favorite Melinda Doolittle, who waited two full years to put out an album after her *Idol* stint, said, "I think that was probably the best part about not winning for me was that I just needed some time to figure out what I wanted to do. I love so many different styles of music. I wanted to see what resonated deep inside me, though, what I wanted to sing and what kind of music I wanted to tell a story with, what kind of vehicle I wanted to use. I did a lot of traveling. I was singing as much as possible. I was out there working, whether it was a corporate date or concerts here and there. I toured twice with Michael W. Smith. I did two Christmas tours with him. I went to Africa twice on behalf of Malaria No More. Once with Mrs. Bush and then once as a presidential delegate, which I never thought I'd get the chance to do. There were a lot of people telling me to hurry. Thank God for my mom and for prayer. I knew that I needed time."

But for many, having experienced that moment of stardom, the expectation that it will continue unabated becomes crippling. Season 6's Phil Stacey went from *Idol* to building an audience for live performances, playing on a circuit across the South. He reflected, "I think the biggest challenge is that a lot of the contestants come off the show and think it's over if they don't get a record deal. They think it's all about the record deal. I came off the show understanding that that wasn't it, that the record deal was actually going to be harder to obtain because I was on *American Idol*. There are already so many people from *American Idol* who have become stars. But even though the record label doors seem closed—the event gigs, the venues, you can go just about anywhere. When you have come off *American Idol* people will always want to see you."

NINE SEASONS IN, the road out of *Idol* has led in more directions than anyone could have dreamed. At the top there are, of course, the three Cs, and one K: Carrie, Chris, Clay, and Kelly, who between them have sold over 33 million albums. A decade after her victory, Clarkson remains one of the most beloved and talked about figures in pop music. Carrie Underwood is the uncrowned reigning queen of country music, selling albums by the millions, filling arenas on her tour, and taking home every award Nashville has to offer. After that group, another handful has managed to chalk up impressive sales for post-*Idol* albums, with Bo Bice, David Archuleta, and Adam Lambert among others earning gold records and putting out hit singles.

The woes of the music industry have, however, taken their toll on *Idol* alum. Since season 5, no winner's debut album has achieved the massive heights of those early efforts. The albums of Jordin Sparks, David Cook, and Kris Allen, while producing hit singles, struggled to cross into platinum status. Nevertheless, there remains a myriad of opportunities for *Idol* alumni outside of the traditional pop/rock charts. Following Carrie Underwood into Nashville, Kellie Pickler, Bucky Covington, and Joshua Gracin, among others, have carved out careers in the country world.

Season 6's Chris Sligh, who is pursuing a career in Christian music, made a name for himself as a songwriter, penning the Rascal Flatts hit "Here Comes Goodbye." The Christian music world has embraced a range of *Idol* stars, from Phil Stacey to Mandisa. RJ Helton has kept working in music continuously since leaving season 1 in one of the most interesting crossover careers, performing both as a gospel star and in gay-themed settings, such as regular work on cruises. Carly Smithson went in a decidedly more hard rock direction, becoming the singer and front woman for We Are The Fallen, a band composed of the original members of Evanescence.

The Asian market, where *American Idol* is watched, if anything, more religiously than it is here, has opened its arms to scores of alumni who have recorded songs and toured, particularly in Japan and the Philippines. Season 3's Jasmine Trias, who relocated her career across the Pacific, remains a major star there.

The birth of iTunes has also opened up opportunities for former Idols to pursue their own careers and capitalize on their notoriety. Since beginning a partnership with iTunes in season 7, *Idol* has sold more than 120 million songs on the online music service. But for many alumni, that online fan base has proved an ongoing source of sustenance, as they are able regularly to put up songs and albums for download. Recording Christmas songs released alone has become a popular route for many.

Then there's Broadway. Season 3 champion Fantasia Barrino most notably headed up the original cast of *The Color Purple*, the musical. In 2009, Constantine Maroulis was nominated for a Tony award for his role in *Rock of Ages*. Season 5 champion Taylor Hicks spent a year with the touring company of *Grease* in the Teen Angel role. Ace Young and Diana DeGarmo headed the cast of a *Hair* revival. In 2010, Justin Guarini appeared in the original Broadway cast of *Women on the Verge of a Nervous Breakdown*. And the list goes on.

Acting has also called out to many former Idols. Most famously, after a few fallow years following her disappointing *Idol* run, Jennifer

Hudson won an Academy Award for Best Supporting Actress for her role in *Dreamgirls*. Katharine McPhee has acted consistently since leaving *Idol*, taking supporting roles in *The House Bunny* and the NBC sitcom *Community*, among other parts. Tamyra Gray went on to a role in *Boston Legal* after leaving *Idol*.

Their ease with the camera has led to careers in TV hosting for many Idols. Justin Guarini has become the face of the *Idol*-affiliated shows *Idol Tonight* and *Idol Chat*, helming the TV Guide Network's programming about *Idol*. A dozen other former Idols have also found work in front of the camera in *Idol*-related shows. Ryan Seacrest's almost cohost, season 1 contender Kristin Holt, can now be seen as a correspondent on nerd central G4 network. Kimberly Caldwell headed up P. Diddy's *Starmaker* show on MTV in 2009. Season 7's Kristy Lee Cook hosts a Nashville-themed show, *Goin' Country*, on the Versus network, described as "hunting with the stars." Alexis Grace found work immediately after *Idol* as a DJ on a station in her hometown of Memphis. Jon Peter Lewis hosts his own online variety show, *The American Nobody Show*, a hilarious romp through *Idol* land built around the misadventures of a singer who, seven years after *Idol*, is still searching to find his place in the industry.

NOT EVERYONE'S ROAD has been smooth. Every few months seem to bring news of another *Idol* alum's brush with the law and infamy. In 2007, season 4's Jessica Sierra was arrested for assault and cocaine possession. She was later the subject of a sex tape released online. Julia DeMato from season 2 was arrested in 2005 for drunk driving and cocaine possession. Season 7's Chikezie Eze was nabbed for identity theft and using a stolen credit card at a Neiman Marcus store in 2010. Season 6's Stephanie Edwards was sentenced to community service for public brawling.

And then there has been the journey of Nikki McKibbin.

As a member not just of the first cast of *American Idol*, but of *Popstars* before it, Nikki could be considered one of the founding mothers of the modern media age. She's certainly plumbed its depths since leaving it. Initially signed by 19 after the *Idol* tour, she eventually stormed out and away from the firm. By her account, she was pressed to record a country album rather than sticking with the hard rock format she felt at home with. With no contract in the offing, Nikki returned to Dallas, where she put together a band and began playing local dates before they eventually broke up. During this period, her alcohol abuse, still relatively mild during her *Idol* stint, began to rage out of control. After the death of her mother, she turned to cocaine and other hard drugs.

Nikki began making the rounds of reality TV as a former *Idol* star, appearing on *Fear Factor* and *Battle of the Network Reality Stars*. When she finally recorded an album in 2007, six years after her *Idol* stint, it failed to take off. Her cycle of depression and drug abuse worsened until in 2008 she was hospitalized and placed in a psychiatric ward. The publicity from that episode brought a call from the team of Dr. Drew Pinsky, who invited her to join the season of *Celebrity Rehab* just about to film. Viewers saw Nikki open up about her childhood history of abuse—"I'll tell people anything. I don't care"—and go through a tortured withdrawal from anxiety medication. She eventually graduated to Dr. Drew's other show, *Sober House*, where she completed the recovery program under the watchful eye of America.

In 2010, she celebrated two years clean and sober, and credits Dr. Drew with saving her life. Married to Craig Sadler, the CTO of a tech company, she lives with him in a Fort Worth subdevelopment, where the pair are raising Nikki's son, seen on television as a four-year-old bringing his mother flowers on the *Idol* stage, and Craig's daughter from a previous relationship.

In the low-key subdivision, the gargoyles that greet visitors on the front steps are the only visible sign of the rocker dwelling within. On the weekends, Nikki works at a memorabilia store, where, she says, customers often point out her resemblance to the young redhead on the *Idol* poster hanging on the wall. But they generally refuse to believe it's her. "I've had a job since I came home from *Sober House* because they tell you you need to have a normal job," she says. "Everybody's gotta work. It doesn't matter if I was on a TV show or what. I come home, I gotta work. That's just the way it is. But it's hard to find a job because everybody looks at you, like, why do you want to work here? You're famous."

In the evenings, she's still singing with the band, this time an ensemble dubbed Wicked Attraction that performs hard rock classics, as well as original songs by Nikki dealing with her recovery and path back. The crowds that turn out for them at local bars and clubs number into the hundreds.

Chapter 20

THE END OF THE DAY

For over five years, Simon Cowell had dreamed of being free of *Idol* and bringing his own show to America. But now that his chance at freedom was at hand, the leap was proving harder than he had imagined. Season 8 had been a watershed for Cowell, a time of very public contemplation as to what his next move would be. Now, entering the final season on his contract, he was being pressed for answers.

In interviews, Cowell had been fairly open about having lost his enthusiasm for *Idol* and wanting to tie his future to his own show, *X Factor*. But the money on the table was staggering. This wasn't some artiste turning his back on filthy lucre for the sake of artistic fulfillment. This was the man who proclaimed his goal in life was to make a lot of money. If he said no, Simon Cowell would potentially be the first man in entertainment history to walk away from a contract worth over a hundred million dollars a year.

There's a Hollywood urban legend that could serve as something of a metaphor for the situation. Jack Nicholson, the story goes, is in the back of a limousine having a meeting with a couple of executives. At some point during the meeting, Nicholson more or less throws himself on the female executive. She slaps his face and storms out of the car, slamming the door in disgust. The other executive—male—says to him, "Jack, how could you do that?" "Lemme tell you something about women," Jack drawls in reply. "There's two kinds of them in the world:

the kind who want to screw Jack Nicholson, and the kind who want to say they turned down a chance to screw Jack Nicholson."

Simon Cowell, of all people, was going to turn down the chance.

And no one was more shocked than he was to find out that, years later—several empires later—it no longer was just about the money. Looking back on his earlier vow that getting rich was the be-all and end-all, Cowell says, "That's the time you find out that's who you really are, I guess. I used to say, It's about the money, and that's what used to drive me. Suddenly, when you're in that position, loyalty comes into it, all sorts of emotions. And funny enough . . . even if the *X Factor* didn't succeed, I'd still say I made the right decision because it was what I wanted to do."

The offer was so overwhelming Cowell initially said yes. But he just couldn't do it. The desire to be the man with the name on the door was too great. After eight seasons of *Idol*, Cowell was done. It was time to move on.

JANUARY 11, 2010 was the first day of shooting season 9's Hollywood Week. It was also Fox's turn to present its lineup at the Television Critics Association meeting in Pasadena. All morning, there had been buzz that something big might happen. Since the *Will Simon Go?* question had been the biggest story in entertainment for months, the assembled press corps wondered if this might be the day of the announcement.

Fox had thrown down the gauntlet.

In the past few days, Cowell had said he would return to *Idol*, then changed his mind and said he would leave. With hints that he was about to change his mind again, the exhausted executives had ordered a contract drawn up and brought to Pasadena, where they told Cowell it was time—once and for all—to sign on the dotted line. And not just sign, but sign before an assembly of press critics, with dozens of cameras rolling and the world's entertainment media observing it all. The room filled with *Idol*'s producers, crew, and even family members who had made the trip to Pasadena for the occasion.

A little after noon, as the assembled media gazed on, a visibly shaken Cowell took the podium. Voice quiet—almost humble—he announced: "There's been a lot of speculation, partly because we didn't have a contract agreement. We reached an agreement formally about half past eleven this morning. Where we have come to is that *X Factor* will launch in America in 2011, with me judging the show and executive producing the show, and because of that, this will be my last season on *American Idol*."

He went on, "I was offered a lot of money to stay on. But . . . I wanted to do something different. I wanted a new challenge."

It was, everyone knew, inevitable.

The moment had been five years in the making. Now that the day was here, the sense of what had been accomplished since this little singing contest had crossed the Atlantic was heavy in the air. Fox might not have been saying good-bye to Cowell, just moving him to another corner of the empire, but the show that had made the network was about to lose the star who had built it. It was the end of something enormous.

For those who were staying with *Idol*, the big question was what would come next, what *Idol* would be without Cowell. No doubt many of the rank-and-file crew thought of moving from *Idol*—an aging giant that had just received its biggest blow yet—to what would undoubtedly be the hotter, fresher production. But before all that there was still a show to put on. Simon Cowell had one more season to go.

SEASON 9 SAW another enormous tweak to the production. This one, anticipating Cowell's decision, had been made months ahead. In those first seasons of *Idol* Paula provided the "heart" of the show, the sense that the kids had someone rooting for them no matter what. With Paula gone, there was a hole in the lineup, and it was clear that Kara wasn't going to fill it. Privately, members of the *Idol* team acknowledged that the audience research on the newest judge was not stellar. "She's the one who broke up the Beatles," said one.

Ellen DeGeneres was a logical replacement choice for many reasons. In the previous decade, she had transformed herself from a slightly caustic boundary-pushing comedian to a fun-loving, dancin'-all-the-time daytime talk show host. In that role, she had been one of *American Idol*'s best friends, a devoted fan who for years would host contestants on her show. She had served two years prior as the remote location host of *Idol Gives Back* and thrown outdoor concerts featuring *Idol* alumni. So, when the year before she had appeared as a celebrity guest judge on

So You Think You Can Dance, a lightbulb had gone off in Mike Darnell's head. Here was a star who was funny, supportive, and beloved. What's more, she had the clout to stand up to Cowell.

On paper, Ellen answered all their prayers. But chemistry isn't something you can plot out on paper. There's a reason it's called lightning in a bottle. And there were lots of reasons this chemistry experiment failed.

While in the past, Simon had enjoyed the give and take, the friendly on-air jousting with Paula, there had never been any question as to who had the upper hand. Simon was the star. Period. This new recruit was a star in her own right, completely independent of *Idol*. Not to mention that despite her just hanging out, nice girl demeanor, Ellen was no slouch in the ego department herself. Privately, she was known as one of the bigger divas in Hollywood, her set rife with horror stories. During the writers' strike of 2008, Ellen had been the only major talk show host to hire scab writers, a fact that, in her ongoing campaign to paint herself as America's best pal, had been swept under the rug.

It remained to be seen how Ellen's ego would stand up to Simon's in this, her first season, and his last. For his part, Cowell might have been heading out, but he wanted to walk away in style. For several years past, his dressing quarters had not been in one of the modest rooms where the rest of the cast prepared, but in more spacious quarters, a trailer located in the parking lot right off the stage, where he could get made up and ready for the show at his leisure. For his final season, however, Cowell decided that would not do—not after he laid eyes on the two-story deluxe trailer that Will Smith used while filming. The multiroom mobile home was delivered to the lot, where it was set up with a little patio area out front. However, with a foot out the door, he was to find there were limits to his powers for the first time. When he requested that *Idol* hire an interior decorator to style his makeup quarters, for perhaps the first time, his request was denied.

COWELL LEFT PASADENA and headed straight to the Kodak Theatre Hollywood Week set for his first day of work with DeGeneres. The aftermath of the announcement found him distracted and notably cranky, even by his standards. The singers trembled as he brought down the axe an one after another, dashing the hopes of some of the brightest talents who had the misfortune to fall on the wrong side of his mood.

Within days, press reports emerged claiming that Simon and Ellen were at each other's throats. "TV Tug of War: It's Ellen vs. Simon" screamed Hollywood's Deadline blog. "It was *American Idol*'s newest judge Ellen DeGeneres's first day of the ninth season's taping of the Hollywood segment, and she was excited and nervous, sources tell us. But then that turned to anger. Because, our insiders say, Simon Cowell was an hour and a half late for the taping. And Ellen stewed while she waited."

For the rest of the season, reporters studied the pair for any sign of strife. To all appearances, the two behaved professionally to each other, but once the cameras stopped rolling they retreated to their own corners. On-screen, they largely ignored each other, with one rarely responding directly to the other's comments, hardly making for good TV. Their one moment of real interaction came when Ellen, in a jesting attempt to dispel the strife talk, climbed in Simon's lap, wrapped her arms around his neck, and began nuzzling his ear. Cowell seemed mortified, and he couldn't even pretend to play along.

As for the rest of the panel, in the Simon/Paula/Randy era, each judge had a very clear roles. Mean judge. Nice judge. Tie-breaking judge. Now you had a mean judge and three others, each of whom were neither clearly nice nor mean but somewhere in between, depending on the day. As the semifinals progressed and the judges came front and center, the ratings plummeted.

The judges struggled to integrate their newest member. On the nights when it was her turn to lead off the panel, Ellen seemed uncertain of which way to turn. A comedian and no music expert, she needed someone to play off, someone to establish the parameters of how a performance went before she felt safe weighing in. The order was shifted, Randy given the permanent first position, and Ellen grew more comfortable. But as the season wore on and her one-liners became familiar, the question of what she added to the panel grew more pronounced.

Now in her second year, Kara had become noticeably confident and was winning critical praise as the most engaged, musically astute of the judges. "Kara DioGuardi has improved from her first season," wrote the *Idol* critic at movieline.com, "now ably diagnosing issues with song choices and artistic intention." She also received a backhanded compliment from her antagonists at Vote for the Worst, who, comparing her to Ellen's early performances, wrote, "At least Kara DioGuardi can finally give away the title of Most Contrived Idol Judge."

Informed though she might have been, Kara's role in relation to the others remained unclear. Offscreen, she seemed eager to take Paula's place by Simon's side. She whispered constantly to him, played with his hair, leaned against him at every moment, and followed him out on cigarette breaks, making it clear—many thought, to Ellen—that she was Simon's number one girl. In fact, Kara seemed to be trying to haze Ellen as Paula hazed her. But there were a couple of problems with the strategy. For one thing, rather than enjoying the banter with Kara as he had with Paula, Simon seemed annoyed and looked as if he was trying to shake her off at every opportunity. As for Ellen, getting in good with Simon seemed to be the last thing she cared about. Kara's gambit fell flat.

IF THE CONTESTANTS in previous years had taken hits, no group had ever been bashed as hard as the contestants of season 9. "The Worst Season Ever?" asked the *Fresno Bee*, in what would become the critics' mantra. Individually, the contestants might not have been so much worse than any given singer on any other season, but coming after the theatrics of Adam Lambert and the other talented season 8 contestants, the current season suffered badly in comparison. None of the group was able to top or even match Lambert's skill at reinventing a song and creating events out of each performance. Halfway through the season, nobody had captured the audience's imagination, nor become a topic of national conversation. That one person who audiences couldn't wait to see never emerged.

Collectively, the group appeared sullen and immature, unable to communicate. Lee DeWyze, the year's surging front-runner, was often nervous to the point he was barely able to get out a sentence when speaking on camera. Siobhan Magnus, hybrid goth/hippie glassblower from Cape Cod, appeared to be in her own world, barely aware of the spectacle unfolding around her. Even the one potential breakout performer was highly problematic. With her missing teeth and dreadlocks, Crystal Bowersox seemed to cultivate the image of a street musician performing on a subway platform. She was definitely not of the *Idol* mold, even with her powerful voice. While Crystal's act was solidly retro, her magnetic charm, which often seemed to shine through despite herself, turned her into the season's only thing approaching a breakout star. Backstage, however, Crystal seemed to resent the requirements of

Idol, and this resentment played itself out in a regular stream of mini-diva fits that provoked huge eye-rolling among the crew. In interviews, she would snap at reporters and mock their questions, and refuse to answer. Halfway through the season, friends shipped Crystal her old mike stand, which she had used in her performances back home, a special contraption fixed up with a glass lamp in the middle, giving it something of a gypsy vibe. When the stagehands brought the stand out for its *Idol* debut, they noticed a thick layer of dust on it and duly wiped it off. Crystal threw a tantrum, proclaiming the dust had been the residue of her whole career and had been swept away.

On a more serious note, coming from a very off-the-grid background, Bowersox arrived at the stage a serious health risk. A lifelong sufferer of diabetes, she had been without health insurance for years. Moreover, she didn't appear to practice a proper diet or treatment regimen for her ailment. Early in the top twelve rounds, Crystal collapsed on the set and had to be rushed to the hospital, where doctors found her dangerously at risk of serious consequences. The medical attention put her on the path to good health at last. "Whatever people say about *Idol*, we saved that girl's life. The show literally saved her life," said one familiar with her condition.

The incident provoked the season's one major piece of public drama when Ryan Seacrest reportedly found an exhausted Crystal wandering outside the set on the brink of quitting the show and convinced her to stay. A few days after the story became public, Crystal's recently eliminated friend Didi Benami reported getting a text reading "Betrayed by Seacrest," a message that was soon to become a catchphrase among the *Idol* press corps. But many believe Crystal's suspicions may have been misplaced. Because the news first appeared on TMZ, a favored spot for on-set leakers, it was speculated that the tidbit had been divulged not by Seacrest but by someone on the production out to milk the one piece of drama that had occurred in the limpid season.

The question many asked was how—of the tens of thousands who auditioned—how could these really be the best? There were the traditional reasons, of course: luck of the draw, talented performers failing to live up to their potential, others who made it through not rising to theirs. But many on the set had other notions. Once Cowell had decided to leave *Idol* and bring over *X Factor*, *Idol* became his competition. And Simon Cowell, by his own admission, was nothing if not competitive. So here was *Idol*'s competitor in charge of choosing its talent. It's impossible to know what was in Cowell's mind as he reviewed each contestant through the auditions, Hollywood Week, and ultimately as he selected the semifinalists. And indeed, although many worried that his boredom would become paralyzing, Cowell appeared more alert in this final season, more focused and serious than he had been in years. Nevertheless, more than a few members of the production broached the theory that season 9's poor crop of talent was due to Simon's not wanting to do his new competitor any favors as he kept his eyes on the future.

F O R T H E F I R S T time since its first season, *Idol* lost a night, garnering lower ratings than a resurgent Kate Gosselin–fueled *Dancing with the Stars*. And amidst all this, the one sturdy, unsinkable ship in the *American Idol* fleet even began springing leaks. Ryan Seacrest, Mr. Smooth, the man who doesn't know the meaning of the word *awkward*, was . . . awkward. On one occasion, pushing his sparring partner Cowell, Seacrest approached the judges' desk and literally got in Simon's face, an inch away from it. Cowell, rather than engaging, pulled back and turned away, creating a bizarrely off-kilter moment. On another night, when Seacrest asked contestant Didi Benami a question about the deceased friend she had just discussed in a video package, Benami suddenly clammed up and murmured that she didn't wish to talk about it, leaving Ryan looking like a ghoul prodding at a tragedy.

The truth was that as host, Seacrest's job was far more complex than it seemed. Derided as a pretty face and reader of cue cards, Seacrest was actually responsible for the most critical element of the live show: its pacing. It's the host who picks up the tempo when it lags, changes the subject, brings up nagging questions, or slows things down to stretch out the tension when that's called for. Watching Seacrest in the early years when his skills were still a work in progress, you can see how the episodes often lurched forward in fits and starts. But Seacrest grew into the role and became the show's true host, keeping the trains—the commercial breaks— running on time, squeezing a few intelligible words out of the often verbally challenged contestants, and making sure he milked every spot of drama.

Nevertheless, while a skilled host can turn lemons into lemonade, he can't make lemonade out of roadkill. Between the judges not jelling and the singers not connecting, Ryan failed to pick up the tempo. Whatever that alchemy had been, the lightning that had bound *Idol*'s inner circle together and made it the most popular television show on Earth was gone.

SEASON 10 WOULD offer a chance to invent the show anew. As the producers pointed out, *Idol* was a hit in dozens of countries without Simon Cowell. The star of German *Idol*, Dieter Bohlen, was, if anything, an even bigger star there than Cowell was here. *Idol* had defied longer odds before and there were still tens of millions of fans who would be tuning in to see what they came up with, ready to give them every benefit of the doubt. It would be something different without Cowell, but it would be something.

Notable at the taping of almost every episode in season 9 was a man who had been only sporadically seen on the set since the early years, *American Idol*'s creator, Simon Fuller. He sat quietly in the last row of the theater, went in and out through a rear staircase, and eschewed any public acknowledgment. While every newspaper, TV news show, and entertainment site on Earth puzzled over the fate of *Idol*, the man who had created it all sat quietly watching each week, unnoticed by reporters sitting a few feet away.

Fuller looked over how far things had come since his hospital revelation nearly a decade and a half earlier. The idea of giving the public the opportunity to create stars was more than a reality: It had become, it seemed, a dying entertainment industry's last hope. In nine years, the products of his empire had sold millions of records, had conquered Broadway, and won an Oscar. One hundred graduates of *American Idol* were making lives in music, whether in national stadium tours or at their local bars, where the *American Idol* name remained a sure draw.

But for Fuller, there was already the next mountain to climb. In the ninth season of *Idol*, he had begun perhaps the most ambitious project ever constructed on the Internet. Over the years working with Paul Hardcastle, with the Spice Girls, not to mention with so many Idols in America, the United Kingdom, and around the world, he had become fascinated with that almost mystical transformation from private person to star. For this very private man himself, that moment had become the subject of his thoughts and reflections, when one life suddenly belongs to something bigger than itself, when it belongs to the people.

Fuller created a house in Beverly Hills where the world would be able to watch this transformation take place, play out as it might over weeks or years; after all he'd been through, he was in no rush. The *If I Can Dream* house was populated with five young aspiring stars, and built with cameras in every nook and cranny, feeding into a Web site that was an amazing technological achievement, where visitors could control their perspective like nothing ever created and where a 24/7 control room monitored and catalogued full-length episodes. Over the next few years, at least one of these young people would become a star, it was hoped, and every moment of that journey would have been captured forever. But just as important, by the very sharing of their process, they would bring the public into their rise, make them partners in their celebrity as they watched them eat dinner, chatted with them on Twitter, became their friends on Facebook. And then, when they made it, their rise would, from the first, be the property of the fans.

The man who had made so many stars was looking for ever newer ways to put that power back in the hands of the people.

IN HIS FINAL days on *Idol,* Cowell seemed notably wistful. On a few occasions he even did the unthinkable and stayed in the theater during commercial breaks to chat with the crowd and sign autographs.

When the finale came, it was a celebration of the Simon era, with the predictable tribute reels and a serenade by a chorus of former *Idol* stars. The emotional high point of the night, however, was not Simon's goodbye speech but a surprise appearance to wish him farewell. Paula Abdul almost didn't go through with her tribute, but when she stepped out on the Nokia stage, the outpouring was incomparable to anything the show had seen. The crowd rose to their feet and stayed on their feet throughout her address—nary a dry eye in the house—as a meandering, tongue-tied, overflowing-with-emotion Paula spoke to the *Idol* faithful once more. To the six thousand people in the room, what she had meant to them would always be a special memory. When she was done, at the commercial break, Simon put his arm around her and, ignoring the show and the other judges, went out for a cigarette break with his old friend. They had come far together, and some speculated that their journey together might continue at the other end of Fox's lineup when X *Factor* debuted. But for now, it was a moment to go out in triumph.

Cowell looked out over the *Idol* crowd one last time. "It felt very weird," he says, remembering the moment. "It's the connection with the audience more than anything else. It's so easy when you get caught up in negotiations that you forget about the people who made it happen, and that's the people who watch the shows. So when you're standing there in front of five thousand, six thousand people and you feel this warmth and emotion, that's when I felt more emotional than I ever thought I would feel. Which is just the fact that we've had this amazing run, and that's what was all going through my mind. And Randy and Ryan, all those things. But still believing—*always* believing—that it's a great show."

SEASON 9 ENDED with what was widely considered a lackluster verdict: Quiet, introverted, often nervous Chicago paint salesman Lee DeWyze continued the rocker boys' dynasty. That summer, the tour became the lowest attended yet. In a miserable summer for the touring industry in general, the promoters were forced to cancel shows for the first time. But for the twelve, even the abbreviated tour remained a dream that a year before they would have never believed possible.

Late in July, the *Idol* team would still be debating how to replace Simon Cowell and the fate of the judges' panel. Meanwhile, in Nashville, Tennessee, sixteen thousand people stood in line before dawn to audition to be the next American Idol. It was the second-highest turnout in *Idol* history, and as the tour went on for the show supposedly on its last legs, the numbers stayed in the stratosphere.

For tens of thousands, the *Idol* dream still meant everything. And for a show looking to renew itself, each one of those tens of thousands was a new story, a new fairy tale ready to be told.

Somewhere in one of those crowds, lined up into the distance before sunrise, there may have stood the person who would change the show, once again in his or her image, and keep the dream alive for yet another generation of dreamers.

SELECTED BIBLIOGRAPHY

★

Archuleta, David, *Chords of Strength*, New York: Celebra, 2010.

Buckles, Justin, *Stage 46*, Portland: Milner Crest, 2008.

Carter, Bill, *Desperate Networks*, New York: Broadway Books, 2006.

Cowell, Simon, *I Don't Mean To Be Rude But . . .* New York: Broadway Books, 2003.

Doolittle, Melinda. *Beyond Me*. Grand Rapids: Zondervan, 2010

Hicks, Taylor, *Heart Full of Soul*, New York: Crown Publishers, 2007.

King, Jonathan, *65: My Life So Far*, London: Revvolution Publishing, 2009.

Malakar, Sanjaya, *Dancing to the Music in My Head*, New York: Pocket, 2009.

Newkey-Burden, Chas, *Simon Cowell: The Unauthorized Biography*, London: Michael O'Mara Books Limited, 2009.